W9-BNN-143

BRAIN POWER

*Train your brain
and improve your memory*

Bath · New York · Cologne · Melbourne · Delhi
Hong Kong · Shenzhen · Singapore

CONTENTS

CONTENTS

INTRODUCTION

THE BRAIN IS THE CENTER OF THE HUMAN NERVOUS SYSTEM, GOVERNING OUR THOUGHTS, FEELINGS, AND MOVEMENTS; IT FILTERS AND PRIORITIZES ALL THE INFORMATION THAT BOMBARDS OUR SENSES EVEN WHILE WE SLEEP; IT CONTROLS OUR AUTONOMIC FUNCTIONS FROM SWALLOWING AND BREATHING TO HEART RATE AND PERSPIRATION; IT CONSTANTLY MODIFIES OUR MEMORIES TO IMPROVE OUR DECISION-MAKING ABILITIES AND FROM EARLY INFANCY IT ALLOWS US TO DEVELOP THE SELF-AWARENESS THAT MAKES US UNIQUELY HUMAN.

Life molds your brain; since you were born it has been developing and fine-tuning the network of connections, the pattern of associations, stitching together the rich tapestry of genetic inheritance and life experience that has brought you to this moment, right here, right now, reading these words.

You will respond to them as only you can because only your brain can occupy this precise point in space-time (although smarter human brains have formulated the theories that accommodate countless other yous in infinite parallel worlds within the multiverse).

Fortunately, brains are spectacularly plastic, meaning they continue to develop throughout our lives; the functional restructuring of brain cells means that it's never too late to learn new information, change your thought processes, and boost your brainpower. Recent research into gamma waves at the Kavli Institute for Systems Neuroscience and Centre for the Biology of Memory at the Norwegian University of Science and Technology (NTNU) has shown that signaling inside the brain isn't restricted to the modification of connections between neurons; the brain is even more flexible than that.

These Norwegian scientists now believe that brain cells use a switching system to literally tune into each other's wavelengths; they receive thousands of inputs and they can choose which to ignore and which to listen to, by tuning into different gamma wavelengths, much like turning the dial on a radio.

Even our memories are more fluid than you might think; they are constantly being updated and changed to inform our current circumstances. Every time we reactivate a memory we reinforce and subtly change it, depending on our current interpretation. Bereavement is a good example of the fluidity of memory and how experiences can be viewed differently over time.

All this flexibility is fantastic news for those who recognize the importance of good brain health, stimulation, and development. This book is a multigym for your mind. It's a brain fitness system made up of a wide range of puzzles, brain teasers, quizzes, and challenges designed for performing different mental tasks to give you a focussed workout.

It is well established that mental exercises during childhood and late adulthood contribute to a slower mental decline in old age, but did you know that a team at Tübingen University in Germany has proposed a theory that healthy old people don't suffer mental decline at all? They just know so much that their brains take longer to process all the information, in the same way that a computer's hard drive slows down when it's full.

The first half of this book covers general brain training. The target areas are concentration, problem-solving, language, numbers, visual perception, and creativity. Each topic introduces a compelling idea in the field of metacognition, followed by a selection of related questions and exercises. The second half of the book then moves on to look in more detail at memory, with techniques and tips on how to improve your mental recall.

Memory training is important as it is memory that defines us, memory that grounds us, and guides us. It is the core of our identity and plays a central role in every aspect of our lives. It informs who we have been and what we want to become. Memory is the basis of love, friendship, thinking, learning, and creating. A life without memory is merely an existence.

But you could still do with a better one, right? Do those tip-of-the-tongue moments come a little too often? Do you find it hard to concentrate when you have to study for a test? Do you struggle to put a name to a face or have to write an order list every time it's your turn to order a round of drinks? Are you worried that your memory will keep on getting worse as you grow older?

You're not alone. But do you think it's possible to train memory? If so, do you believe long-term memory has a limited storage capacity or is limitless?

Fortunately, memory science places no limitation on the capacity of memory because brains are spectacularly plastic, meaning they continue to develop throughout our lives. The functional restructuring of brain cells means that it's never too late to learn new information, change your thought processes, and boost your memory.

The human brain is so big and nutrient hungry that an estimated 25 percent of all our energy expenditure is used to power its 85 billion neurons; new connections are formed between them every time you make a memory. All this brain size and flexibility is fantastic news for those who recognize the importance of good brain health, stimulation, and development. Did you know that the hippocampus—a region of the brain associated with the consolidation of information from short-term to long-term memory and spatial navigation—continues to grow new brain cells well into old age?

The sections on improving memory in this book show how to improve your mental recall and actually grow your brain. It's a neurogenetic memory system made up of a wide range of puzzles, quizzes, and challenges designed for performing different memory tasks to give you a focussed workout. The target areas are nutrition, attention, concentration, visual, auditory, kinesthetic, spatial, musical, intuitive, deliberate practice, and more than a dozen powerful mnemonic techniques.

Pages 134–196 explain how the memory works and details the major different types that form a complex memory matrix. Then pages 197–267 introduce you to lots of strategies and tips that will expand your memory capacity.

Currently, some of the world's top memory athletes can recite the first 65,000 digits of Pi or memorize 60 shuffled packs of playing cards after viewing them only once. None of them were born with this ability. They use memory techniques and have spent years practicing. You too can improve your memory. There's no secret. You don't have to be a genius. You just need a few techniques and you will start to see results within hours. Even now, you remember more than you think and often failures of memory are caused by a simple lack of attention.

If you are serious about training your brain and improving your memory you should read this book cover to cover. But if you want to focus on specific issues, you can dip in and out as you please since most of the topics are self-contained, although some of them refer back to earlier sections.

LIFE IS A ROUGH BIOGRAPHY. MEMORIES SMOOTH OUT THE EDGES.

(TERRI GUILLEMETS)

1#
<u>TRAIN YOUR</u>
<u>BRAIN</u>

CONCENTRATION AND FOCUS
SKILLS TEST

This quiz is designed to assess your concentration levels.

Strongly Agree	Agree	Neutral	Disagree	Strongly Disagree
1	2	3	4	5

1. My mind often wanders when I am trying to concentrate.

2. When concentrating I quickly become tired.

3. I rarely use strategies and motivational techniques to help me achieve boring or challenging tasks.

4. Other people always seem to be disturbing me.

5. When I most need to concentrate is when I feel most distracted.

6. I don't know which times of day are my most productive so I don't arrange my schedule to tackle difficult tasks at optimum times.

7. I try to do several things at once and flit between them.

8. I don't set goals and objectives before starting a project.

9. I regularly check social media while I'm working.

10. I repeat the same things over and over again because I lose track.

11. I can't concentrate if someone is talking nearby.

12. I feel rushed.

13. I get bored easily.

14. I push on through tasks and rarely take short breaks.

15. My working environment is not conducive to concentration.

16. The task takes as long as it takes, so I don't set time goals.

17. I always feel like the fun is happening somewhere else and I'm missing it.

18. I often forget what I am supposed to be doing or what comes next.

19. I can only stay focussed on something if it's really interesting.

20. I suffer from intrusive thoughts.

21. This quiz is boring.

22. My study area is tidy and uncluttered.

23. I rarely work in a place free from auditory and visual distractions.

24. I fidget and/or find it hard to sit still.

25. I procrastinate.

Total score:

RESULTS

25–50

You are in urgent need of some strategies to aid your concentration. You may have problems beginning tasks and may suffer from anxiety as a result of your lack of focus. You tire easily, are easily distracted, and never seem to have enough time to complete your work. You have a low boredom threshold and often blame others for your inability to concentrate.

51–75

You sometimes use strategies to aid your concentration but would benefit from setting goals, structuring your work environment, and setting time limits to increase your focus. You should also take short breaks when your attention wanders. You take some responsibility for your own concentration but still prefer gossiping around the water cooler to committing yourself to some serious focussed work.

76–100

On the whole you have good concentration and usually take full responsibility for structuring your work environment and minimizing distractions. However, you still have moments when you lose it and just can't seem to focus, which means you would benefit from taking breaks and using some of the techniques in this chapter to give you extra motivation when your energy is flagging.

101–125

Your mind is laser sharp and your focus and self-discipline are in the top percentile. You have a wealth of strategies and inner resources to draw upon when the going gets tough. You can stick to even the most thankless tasks because you set clear goals, use your time efficiently, and always take full responsibility for structuring your work environment and minimizing distractions.

INCREASE PRODUCTIVITY

Staying focussed can be a big challenge and isn't always about working harder or blitzing a problem with extra resources. Software developers are familiar with Brook's law which states that "adding manpower to a late software project makes it later." Increasing productivity involves acting smarter to maximize your cognitive assets: You can't change the number of hours in the day but you can transform the way you use them.

1. Scientific studies have linked ambient temperature to productivity and show that the "comfort zone" is between 72°F (22°C) and 77°F (25°C).

2. Make a plan for the day. Set ambitious but realistic goals. If your goals are overambitious you are setting yourself up to fail and destroying your future motivation.

3. Now just start and your fears of failure/lack of time will greatly reduce. If a huge project overwhelms you, break it down into manageable chunks.

4. Trust in the competence and sincerity of others. Ask for help when you need it and share your expertise with others in return.

5. Less is more. Productivity is not measured by how long you sit at your desk. Work in short bursts with maximum focus and take short breaks when your attention wanders.

6. Tell other people about your goals so that you feel more accountable for them.

7. Find your most productive time of day and start work then, even if it is 5 a.m. or 11 p.m. If it feels right to you, don't worry about conforming with the nine-to-fivers.

8. Change your environment. Sometimes just moving into another room and working with pen and paper instead of a computer can remotivate you and promote creativity.

9. Follow the Pareto principle (devised by Italian economist Vilfredo Pareto and also known as the 80–20 rule), which states that for many events, 80 percent of the effects come from 20 percent of the causes. What 20 percent of fruitless activities are wasting 80 percent of your time?

10. Focus on one thing at a time. Research has shown that multitasking is inefficient.

Less is more: The solutions to these puzzles are easier and require less work than you might think.

KEG OF BEER

Is the keg of beer more than half full or less than half full? There is a way you can tell without using any additional equipment.

THREE LIGHTBULBS

The three switches on the wall outside the windowless room are connected to three bulbs inside the room. How can you work out which switch is connected to which bulb if you are only allowed to enter the room once?

GOOD SAMARITAN

The Pareto principle is the idea that in many systems there is inequality between causes and effects. In this puzzle, one choice you make is vital while the others only offer small returns.

You are driving down the road in your car on a wild, stormy night, when you pass by a bus stop and you see three people waiting for the bus:

1. *An old lady who looks like she is about to die.*

2. *An old friend who once saved your life.*

3. *The perfect partner of your dreams.*

You can only fit one passenger in your car. Who should you choose?

ATTENTIONAL CONTROL

Attention and focus are critical skills that help us to absorb, process, and memorize information. Attentional control (AC) is the capacity to choose what to pay attention to and what to ignore, how effectively we can engage and disengage our focus. In many ways it defines who we are. The Spanish philosopher José Ortega y Gasset said, "Tell me to what you pay attention, and I will tell you who you are."

AC primarily involves the frontal areas of the brain, including the anterior cingulate cortex, and it is closely related to working memory. It is greater in adults than children because their frontal lobes are still developing, but even in adulthood you can greatly improve this crucial cognitive skill. Disrupted AC is related to conditions such as Attention Deficit Hyperactivity Disorder (ADHD) and autism.

It is also adversely affected by anxiety, but impaired AC has been identified as one of the primary cognitive factors underlying the origin and maintenance of anxiety. In other words, reducing your anxiety will improve your AC but also, improving your AC and focussing on the task at hand will reduce your anxiety.

The best way to improve your AC is that by practice: Performing tasks with the prime motivation of refusing to let yourself become distracted. However, setting up your environment and mindset is also essential. Remember, research has shown that self-discipline is more important than IQ in predicting academic success:

1. Eliminate distractions: Turn off the TV and music, and remove devices such as your cell phone. Simplify your visual field (e.g. when doing desk work, remove sticky notes and all other clutter from your desk).

2. Work in manageable chunks of time: 15–45 minutes with a short break in between.

3. Understand WHY you are doing the task and how it will benefit you or others.

4. Set a clear goal so you understand WHAT you are doing and monitor your behavior toward that goal.

5. Break tasks down into components, so you don't become overwhelmed and demotivated by the size of the whole task. Work on one task at a time.

MIXED SIGNALS

This exercise involves blocking out one or more stimuli to focus exclusively on another. Many people are already very skilled at this when they so choose (we all have friends and family who won't acknowledge our existence while they watch television, play video games, or text).

Pick one or more competing stimuli (aural, tactile, visual, olfactory, taste), e.g.: Blazing television/radio, lights flashing on and off (get a friend to help), sucking a lemon, being hit on the head at random intervals by a balloon, sitting in a cold bath, etc. Now tune a second radio onto a speaking station. During a five-minute period, count the number of times the speakers say the word "the." Notice how the "game" aspect reduces the negative emotional component (i.e. irritation).

COUNT THE SQUARES

How many squares are there in this picture?
92 percent of people fail this simple attention test!

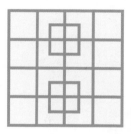

HOW MANY Fs?

How many "F"s are there in each of these sentences? Read them only once and write down your answers within sixty seconds.

1. Finished files are the result of years of scientific study combined with the experience of years.

2. For a strange definition of fun, consider that all that fun means is that four out of five people enjoy counting Fs.

3. It is easy to miss the finer points in life; folk are frequently guilty of falling into this trap.

HOW TO DEAL WITH
INTRUSIVE THOUGHTS

Intrusive thoughts are almost always created by anxiety and/or negative emotional experiences. They hinder your concentration, encourage you to procrastinate, distract you from the task in hand, and inevitably increase your anxiety, which can lead to an increase in intrusive thoughts.

Trying to block out unwanted thoughts is actually counterproductive. Close your eyes right now and set a timer. Your aim is to spend a minute without thinking of a white bear.

How did you get on? How many seconds did you last before the white bear appeared in your thoughts? And why do we think of a white bear when we have expressly told ourselves not to?

Daniel Wegner, a psychology professor at Harvard University, pioneer in the field of thought suppression and author of *White Bears and Other Unwanted Thoughts*, has shown that trying to suppress thought leads to obsession.

So, don't block out unwanted thoughts or earworms (the name given to snippets of a catchy song playing on a loop in your head). Instead, congratulate yourself for recognizing that you are experiencing them and realizing that your concentration is wandering.

Wegner offers several strategies to deal with your white bears:

1. Focus on something else instead! If you are cognitively engaged, it limits the ability of intrusive thoughts to enter your head.

2. Try to postpone the thought. Write a list of the things that are bothering you and then set it aside to be dealt with at an assigned point later in the day. This means that you don't have to hold the thoughts in your memory and you know that you will deal with them later.

3. Wherever possible, avoid multitasking, which can reduce productivity by approximately 40 percent according to some researchers, as well as increasing stress and anxiety.

4. Exposure: "This is painful," Wegner says, "but it can work." Allow yourself to think about the unwanted thought, so that it is less likely to pop up unwanted at other times.

5. Meditation and mindfulness strengthen mental control and help to control unwanted thoughts.

REMOVE EARWORMS

Dr. Ira Hyman, a music psychologist at Western Washington University, claims the best way to stop earworms is to solve some tricky anagrams.

FINE IN TORN JEANS	Actress (F)
NARCOLEPTIC	English musician (M)
CRAZED I MOAN	Actress (F)
ERROR ON BIDET	Actor (M)
ELITE BRAIN NEST	Theoretical physicist (M)
I DEMAND TV LATER	Television host (M)
A FAMOUS GERMAN WALTZ GOD	Composer of the Classical era (M)
MORMON IDEAS	Singer (F)
I RULE STAR JOB	Actress (F)
HE'S GROWN LARGE N CRAZED	Actor turned politician (M)
LEAN WAR MISSILE	Tennis champion (F)
USE MY LYRIC	Actress and recording artist (F)

OBJECT FOCUS

Take a small simple object such as a glass or a piece of fruit. Concentrate on and explore it. Turn it over in your hands to experience the object without using thoughts. See if you can shift all your focus on to the object with a quiet, nonjudgmental mind.

CLOCK WATCH

This exercise was suggested by Vanda North and Richard Israel, the authors of *Mind Chi*. Focus on the second hand of a clock on the wall, while repeating the word "one" until a stray thought pops into your mind. Then say "two" over and over until you spot the next thought, and then start saying "three." See how low you can keep your score during a one-minute clock watch.

AWAKEN YOUR SENSES

It is all too easy to neglect our five senses and miss out on a plethora of fun ways to boost brain performance. Stimulating taste, touch, smell, hearing, and vision immediately before applying yourself to a specific task can improve concentration and alertness.

SIGHT

Research at the University of Hiroshima in Japan has found that looking at pictures of cute animals improves concentration. Tests on 132 university students showed they performed better in cognitive tests after looking at photos of baby animals, but not after viewing their adult counterparts. Students who viewed cute animals improved their performance in an Operation-style game (which tests hand–eye coordination and fine motor skills) by 44 percent. The researchers concluded, "Cute images are considered to induce positive affect with high approach motivation because they are evolutionarily related to caregiving and nurturing or because they prime social engagement."

Exposure to color has an important effect on moods and feelings, which impact concentration. Green is considered to be the color of concentration. If you haven't already painted your study area green, place some green objects on your desk and set aside a particular favorite article of green clothing to wear only when you need to concentrate. Best of all, spend ten minutes walking in nature before you start work.

SMELL

Several studies have shown that peppermint aroma improves memory, focus, and concentration. In one study in Cincinnati, Ohio, a group of students who were exposed to the aroma of peppermint oil before a test showed an improved accuracy of 28 percent.

Lemon balm can also boost memory and mood. Its cognitive benefits have been extolled for centuries. In the sixteenth century, herbalist John Gerard offered it to his students to "quicken the senses." Laboratory tests on this common weed have found it increases the activity of acetylcholine, a chemical messenger linked to memory.

Other scents that aid concentration include jasmine, cinnamon, vanilla, vetiver, cedarwood, and rosemary (which increases blood flow to the head and brain). Care should be taken when using essential oils to provide these scents.

TASTE

Instead of reaching for your customary cup of coffee, suck on a lemon or sip a glass of iced lemon or lime juice, which will hydrate you while the sourness increases your alertness.

Research published in the journal *Psychological Science* by scientists at the University of Georgia indicates that just the taste of sugar (gargling with lemonade made from real sugar) improved the focus and self control of test subjects. Coauthor Leonard Martin explains: "After this trial, it seems that glucose stimulates the simple carbohydrates sensors on your tongue," which "signals the motivation centers of the brain."

TOUCH

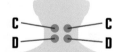

Several acupressure points improve memory and concentration, relieve headaches, and aid relaxation. Self-massage or apply gentle fingertip pressure at these points.

(A) One Hundred Meeting Point (on the crown of the head in between the cranial bones)

(B) Sun Point (in the depression of the temples)

(C) Gates of Consciousness (the hollows below the base of the skull)

(D) Heavenly Pillar (half an inch below the base of the skull on muscles one-half inch either side of the spine)

(E) Three Mile Point (four finger-widths below the kneecap, one finger-width outside of the shinbone)

(F) Bigger Rushing (in the dimple between the big toe and the second toe)

HEARING

Binaural beats are an intriguing way to change your brain waves to aid concentration (or send you to sleep, depending on your requirements). They involve playing tones of slightly differing frequencies into each ear via stereo headphones before or even while you work. Search YouTube for " binaural beats concentration."

DIGITAL DISTRACTIONS

It is a fact of life that most of us are becoming increasingly reliant on technology, from smartphones to the Internet, but while technology and social media have many benefits, research psychologists such as Dr. Larry Rosen believe that our overuse of smartphones, tablets, and computers is creating widespread mental health issues.

In his book *iDisorder: Understanding Our Obsession with Technology and Overcoming Its Hold on Us*, Rosen warns that "many of us are on the verge of an iDisorder" caused by "the way we all relate to technology and media" which expresses the symptoms of several psychological disorders, "including narcissism, obsessive-compulsive disorder, depression, attention-deficit disorder, social phobia, antisocial personality disorder, hypochondriasis, body dysmorphic disorder, schizo-disorders, and voyeurism." If you are "plugged in" you may already recognize unhealthy aspects of your own relationship with technology: Wasting an hour online when you only intended to send an email; checking your text messages during the middle of the night; mentally rehearsing a twitter update instead of experiencing the moment.

Do you have an iDisorder?

If you can answer yes to five or more of these questions, you may have a problem:

1. Do you feel anxious that you're missing out if you can't regularly check your emails/social media?

2. Do you lie in bed checking your phone/tablet before you go to sleep?

3. Do you often bring your laptop when you sit on the toilet?

4. Do you refresh your inbox over and over in case someone emailed you in the last 30 seconds?

5. Do you change your Facebook profile picture more than twice in a month?

6. Do you say things online that you wouldn't dream of saying to someone's face?

7. Do you regularly think your phone is vibrating in your pocket even when it isn't?

8. Do you interrupt tasks in order to check your emails/social media?

9. Do you use your cell phone while driving (not hands free)?

10. Do you tweet/post on social media in the middle of the night to announce that you can't sleep?

Studies show that students who checked Facebook just once during a 15-minute study period performed worse. Constantly checking our devices becomes an obsessive feedback loop, often driven by what MTV called FOMO (*fear of missing out*) and Jim Taylor from the University of San Francisco calls DA (*disconnectivity anxiety*).

The anxiety experienced when those technologies are not available (having to switch off a smartphone in the movies, the internet goes down), the disruption to sleep caused by interacting with technology before bedtime, not to mention the narcissistic obsession with how one presents oneself online, all add up to iDisorder.

So how do we maintain focus when technology and social media constantly threaten to distract us? Here are three ways to reduce your dependence on technology:

SPEND MORE TIME WITH NATURE

Spending even a few minutes interacting with a natural environment helps to calm and reset the brain and improve its ability to function. Scientists at the University of Michigan have even discovered that ten minutes spent looking at photographs of nature offers the same restorative effects as the real thing.

LISTEN TO MUSIC

Dr. Larry Rosen says, "music activates the same reward circuits in the brain that react to food and sex, and brain scans have shown that just listening to music for a short time can help reset the brain."

RETHINK, REBOOT, RECONNECT, AND REVITALIZE

Science and technology journalist Daniel Sieberg's four-step plan encourages you to:

Rethink: Work out how much time you spend interacting with technology.
Reboot: Disconnect for a period to break your habitual behaviors.
Reconnect: Gradually reintroduce technology, but now with a greater awareness; restructure your environment so that you control the technology (e.g. place your tablet/cell phone in another room while you focus exclusively on an important task without interruption).
Revitalize: Prioritize human contact.

THE "FIVE MORE" RULE

HOW MUCH WILLPOWER DO YOU HAVE?

1. When I am performing a difficult task I
   a) try to finish as quickly as possible so that I can put my feet up
   b) enjoy the challenge
   c) worry that I won't be able to complete it/lose my temper/pay someone else to do it

2. When trying to stick to a new regime (diet, work schedule, financial budget) I
   a) stick rigidly to the rules
   b) allow myself the occasional lapse without beating myself up about it
   c) quickly cave in to temptation/quit after a few days

3. Other people seem to have it easier than me
   a) sometimes
   b) rarely
   c) always

4. I keep promises I make to myself
   a) sometimes
   b) always
   c) rarely

5. Hard work pays off
   a) sometimes
   b) always
   c) rarely

6. The most useful question I can ask is
   a) why?
   b) why not?
   c) why me?

7. When something isn't working out I
   a) keep plugging away
   b) review the situation and I'm not afraid to change direction if required
   c) get stressed out/give up/blame someone else

8. I would best describe willpower as
   a) a finite resource that runs out and needs refilling (like a rain barrel)
   b) a self-renewing supply that always gives as much as I need (an underground lake)
   c) something only other people seem to possess

RESULTS

Mostly As

You have some willpower but it's all or nothing with you. Sometimes you aren't prepared to put in the consistent work to get the results that you want and shirk responsibility for your failures. You have a tendency to think something or someone else is responsible for your problems and their solutions.

Mostly Bs

You have the traits of a highly successful person, combining willpower and consistency with the ability to admit your own failings. You have the confidence and flexibility to change tack when a new strategy is needed. You take pleasure in being creative and seeing where opportunities can take you, without being too much of a perfectionist.

Mostly Cs

You need to learn to take responsibility for your future by getting busy in the present moment. You lack self-reliance because your previous setbacks have dented your motivation and spirit of adventure. The good news is that you can improve your prospects instantly by asking a little bit more from yourself with the "five more" rule.

When you feel your attention wandering or you want to quit, just do FIVE MORE—stay with it for five more minutes, read five more pages, do five more reps in the gym, do five more math problems.

It is important to recognize that the prevailing belief that willpower is a finite reserve is actually untrue and unhelpful. It is not a well that runs dry (unless you believe that it is). Stanford University psychology professors Greg Walton and Carol Dweck followed 153 college students over five weeks and found that students who had been taught that willpower was unlimited and self-renewing exhibited increases in willpower and reported eating less junk food and procrastinating less than students who had been taught that willpower was finite. Subsequently they also earned better grades.

Walton and Dweck's explanation is: "People who think that willpower is limited are on the lookout for signs of fatigue. When they detect fatigue, they slack off," whereas people who are taught that willpower is unlimited learn to view fatigue not as a reason to quit, but "a sign to dig deeper and find more resources." So the more you follow the five more rule, the easier you will find it to follow the five more rule! You can push beyond what you thought biologically and mentally possible by incrementally increasing your commitment and stamina.

IMPROVE YOUR
REACTION TIME

Although reactions decrease with age, they are a consistent indicator of general fitness, health, and how well you are taking care of yourself. The best ways to improve your reaction time are to get adequate sleep, eat healthily, do plenty of exercise, and avoid drugs and alcohol.

Your reactions change throughout the day, so you can use these two tests to gauge when you are at your most productive. Also, keeping track of your reaction time over several weeks can be a big motivator if you are trying to improve your mental and physical fitness.

One of the best ways to improve your reaction time is to relax. Using your imagination to "go through the motions"—visualizing the physical movements that your body needs to perform for a given task—has also been shown to speed up reaction times in real-life situations. Sports people spend a lot of time training their muscle memory to increase their speed and accuracy.

Sugar and high glycemic foods can cause drowsiness and slow down reactions, while a little shot of caffeine will boost your performance (although overdo the coffee and it will quickly decline). If you need an energy boost, avoid sugary foods and drinks, and chew a stick of gum instead. A team of scientists at Japan's Chiba University found that students improved their reaction times by seven percent by chewing gum. This may be because the jaw muscles stimulate areas of the brain, including the premotor cortex within the frontal lobe, which is involved in preparing and executing limb movements.

LEFT RIGHT UP DOWN

1. Working from left to right, top to bottom, call out the direction that the eyes are looking (from your perspective). Time yourself. Keep practicing until you can do it in only 15 seconds.

2. Now add a layer of complexity by calling out the direction from the face's perspective.

3. Finally, call out the opposite direction (from your perspective, or if you are a real masochist, from the face's). This is the ultimate challenge but that feeling that you are tying yourself in knots works wonders inside your brain.

BALL DROP

A helper holds a ball out to the side of their body at shoulder height. When s/he drops the ball, you must sprint to catch it before it bounces for a second time. Vary the sprinting distance according to your ability so the drill is challenging without being impossible.

IMPROVE YOUR BRAIN'S
PROCESSING SPEED

Brain processing speed is how fast your brain can process information and perform cognitive functions over time and it is one of the ways that intelligence is measured. Your brain has about 100 billion cells called neurons which receive and transmit electrochemical signals. Each neuron contains branched projections called dendrites which receive electrochemical messages from other neurons, which then travel through a cable-like structure in the cell called an axon before jumping to other neurons across junctions called synapses.

The brain needs optimum nutrients and daily training to attain maximum performance. Physical exercise and healthy dietary choices are the best ways to improve cognitive speed. Exercise stimulates blood circulation, increases blood flow to the brain, and stimulates hormones that are responsible for cell repair and generation. The best physical exercise, such as sport and dancing, engages your mind as well as your body and requires advanced coordination.

The neural axons are protected and insulated by a material called myelin (which looks like a string of sausages). The myelin increases the speed at which impulses are transmitted (impaired myelin is present in many neurodegenerative diseases such as multiple sclerosis and Guillain-Barré syndrome). Myelin sheath function declines with age, which is one of the reasons that processing speed also declines with age. But, according to the clinical nutritionist Byron Richards, three dietary supplements may provide nutritional support for myelin sheathing: Calcium AEP (amino ethanol phosphate), Phosphatidylserine (also present in soy lecithin, Atlantic herring, chicken heart, and other variety meats), and fat-soluble antioxidants, such as the tocotrienol form of vitamin E (also present in low levels in select rice bran oil, palm oil, wheatgerm, and barley).

Games with time limits are excellent brain-speed boosters because they force you to perform an activity within a set time. For brain-speed training, choose puzzles and games where the goal is speed and accuracy rather than open-ended puzzles where simply solving the problem is the main focus. Rhythm games are also useful because they force you to make decisions quickly. Just as lifting heavy weights builds muscle strength, doing daily brain exercises where speed is essential increases brain speed.

SAY MY NAME

Time yourself to see how quickly you can:

a) say the number of letters of the word (five, four, five . . .)

b) add consecutive numbers horizontally (eight, twelve, seventeen, eighteen . . .)

c) add consecutive numbers vertically (ten, sixteen, eleven, ten . . .)

3	5	7	10	8	5	10	3	4	10
7	10	8	2	3	4	10	5	10	8
9	8	10	2	10	10	2	6	3	7
2	1	9	1	5	1	3	9	5	5
8	1	2	3	2	7	1	9	8	4
9	5	9	7	7	2	7	9	7	1
10	9	5	1	4	5	8	7	5	1
4	5	1	9	8	3	7	6	8	10
5	5	1	7	1	6	9	6	2	2
7	3	8	9	10	9	6	6	3	10

SLAP, CLAP, SNAP, SNAP

Establish a slow rhythm by slapping your legs with both hands once (slap), clapping once (clap), and then clicking right and left fingers one after the other (snap, snap).

Pick a topic (animals, cars, flowers, etc.). When you slap your legs, call out an example of your chosen topic that begins with the letter "A," then on the next leg slap, one that begins with "B," and so on. Slow down the rhythm so you can get through the alphabet without stopping. If you falter, keep the rhythm going and resume on the leg slap. You may repeat a topic and speed up the rhythm to test your memory and challenge your brain to process more quickly.

COLOR MATCH "SNAP"

Playing on your own (or with another player) and using a standard 52-card deck, deal cards face up one by one (so that each card covers the next) and shout out "snap" whenever the current card matches the color of the previous one (i.e. both red or both black).

SOLUTION-FOCUSSED
THINKING

Understand the problem, then focus everything on the solution. It sounds easy, but many of us just focus on the problem, are often overwhelmed and filled with anxiety by its negative consequences, and end up procrastinating. Others dive into the solution without fully understanding or addressing the problem. This risks seeking a solution to the wrong problem or a problem that doesn't even exist.

UNDERSTAND THE PROBLEM

Successful companies look at what their customers need—their problems—and try to solve them with their products. Unsuccessful companies design solutions for the wrong problems or problems which don't even exist, or they launch products that don't fill a need. A new product flops when its designers focus on the solution without considering the problem.

In the seventies, a leading brand of shampoo famously bombed because its unique selling point—that it contained yogurt—just didn't wash with its customers. The high-profile launch of a ready-to-drink coffee product also tanked because it promised convenience (just pop in the microwave) but the solution didn't solve the problem (if pouring boiling water on coffee beans/ granules was ever a problem in the first place) because the carton itself could not be heated in the microwave.

Apple's global success has been based on making a few products really well, rather than lots of products less well. Apple identifies a need/problem and then designs a simple paradigm-shifting solution that blows the competition out of the water. Its solutions have been so appropriate that Apple sometimes appears to invent things we couldn't have imagined and didn't even know we needed.

One of the most vital considerations at the problem-understanding stage is to examine your assumptions about the problem. This is especially important when you are working in a group: Conflicting assumptions will always suppress a solution because they indicate a failure to understand and agree on the problem.

FOCUS ON THE SOLUTION

Your mind works best when it is directed on one thing. You can either move in the direction of the problem or the solution, but not both at the same time. Once you've understood the problem it is time to change direction toward the solution, because as we all know, problems grow bigger when we brood on them.

No one understands this better than Dr. Aaron Beck, the father of Cognitive-Behavioral Therapy and cofounder of the Beck Institute. He discovered that "every disorder has some degree of self-focus" and that focussing on the problem inevitably makes it worse. He has helped many social anxiety sufferers to take their focus away from themselves so that they can socially engage and counter the self-reinforcing belief that was perpetuating their social isolation. He observes that people suffering from chronic pain experience a reduction in pain when their focus is directed toward something else: "Get them into a conversation . . . they are no longer grimacing . . . the pain is greatly diminished . . . their emotional or psychological investment for the time being has been diminished." The long-term solution is to set new goals and focus on these precisely because the goals are the solution.

Focussing on the solution lights a fire under you and drives you into a decisive action; focusing on the problem leads to inactivity and paralyzing fear. Problems rarely solve themselves; they are usually resolved by action.

ARE YOU PROBLEM-ORIENTED OR SOLUTION-ORIENTED?

1. When I look at problems, situations, and people, I work from the assumption that

   a) many people can't be trusted

   b) the vast majority of people are basically good and trustworthy

   c) the relationships and connections I make are more important than finding a solution

2. All problems can be solved if we have the will

   a) I strongly disagree

   b) I strongly agree

   c) it depends on the problem

3. When faced with a new challenge I feel
    a) anxious
    b) excited
    c) both

4. When I have to perform an unpleasant but necessary chore I
    a) think about all the reasons why I hate it and ways I can avoid doing it
    b) get right on and do it, so I can focus on doing something else that I do enjoy
    c) moan a bit, put it off as long as possible, then find it's not as bad as I thought it would be

5. When I have to perform an unfamiliar task I
    a) spend so much time feeling worried and unprepared that when I do begin, I feel rushed
    b) focus on completing the task to the best of my ability after a short preparation
    c) usually only feel ready to begin after considerable preparation

6. I evaluate the usefulness or nonusefulness of a task
    a) before, during, and after
    b) before
    c) rarely

7. I begin tasks without knowing why I am doing them
    a) always
    b) never
    c) sometimes

8. I have more than my fair share of problems
    a) strongly agree
    b) strongly disagree
    c) sometimes

RESULTS

Mostly As

You are highly problem-oriented. Life frequently feels like a succession of obstacles and inconveniences, often caused by other people. You regularly firefight instead of planning ahead. Sometimes you experience high levels of doubt and anxiety which prevent you from beginning and completing projects, and you often feel rushed. You rarely focus fully on a solution because you are distracted by the problem, ways to avoid it, and doubts about the usefulness of the task.

Mostly Bs

You are highly solution-oriented. You like and trust others and see problems as opportunities. You understand the importance of good preparation but you recognize that results are more important than the process. You establish the importance of a task at the start, so your motivation to complete it isn't hampered by doubts. You set clear goals and believe that you can achieve them.

Mostly Cs

You are a conscientious and fairly positive person but you experience bouts of self-doubt and procrastination. You can enjoy a challenge but sometimes you invest a little too much energy into preparation and reading around the subject, and rarely feel ready enough to tackle a new situation. When you finally start a project you have a tendency to enjoy the process more than finding a solution.

DIGITAL DILEMMA

You have 15 minutes to find a solution to this problem. While you work, try to be aware of the thoughts, positive and negative, that pop into your head and HOW you approach the problem, with respect to the issues raised in the questionnaire about being solution-oriented, anxiety levels, your motivation or lack of it, and your ability to stay focussed on the solution rather than being distracted by the usefulness of the task.

How can you use all the ascending consecutive digits 1, 2, 3, 4, 5, 6, 7, 8, 9, combined with any combination of just six plus or minus signs, to reach the total 100? (e.g. 1 + 23 - 4 + 5 . . .)

___ +/- ___ +/- ___ +/- ___ +/- ___ +/- ___ +/- ___ = 100

LOGICAL REASONING

IN ITS SIMPLEST DEFINITION, LOGICAL REASONING INVOLVES COMBINING A SET OF PREMISES TO REACH A LOGICALLY VALID CONCLUSION. IF THE PREMISES ARE TRUE, THEN THE CONCLUSION MUST ALSO BE TRUE.

Logic was studied and developed in many ancient civilizations, including India, China, and Persia, but the greatest influence on Western thought has been Aristotle, the ancient Greek philosopher, born in 384 BC, who is credited with inventing the formal discipline of logic.

Aristotle's followers (the Peripatetics) grouped together six of Aristotle's treatises under the title *Organon* (*Instrument*), which formed the basis of the earliest formal study of logic until the collapse of the Roman Empire 800 years later.

Islamic and Jewish scholars continued to translate and study the Greek texts during the Early Middle Ages, but most of Aristotle's logical works had to wait until the twelfth century to be translated into Latin (a revival known as the "Recovery of Aristotle"). Christian scholars such as Albertus Magnus and Thomas Aquinas then began to assimilate Aristotle's teaching into Christian theology, so by the sixteenth century his work had become intricately bound up with the Catholic Church, as sacred and untouchable as the Bible; anyone who challenged the authority of his teachings was persecuted as a heretic. The heresy of the Italian astronomer Galileo included the rejection of Aristotle's dynamics concerning the arrangement and movement of heavenly bodies and the notion of the heavens as a perfect, unchanging substance.

The Scientific Revolution and the Enlightenment challenged the authority of Aristotle and the Church in favor of reason and the advancement of knowledge through the scientific method. Despite this, Aristotle's logic remained the dominant form in the West until nineteenth-century advances in mathematical logic (most notably, the propositional calculus invented by the English mathematician George Boole—*see* page 44).

Logic is often broadly divided into three types: deductive reasoning, inductive reasoning, and abductive reasoning.

DEDUCTIVE REASONING

The basis of Aristotle's deductive argument was the syllogism, which has three parts: Major premise, minor premise, and conclusion. For example,

Premise 1: All A = B

Premise 2: All C = A

Conclusion: C = B

Major premise: All humans are mortal.

Minor premise: All Greeks are humans.

Conclusion: All Greeks are mortal.

Premise 1: No reptiles have fur.

Premise 2: All snakes are reptiles.

Conclusion: No snakes have fur.

In *Organon*, Aristotle gives the following definition: "A syllogism is discourse in which, certain things being stated, something other than what is stated follows of necessity from their being so. I mean by the last phrase that they produce a consequence, and by this, that no further term is required from without in order to make the consequence necessary."

In syllogistic logic, there are 256 possible ways to construct categorical syllogisms but only 24 of them can be described as "valid" (conclusion necessarily follows from the premises) and 19 of these are valid and "unweakened" (it is not possible to strengthen them by the substitution of a particular sentence [some] for a universal one [all] in the conclusion).

In all valid syllogisms, at least one of the two premises must contain a universal form (i.e. using the word "all"). If both premises are particulars (using the word "some"), then no valid conclusion can result from them. Also, at least one of the two premises must be affirmative.

Premise 1: Some dogs are dangerous.

Premise 2: Some dangerous things are volcanoes.

It does not follow that "some dogs are volcanoes" (because both premises are particulars).

However, a syllogism can still be logically valid without being true. For example, the conclusion in the following syllogism is logically valid and internally consistent, but untrue because it contains a "false premise" (since unicorns don't exist).

Premise 1: All unicorns are animals.

Premise 2: Some unicorns are invisible.

Conclusion: Some animals are invisible.

Try these syllogisms out for size (follow the logic, not the truth). Here is one example of each of the 19 valid and unweakened modes of the classical syllogism (which were each given a mnemonic name by medieval scholars):

Barbara

Premise 1: All birds have beaks.

Premise 2: All penguins are birds.

Conclusion: _____

Celarent

Premise 1: No birds have teeth.

Premise 2: All penguins are birds.

Conclusion: _____

Darii

Premise 1: All birds have feathers.

Premise 2: Some pets are birds.

Conclusion: _____

Ferio

Premise 1: No birds are dogs.

Premise 2: Some animals are birds.

Conclusion: _____

Cesare

Premise 1: No horse is a building.

Premise 2: All hotels are buildings.

Conclusion: _____

Camestres

Premise 1: All horses have hooves.

Premise 2: No carrots have hooves.

Conclusion: _____

Festino

Premise 1: No bald people are fat.

Premise 2: Some women are fat.

Conclusion: _____

Baroco

Premise 1: All carrots are vegetables.

Premise 2: Some pink things are not vegetables.

Conclusion: _____

Darapti

Premise 1: All fruit is nutritious.

Premise 2: All fruit is tasty.

Conclusion: _____

Disamis

Premise 1: Some butterflies are colorful.

Premise 2: All butterflies are delicate.

Conclusion: _____

Datisi

Premise 1: All gorillas are agile.

Premise 2: Some gorillas are endangered.

Conclusion: _____

Felapton

Premise 1: No fruit in this bowl is fresh.

Premise 2: All fruit in this bowl is yellow.

Conclusion: _____

Bocardo

Premise 1: Some cats have no tails.

Premise 2: All cats are animals.

Conclusion: _____

Ferison

Premise 1: No snakes have wheels.

Premise 2: Some snakes are green.

Conclusion: _____

Bramantip

Premise 1: All the socks in my drawer are purple.

Premise 2: All purple clothing is ostentatious.

Conclusion: _____

Camenes

Premise 1: All colored flowers are scented.

Premise 2: No scented flowers are grown indoors.

Conclusion: _____

Dimaris

Premise 1: Some big dogs like cheese.

Premise 2: All dogs that like cheese are friendly.

Conclusion: _____

Fesapo

Premise 1: No Hollywood actors are happy.

Premise 2: All happy people are neighborly.

Conclusion: _____

Fresison

Premise 1: No humans are pandas.

Premise 2: Some humans are evil.

Conclusion: _____

INDUCTIVE REASONING

Inductive reasoning involves deriving the general from the particular. It is the exact inverse of deduction, which involves deriving the particular from the general. Inductive reasoning requires guesswork to observe patterns in specific data, formulate a generalization from them, and then test this hypothesis to reach the most credible conclusion.

Unlike deductive reasoning, inductive reasoning provides a conclusion that is neither watertight nor inevitable, merely the most credible. Inductive reasoning relies on one or more premises that are generalizations rather than absolutes, so the conclusions merely give a strong indication of the truth rather than absolute certainty. There is always a possibility that the conclusion is false.

Statistical syllogisms are examples of inductive reasoning.

Premise 1: *Almost all A are B.*
Premise 2: *C is A.*
Conclusion: *Therefore C is almost certainly B.*

Premise 1: *Almost all birds can fly.*
Premise 2: *An eagle is a bird.*
Conclusion: *Therefore an eagle can almost certainly fly.*

Pick a breed of bird at random to replace eagle and you stand a good chance of your conclusion being correct. However, there are about 40 species of flightless birds in existence today (e.g. penguin, ostrich) and all baby birds are initially flightless, so even an eagle cannot be said with complete certainty to fly.

Inductive reasoning has been criticized by many logicians and philosophers. Philosophical Skepticism argues that nothing can be absolute or true with unconditional certainty because all human experience is subjective and incomplete. However, Immanuel Kant argued in his masterpiece *The Critique of Pure Reason* that this is precisely the reason why we must rely on both inductive and deductive reasoning, in his famous statement: "thoughts without content are empty, intuitions without concepts are blind." In other words, our subjective understanding of the external world is founded on experience (inductive reasoning) and *a priori* concepts (deductive reasoning).

Inductive reasoning is necessary because we don't know all the fundamental laws of nature so we have to guess and formulate generalizations from observation and then test them—this is the basis of the modern scientific method.

If all this philosophy is making your head spin, you can at least thank inductive reasoning for helping us all to stay sane! For example, we inductively reason that the sun will rise tomorrow because that's what it has done for every previous day of our lives and back through written history. When you take a trip in an airplane you invariably use inductive reasoning to reassure yourself that you will survive the flight, although you can't be 100 percent sure.

Premise 1: *The vast majority of plane flights do not result in a crash.*

Premise 2: *This is a plane flight.*

Conclusion: *It almost certainly will not result in a crash.*

Your plane NOT crashing is the pattern that best fits the observable data. How comforting!

INDUCTIVE REASONING TESTS

An inductive reasoning test is a common form of psychometric aptitude test used by employers, along with numerical and verbal reasoning. The most common form of inductive reasoning test involves spotting patterns in a series of graphics and finding the best match for the next in a sequence. Unlike deductive puzzles (such as Sudoku) where you can examine and discount possible outcomes one by one, inductive puzzles (such as cryptic crosswords) require you to create general conclusions from observable events and then test them. The reasoning is open and explorative.

Visual reasoning tests often include similar features: Items rotating, items being mirrored, details of a shape being added or subtracted (e.g. shapes adding or losing a side). Also, there may be as many as five separate rules governing the behavior of the items to create the pattern. If you can break down each puzzle into its components to identify individual rules, you can quickly narrow down possible solutions.

Here, there is only one rule: The shape loses one straight line every time.

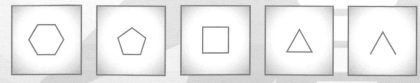

So the next in the series is

Now another rule has been added: The small shape alternates between being a triangle and a square.

So the next in the series is

Finally, a third rule has been added: There is a cross when both shapes have the same number of sides and a zero when they have different numbers of sides.

So the next in the series is

WHICH COMES NEXT IN THE SEQUENCE?

Look at the first five boxes then choose the next in the series from boxes A–E.

1.

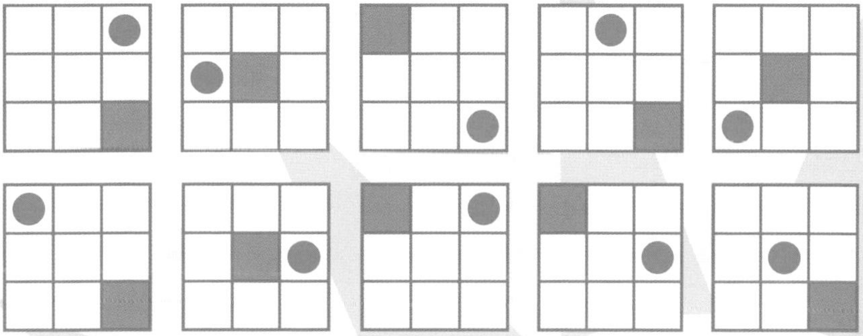

A   B   C   D   E

2.

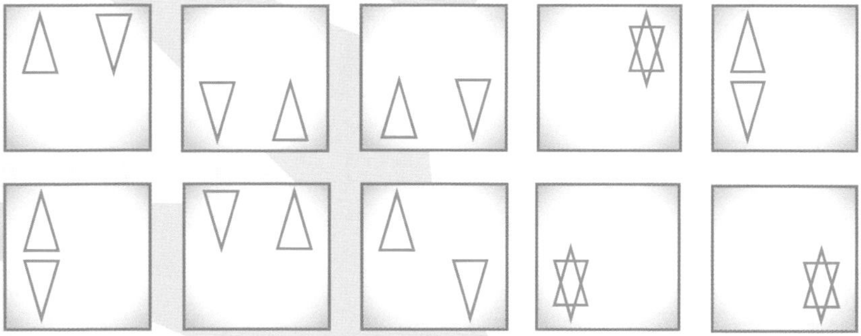

A   B   C   D   E

3.

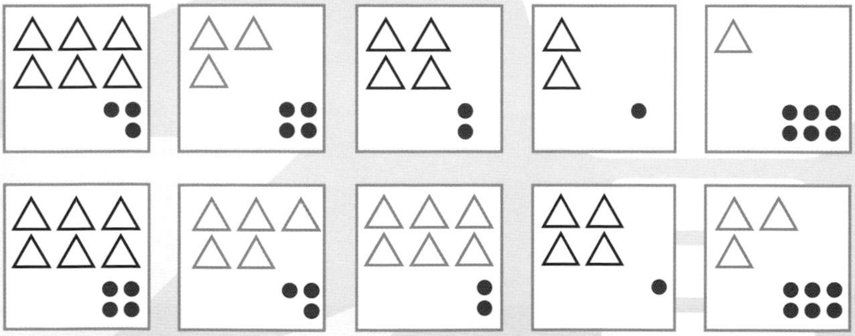

A   B   C   D   E

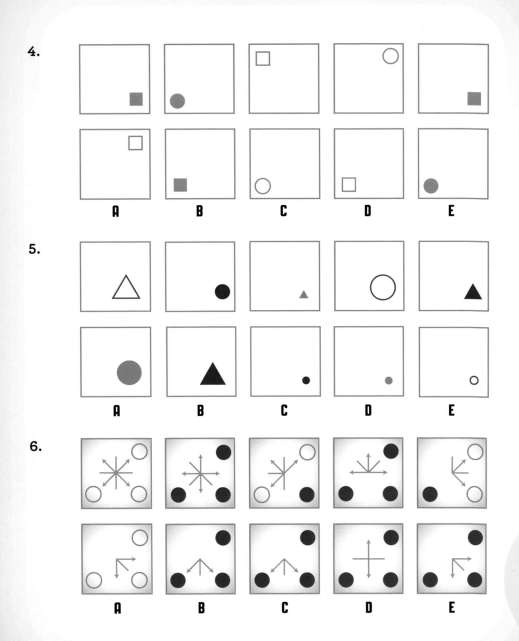

4.

A   B   C   D   E

5.

A   B   C   D   E

6.

A   B   C   D   E

7.

8.

9.

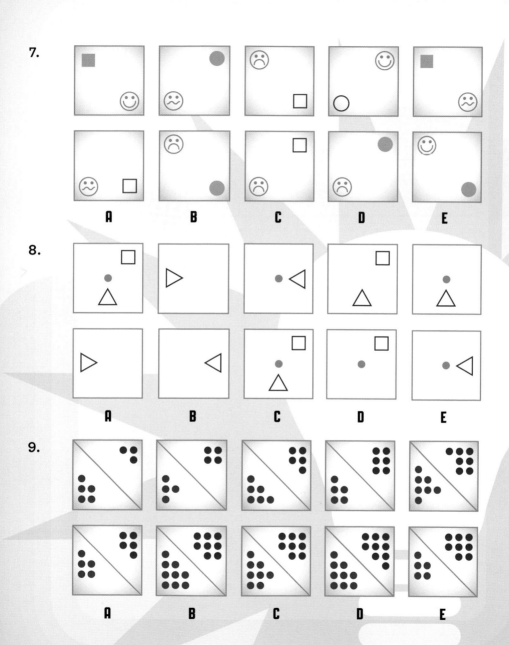

ABDUCTIVE REASONING

Abductive reasoning involves using observation of data to theorize the best explanation as to the cause of an observable set of data. Unlike deductive reasoning, conclusions from abductive reasoning may be false because there may be other causes.

For example, if the lawn is wet you may use abductive validation to theorize that it has recently rained, since it is a known rule that when it rains the grass gets wet. However, this may be a false conclusion. The lawn may be wet from dew or someone may have watered it with a hose. However, rain still remains a highly plausible solution. If you do not own a hose and it's winter, your rain hypothesis becomes even more plausible—it remains the simplest, most economical, and elegant explanation.

Despite infinite possible explanations for the hundreds of events that take place each day of our lives, we constantly use abductive reasoning to orient ourselves in our surroundings. It's a reasoning shorthand that encourages us to disregard the irrelevant causes of events, otherwise we would be unable to function. On a purely functional level, it wouldn't benefit us to infer from a wet lawn that aliens landed in a spaceship with water pistols; it's imaginative, but from an abductive perspective it's a highly implausible explanation. More valid hypotheses are given priority to save time and effort so we can get on with our busy lives.

A syllogistic representation of abductive reasoning is:

The fact C is observed;

But if A were true, C would be a matter of course,

Hence, there is reason to suspect that A is true.

The most direct application of abduction is to find faults in systems. When a problem is observed, abduction can be used to derive a set of faults that are likely to have caused it. It is used in medical diagnosis and in legal reasoning, although watch out for errors caused by, for example, "base rate fallacy" and "prosecutor's fallacy."

BASE RATE FALLACY

1. Police officers use roadside breathalyzers that show a false drunkenness five percent of the time but they are 100 percent reliable at detecting a genuinely drunk driver. One in two thousand drivers is driving over the legal limit. If a policeman has stopped a driver at random and the breathalyzer indicates that he or she is over the legal limit, what is the probability that this reading is genuine?

   a) lower than 1 percent

   b) 95 percent

   c) 96 percent

2. A city has 1 million inhabitants of which 100 are terrorists. Facial recognition surveillance equipment in the city is designed to trigger an alarm every time it detects a terrorist. However, there are two bugs in the software:

   Bug 1: False negative: If the camera scans a terrorist it will only trigger the alarm 99 percent of the time.

   Bug 2: False positive: If the camera scans a non-terrorist it will incorrectly trigger the alarm 1 percent of the time.

   The alarm sounds. What is the approximate probability that the inhabitant is a terrorist?

   a) 99 percent

   b) less than 1 percent

   c) 98 percent

PROSECUTOR'S FALLACY

A man is on trial for murder. The defendant shares the same rare blood type as the perpetrator (blood was found at the crime scene) and just 1 percent of the population of 300 million. Setting all other evidence aside, what is the probability that the man is guilty based on the blood type match alone?

a) 10 percent

b) 99 percent

c) 0.00003333 percent

BOOLEAN LOGIC

Boolean logic is a subarea of algebra that was originally developed in the nineteenth century by the English mathematician, philosopher, and logician, George Boole.

The elementary algebra we learn at school uses variables to denote mainly numbers (e.g. x^2 + 2y = z) and the main operations are addition, subtraction, multiplication, and division. In Boolean algebra, the variables are the truth values TRUE (1) and FALSE (0) and the three fundamental operations are AND (∧), OR (∨), and NOT (¬).

AND (∧)

This operator takes two inputs and returns a "true" (1) output only when BOTH of the inputs are true (1).

So if you have the inputs A and B and perform the operation AND on them (A ∧ B) there are four possible combinations, but only one of them produces a "true" (1) result.

A	B	A ∧ B
False (0)	False (0)	False (0)
False (0)	True (1)	False (0)
True (1)	False (0)	False (0)
True (1)	True (1)	True (1)

OR (∨)

This operator takes two inputs and returns a "true" (1) output when ONE or BOTH of the inputs are true.

A	B	A ∨ B
False (0)	False (0)	False (0)
False (0)	True (1)	True (1)
True (1)	False (0)	True (1)
True (1)	True (1)	True (1)

NOT (¬)

This operator takes an input and returns the OPPOSITE, so a "true" (1) input returns a "false" (0) output, and a "false" (0) input returns a "true" (1) output.

A	A¬
False (0)	True (1)
True (1)	False (0)

These three operators are then combined to create more complex digital circuits.

So, for example, the statement "If A and B are true or C is true, then Q is true" could be expressed with this truth table, showing all the possible combinations:

A	B	C	Q (A ∧ B ∨ C)
False (0)	False (0)	False (0)	False (0)
False (0)	False (0)	True (1)	True (1)
False (0)	True (1)	False (0)	False (0)
False (0)	True (1)	True (1)	True (1)
True (1)	False (0)	False (0)	False (0)
True (1)	False (0)	True (1)	True (1)
True (1)	True (1)	False (0)	True (1)
True (1)	True (1)	True (1)	True (1)

So what is the practical application? Boolean logic is the basis for modern digital computers. Here are two examples of Boolean logic at work:

SODA DRINK DISPENSER

A = Coin is inserted

B = Drink button is pressed

The program inside the machine knows that when A and B occur (A ∧ B), it should dispense a drink (Q). The circuit uses a simple AND operation to decide whether or not to dispense a soda. Both events must be true for Q to take place.

THE FAMOUS TWO DOORS PUZZLE

You are faced with two doors and two guards. One guard always tells the truth and the other guard always lies. You don't know which guard is which. One door leads to Heaven, the other to Hell. You must choose a guard and may ask just one question to which the guard may only reply "Yes" or "No."

Most people are familiar with this puzzle. It has appeared in various forms in popular culture including the *Doctor Who* story "Pyramids of Mars" and the film *Labyrinth*. The question you should ask is "If I asked the other guard if this door leads to Heaven, what would he tell me?"

Using the AND operation, it is clear that you will only get a true result when all the constituent variables are true and a false result otherwise. In other words, the only way you can guarantee a truthful answer is if both guards told the truth. Since you know this isn't the case and also, that both guards can't be liars, the only remaining options return a False result. So, if the guard says "yes," you should choose the other door; if the guard says "no," you should choose that door.

Guard A	Guard B	A ^ B
False (0)	False (0)	False (0)
False (0)	**True (1)**	**False (0)**
True (1)	**False (0)**	**False (0)**
True (1)	True (1)	True (1)

THESE PUZZLES CAN ALSO BE SOLVED USING BOOLEAN LOGIC

1. Inspector Hercule Poirot interrogates two suspects of the theft of the Hope Diamond.

    Bonnie declares: "Both Clyde and I are guilty."

    Clyde protests: "Bonnie stole it."

    If one of them is lying and the other one is telling the truth, who stole the diamond?

2. John says: "My wife and I are both liars."

    Who is what?

3. There are three boxes. One is labeled "NUTS," another is labeled "BOLTS," and the third is labeled "NUTS AND BOLTS." You know that each box is labeled incorrectly. You may pick just one item from one single box. How can you label the boxes correctly?

GEOMETRIC REASONING

Geometry is a branch of mathematics that focusses upon shape, size, relative position of figures, and the properties of space. It first developed in several ancient cultures to deal with everyday issues such as lengths, areas, and volumes, and it began to emerge in the West as a formal mathematical discipline in the sixth century BC with Thales, one of the Seven Sages of ancient Greece. The word "geometry" derives from the Greek *geo* (earth) and *metron* (measure).

The acknowledged Father of Geometry was the Greek mathematician Euclid, who worked in Alexandria, Egypt, in the third century BC. His 13-volume *Elements* is one of the most important books in the history of mathematics. Euclid was the first mathematician to write down a small group of axioms and then use them to deduce many other propositions. An axiom is a statement which is regarded as being self-evidently true and it is the product of inductive reasoning (*see* page 36). Euclid based his entire system of geometry on just five axioms and five "common notions."

AXIOMS

1. A straight line can be drawn between any two points.

2. A finite line can be extended infinitely in both directions.

3. A circle can be drawn with any center and any radius.

4. All right angles are equal to each other.

5. Given a line and a point not on the line, only one line can be drawn through the point parallel to the line.

COMMON NOTIONS

1. Things which are equal to the same thing are also equal to one another.

2. If equals are added to equals, the wholes are equal.

3. If equals are subtracted from equals, the remainders are equal.

4. Things which coincide with one another are equal to one another.

5. The whole is greater than the part.

The fifth axiom, known as the "parallel postulate," became famous because mathematicians spent the next two thousand years trying to prove it. Finally, in the early nineteenth century, a young Hungarian prodigy named János Bolyai moved beyond the parallel postulate and the results were quite literally explosive.

Bolyai had spent more than ten years obsessed with Euclid's parallel postulate. In 1832, at the age of 30, he published a treatise describing his system of revolutionary non-Euclidian geometry based on a different description of parallel lines. "I created a new, different world out of nothing," he wrote to his father, which was an understatement.

Russian mathematician Nikolai Lobachevsky had also published a similar piece of work three years earlier. The Bolyai–Lobachevsky departure from Euclid, along with the work of the contemporary 55-year-old German genius Carl Friedrich Gauss (who had also been obsessed with the problem for 35 years), was a colossal mathematical breakthrough.

Thanks to Bolyai-Lobachevsky and Gauss, the mathematical tools existed to enable Einstein to develop the idea of curved space-time and his Theory of General Relativity, which in turn led to the creation of the atomic bomb.

GEOMETRICAL MAGIC

Geometry is an awesome tool that allows mathematicians to become the creators and destroyers of worlds. Or for those whose ambitions are more modest, it allows us to create and perform some baffling magic tricks, including the famous 64 = 65 Geometry Paradox:

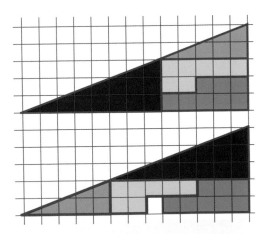

Where does the hole in the second triangle come from (the partitions are the same)?

Geometry can explain the apparent paradox. In fact, the edges of the four shapes do not lie along a straight line. The diagonal line is not a line at all; it is a shape—a lozenge (diamond-shaped figure)—whose area exactly matches the so-called "missing" square.

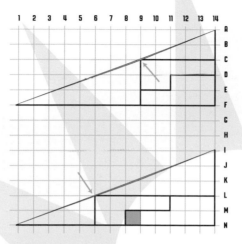

SEVEN GEOMETRY PUZZLES

Try tackling these geometric brain teasers. Don't worry—you don't need to have any prior knowledge of geometry.

1. A castle is surrounded by a moat that is 4 yards wide with a 90-degree turn. You have only two planks, each of which is 3.9 yards long. How can you cross the moat right now using just the planks laid flat?

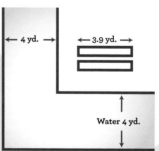

2. Place 10 balls in 5 lines in such a way that each line has exactly 4 balls on it.

3. Why is it better to have round manhole covers than square ones?

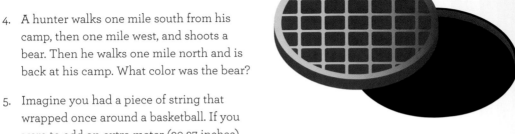

4. A hunter walks one mile south from his camp, then one mile west, and shoots a bear. Then he walks one mile north and is back at his camp. What color was the bear?

5. Imagine you had a piece of string that wrapped once around a basketball. If you were to add an extra meter (39.37 inches) of length to the string, there would be a gap of 15.92 cm (6.27 inches) between the ball and the string.

   Now imagine you had a piece of string that was long enough to wrap around the equator of the earth (40,075 km/24,901 miles). If you were to add another 1 meter in length to this string, how high off the ground would the string be now?

   a) 15.92 cm (6.27 inches)

   b) 0.00000000000000001 cm

   c) 0.0000001 cm

   Hint: The only equation you need to solve this problem is $r = c/2\Pi$ (where r is the radius, c is the circumference, and Π is 3.14).

6. How can you create 8 equilateral triangles with 6 popsicle sticks (without breaking any)?

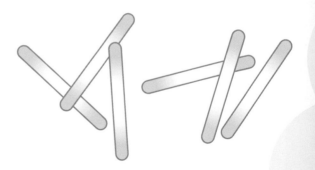

7. Four people go out for lunch and share a large pizza. They divide it into equal parts with five straight cuts and each gets three pieces. How?

SPATIAL THINKING

Spatial thinking is the ability to visualize with the mind's eye, to solve spatial problems, imagine and manipulate objects in space. It is crucial to problem solving and deeply embedded in the activities of daily life, from filling the dishwasher to fitting a child safety seat into a car.

Some of the greatest thinkers in history possessed staggering powers of spatial visualization. Nikola Tesla, one of the greatest electrical inventors who ever lived, is reputed to have been able to visualize every part of a working engine in his mind and mentally test each component. Watson and Crick discovered the molecular structure of DNA by imagining and building a three-dimensional model to reveal that the long chain molecules form a double helix—marking one of the greatest achievements of twentieth-century science.

Research has shown that children and adults alike can improve their spatial thinking with practice. Even playing the block-manipulating computer game Tetris creates dramatic improvements in spatial thinking that are long-lasting and transferable to other situations.

1. TWO-DIMENSIONAL SPATIAL VISUALIZATION

Choose the drawing that matches the shape after it has been rotated 180 degrees.

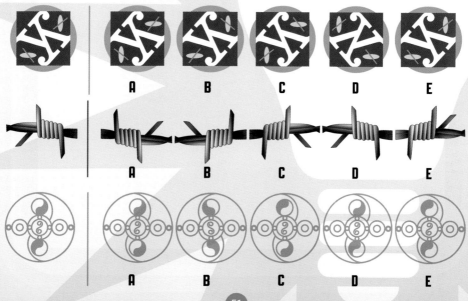

A   B   C   D   E

A   B   C   D   E

A   B   C   D   E

2. THREE-DIMENSIONAL SPATIAL VISUALIZATION

Which of the five objects can be assembled from the flat cardboard?

(Fold so the dotted lines are on the outside of the 3-D shape).

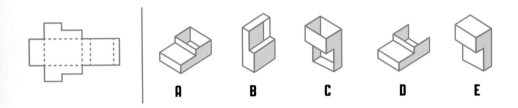

Only two of the shapes are identical to the original. Which are they?

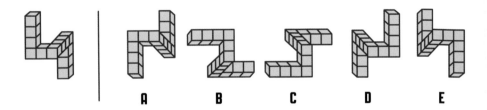

Which shape matches the original?

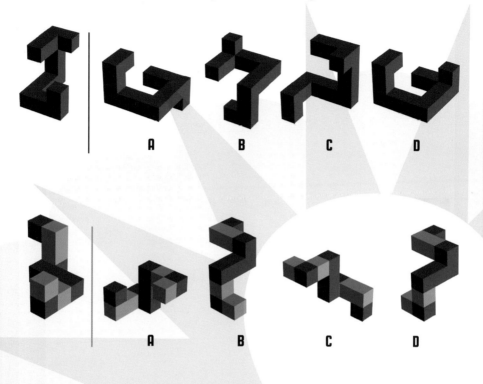

A   B   C   D

A   B   C   D

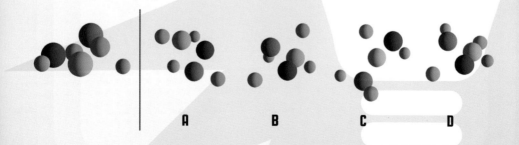

A   B   C   D

The three shapes below are standing on a glass table—what is
the view looking up from below the table?

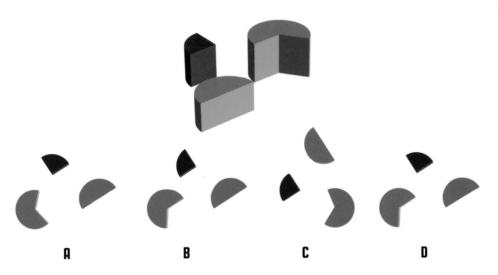

A   B   C   D

Which is the odd one out?

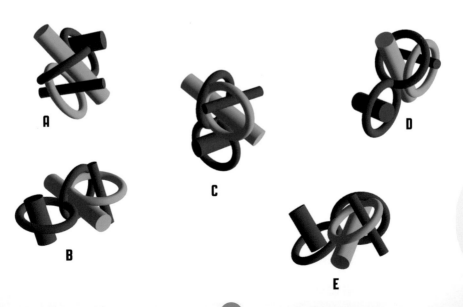

A

B

C

D

E

LATERAL THINKING

According to its inventor, the Maltese doctor and author Edward de Bono, the term "lateral thinking" was created in 1967; it first appeared in his worldwide bestseller *The Use of Lateral Thinking*.

The key principle behind lateral thinking can be summed up by his maxim: "You cannot dig a hole in a different place by digging the same hole deeper," which means that you cannot solve a problem by repeating the same strategy (because the creative breakthrough is often the result of effort focussed in a different direction). This requires you to change concepts and preconceptions: "We assume certain perceptions, certain concepts, and certain boundaries. Lateral thinking is concerned not with playing with the existing pieces but with seeking to change those very pieces."

In school we are taught to face problems head-on using what de Bono calls "vertical thinking" but the brain is "a self-organizing information system" which "forms asymmetric patterns" and "in such systems there is a mathematical need for moving across patterns." Lateral thinking aims to address this need.

LATERAL THINKING TECHNIQUES

Alternatives: Look for alternative solutions and concepts even when doing so isn't urgent. Looking beyond the obvious systemic solutions generates a network of creative branches to explore.

Focus: Make a deliberate effort to focus on areas that no one else has thought about.

Challenge current thinking: The "If it ain't broke, don't fix it" mentality means that we don't question the status quo; we assume that the existing solutions are adequate because they appear to be working satisfactorily. However, if you break the inertia by working from the assumption that the current solution is not optimal, you can find a better solution that no one has bothered to consider before.

Random entry: Introduce random input to encourage new associations. For example, when brainstorming a problem or idea, open a book at a random page, pick a word, and introduce that word into the thinking process; often the juxtaposition of the new word can unlock your creativity.

Provocation: Generate deliberately unreasonable, provocative, or hyperbolic statements and use them to build new ideas.

Here is a classic example of a lateral thinking brainteaser with which you may already be familiar:

> *A father and his son have a car accident and the son is rushed to the hospital for emergency surgery. The surgeon looks at him and says, "I can't operate on him, he's my son." Explain.*

The surgeon is, of course, his mother. It is a classic illustration of how we can solve problems by challenging our assumptions and prejudices. Many lateral thinking problems are designed to exploit one or more assumptions, or they establish an initial detail that is overlooked when reading the whole problem. Here's a slightly different problem:

> *A trainee airline pilot had just completed a long-haul flight to Sydney, Australia, when he met the captain wearing a dress in the hotel bar. What should he do?*

Join her for a drink, maybe? Did you make the same gender stereotype mistake again? Different problem, same assumption!

> *Romeo and Juliet lie dead on the floor. There is water and glass strewn around their unclothed bodies. Why did they die?*

Here we make the assumption that Romeo and Juliet are humans, which is reinforced by the word "unclothed." They are goldfish.

It's also important to read the question carefully. Many lateral thinking problems rely on the reader missing obvious details:

1. To the nearest cubic inch, how much soil is there in a 3 yards x 2 yards x 2 yards hole?

2. A farmer has 15 cows; all but 8 die. How many does he have left?

3. John's mother has three children. One is named April, one is named May. What is the third one named?

If your answers are 12 cubic yards, 7, and June, reread the questions—slowly.

Our assumptions are usually the product of abductive reasoning (*see* page 42) which is useful in day-to-day situations, but a hindrance when trying to think laterally.

Can you solve these conundrums with some lateral thinking? Beware—some of the answers are rather outlandish!

1. Name an ancient invention still in use in most parts of the world today that lets people see through walls.

2. Deep in the forest a man's body was found. He was wearing only swimming trunks, snorkel, and facemask. The nearest lake was 10 miles away and the ocean was 100 miles away. How did he die?

3. A man dies of thirst in his own home. How?

4. How could a toddler fall out of a thirty-story building onto the ground and survive?

5. A man wants to build a house, so he asks for quotes from one hundred builders, each of which claims to be the best builder in the area. Getting the best builder possible is more important to him than price, so how does he choose between them?

6. A seven-foot-tall man is holding a glass mug above his head. He drops it on the carpet without spilling a single drop of water. How?

7. A traffic cop sees a truck driver going the wrong way down a one-way street, but doesn't arrest him. Why?

8. A man is found dead in a field. He is holding a broken match. What happened?

9. There are six eggs in the basket. Six people each take one of the eggs but one egg is left in the basket. How can this be?

10. A man drank some of the punch at a party, then he left early. Everyone else who drank the punch died of poisoning, but the man was unharmed. Why?

11. When Archduke Ferdinand was shot, his attendants could not undo his coat to stop the bleeding. Why not? (True story.)

12. A man lies dead in a room. There is a net basket on the floor containing gold and jewels, a chandelier attached to the ceiling, and a large open window. How did he die?

13. Tommy's mother told him never to open the cellar door. One day while she was out, the cellar door opened and Tommy saw a man kneeling and smiling at him. What was the man wearing?

14. A woman called the waiter in a restaurant. She told him there was a fly in her tea. The waiter took it away and brought her a fresh cup. After a few moments the woman knew it was the same cup of tea. How?

15. What happened in the year 1961 that won't occur again for almost another 4,000 years?

16. A man was walking downstairs in a building when he suddenly realized that his wife had just died. How?

17. How long is a piece of string?

18. Acting on an anonymous tip-off, police raid a house to arrest a suspected terrorist. All they know is that his name is Joaquín and that he is inside the building. Inside the house they find a carpenter, a truck driver, a mechanic, a wrestler, an astronaut, and a man with a beard all playing poker. They immediately arrest the bearded man. How did they know he was the terrorist?

19. Two drivers stop at a traffic light which is on red. A nearby police officer immediately arrests one of the drivers. Why?

20. Why does an old lady always answer the door wearing her hat and coat?

21. A blind beggar had a brother who died. What relation was the blind beggar to the brother who died? (Brother is not the answer.)

22. If a plane crashes on the Italian/Swiss border, where do you bury the survivors?

23. As I was going to St. Ives, I met a man with seven wives; Each wife had seven sacks; Each sack had seven cats; Each cat had seven kits: Kits, cats, sacks, and wives; How many were going to St. Ives?

24. A man is lying dead in a field. Next to him there is an unopened package. There is no other animal in the field. How did he die?

25. The music stopped. She died. Explain.

26. A man walks into a bar and asks for a glass of water. The barman pulls out a gun and points it at the man. The man thanks him and walks out. Why?

27. The most boring man in the world was on his way home in a taxi. The taxi driver pretended to be deaf and dumb so he wouldn't have to engage him in conversation. They reached the destination, the most boring man in the world paid the fare and opened his front door. Then he realized that the taxi driver had been pretending. How?

28. Alison lives in a remote part of the Australian outback. She wants a tattoo so she visits the only two tattoo artists for 500 miles. Both of them are covered in impressive tattoos, but the clincher is a magnificent eagle, with wings outstretched between the shoulder blades of the second tattoo artist. Despite this demonstration of breathtaking artistry, she decides to hire the first one instead. Why?

PARALLEL THINKING

Parallel thinking is another technique that was invented by the Maltese doctor and author Edward de Bono. The system is the direct opposite of dialectic or adversarial methods which take the form of argument and counterargument, the most famous of which is Socratic debate.

In Socratic debate, a discussion takes place between two or more individuals, based on asking and answering questions that challenge and explore beliefs in an attempt to highlight inconsistencies within a particular viewpoint. This leads to better hypotheses that are based on reason, rather than what the classical Greek philosopher Socrates considered to be the rhetoric and clever oratorical and philosophical tricks employed by the sophists, who preceded him.

Parallel thinking is more collaborative and nonconfrontational. Several thinkers put forward hypotheses and ideas in parallel, helping to guide the discussion in one direction at a time so that each issue can be explored more fully, rather than try to score points over opponents or charm them with clever oratory.

The most famous parallel thinking (or multiperspective analysis) system is de Bono's "Six Thinking Hats" method. When faced with a problem, one by one put on each of the differently colored thinking hats and approach the problem from a different viewpoint.

White Hat: Facts and figures

This is the number crunching, data collecting, researching hat that gathers all the available information related to the issue. It looks at past trends and analyzes previous results/performance. It asks what information you have and what more information you need.

Red Hat: Emotions and feelings

The wearer of this hat approaches the problem using intuition, emotion, and gut instinct. It also looks outward to other people and empathizes with their feelings and opinions.

Black Hat: Cautious and careful

Wearing the black hat makes you anticipate obstacles, negative consequences, and risks, and explore contingency plans. It focusses solely on weak points, failures, and underperformance. De Bono has said that within the context of the other five hats, the black hat can be the most productive, and help to counter too much yellow hat thinking.

Green Hat: Creative thinking

The green hat looks for creative solutions, alternatives, new ideas, and possibilities. It is nonjudgmental and does not self-censor.

Yellow Hat: Speculative-Positive

Wearing the yellow hat makes you see only the positives and the benefits; it mitigates risks, and views obstacles as challenges to be overcome. However, it isn't just blind optimism, since it should still be supported by analytical and strategic thinking.

Blue Hat: Control of thinking

The blue hat is process control. It sets out the agenda, maintains group focus, oversees the other hats, and acts as a chairperson, helping to consolidate information, note conclusions, and formulate action points.

HERE ARE TEN QUESTIONS TO WHICH YOU SHOULD APPLY PARALLEL THINKING TO FIND A SOLUTION:

1. How can I get myself a 25 percent raise in pay?

2. How can I improve by two levels at school?

3. How can I find someone to spend the rest of my life with?

4. Should I stay in this marriage and try to work things out?

5. What's the best way to improve my health and wellbeing?

6. Should we have another baby?

7. How can I free up some leisure time?

8. What are five effective ways to do my bit for the environment?

9. Where should I go for vacation next year?

10. Should I buy a dog?

SIMPLE SOLUTIONS
ARE BEST

Human delight in simplicity is ubiquitous and is expressed in every discipline from philosophy, epistemology (the study of the theory of knowledge), and theology, to science and art. According to St. Thomas Aquinas, "God is infinitely simple." The Italian Renaissance polymath Leonardo da Vinci considered simplicity to be "the ultimate sophistication." Scientists often talk about scientific and mathematical theories being beautiful and simple, and they aim to make them as simple as possible without sacrificing accuracy or crucial meaning.

Albert Einstein famously said, "If you can't explain it to a six-year-old, you don't understand it yourself." This is worth bearing in mind whenever you are grappling with complex ideas.

The heuristic argument that simple solutions are the best is often referred to as "Occam's Razor," named after William of Ockham, the medieval English Franciscan friar who invented it. It is the principle that when you have competing hypotheses, you should choose the one with the fewest assumptions and variable parameters. The more assumptions that you make and the more adjustable parameters you introduce, the greater the possibility for error and inaccuracy in the end result.

As we have seen in earlier chapters (*see* pages 36 and 42), our preference for simplicity is a fundamental component of inductive and abductive reasoning, but just because something is simple doesn't mean that it is always right and, conversely, just because something is complicated doesn't mean we should dismiss it outright. One of the main arguments that Creationists make against the theory of evolution is that it couldn't create creatures of such variety and detail. Of course, the irony is that the theory's simplicity is its greatest strength, and accounts for why nature can be so complicated and how life on earth has developed from single-celled organisms to creatures of increasing complexity.

Isaac Newton's Theory of Gravity has been superseded by Einstein's Theory of General Relativity and ever more complex theories such as Superstring Theory, but it is still used because it is simpler and still gives sufficiently accurate results for many gravitational calculations. So even when a simple solution is replaced by a more complex one, we have a preference for simplicity over accuracy to solve everyday problems.

So, despite its limitations, Occam's Razor or the acronym KISS (keep it simple, stupid) still remain useful principles to follow when you are trying to solve problems and puzzles. But if a more complex system does a better job, use that one instead. Don't get so hung up on simplicity that you avoid complexity. Maybe the best way to approach Occam's Razor is to follow the advice of twentieth-century English mathematician and philosopher Alfred North Whitehead, the founder of the philosophical school known as process philosophy, who advised: "Seek simplicity and distrust it."

THE SEVEN BRIDGES OF KÖNIGSBERG

The old town of Königsberg, now Kaliningrad in Russia, has seven bridges. Can you take a walk through the town, fully crossing each bridge once and only once? (You may only cross a river by bridge. No jumping or swimming allowed!)

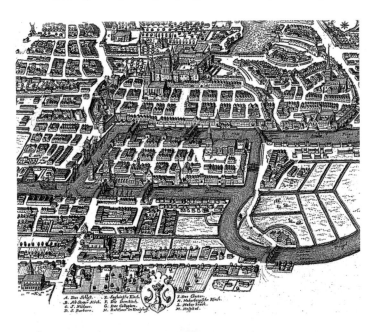

FIVE ROOM PUZZLE

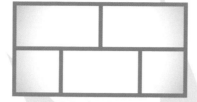

A large rectangular house is divided into five rooms. Can a ghost walk through each wall in a continuous line only once?

FOUR FORWARD-THINKING CAMELS

Four forward-thinking camels were traveling along a very narrow mountainside ledge when they encountered another four forward-thinking camels approaching from the opposite direction. Everyone knows that forward-thinking camels have no reverse gear, but they will climb over another camel, as long as there is a camel-sized space on the other side.

Both camel quartets stop, facing each other, with exactly one camel's width between them. How can all the camels continue on their journey without any camel reversing (or jumping off the ledge)?

These puzzles are a good illustration that simple solutions are the best. The smarter you are and the higher your level of formal education, the more difficulty you will have calculating the answer. So keep your reasoning simple.

1. How can you throw a ball as hard as you can and ensure that it comes back to you even if it doesn't hit anything, there is no string or elastic attached to it, and no one else throws or catches it?

2. What is the pattern here? bun, stew, ghee, pour, chive, mix, leaven, weight, dine, hen.

3. Copernican Revolution

The first roll of the dice scores two.

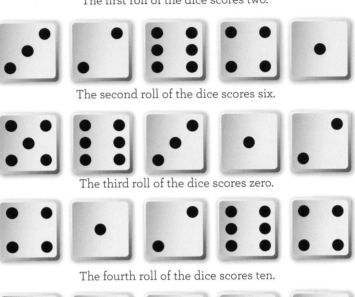

The second roll of the dice scores six.

The third roll of the dice scores zero.

The fourth roll of the dice scores ten.

The fifth roll of the dice scores four.

What does this score?

VERBAL REASONING

Verbal reasoning is thinking with words, the ability to understand written information and to make reasoned conclusions using concepts framed in language. The ability to think constructively is even more important than language fluency (*see* page 69) and vocabulary knowledge (*see* page 74) and it is more than simply being good at literacy.

Verbal reasoning tests are widely used by employers and you can significantly improve your score with practice; there are scores of sample tests available online (google "verbal reasoning tests"). The tests are time restricted, so familiarity with the format will allow you to focus solely on your performance and give you a distinct advantage over more confident candidates with innate ability but less preparation.

When completing a verbal reasoning test, follow these five tips:

1. KEEP CALM

Verbal reasoning tests are usually timed, which adds pressure, so apart from practice, staying calm is the single most important way to maintain focus and boost your performance. No one can concentrate when they are agitated, so control your emotions.

2. READ THE STATEMENT TWO OR THREE TIMES

Don't rush. If you rush the reading stage and start answering the questions too early, you will waste more time rereading because you haven't assimilated the finer details. It's more time efficient to read the passage three times at the beginning, rather than have to keep returning to the text later. However, you may benefit from quickly skimming the passage once, to pick out key words and to provide context, before making your two to three detailed readings.

3. MAKE SENSE OF CONVOLUTED TEXT BY STARTING AT THE END OF THE SENTENCE

This trick helps you understand complicated sentences containing several subclauses.

4. DON'T WASTE ALL YOUR TIME ON ONE QUESTION

If you are really stuck, move on to the next question; it's better to drop one point than ten. You don't lose a grade for skipping questions.

5. MAKE NO ASSUMPTIONS

Base your reasoning only on information contained within the text. This is NOT a test of your general knowledge.

1. Three words are related and two do NOT go with the other three—which two?

   angle, fish, pushover, tackle, rugby   Answer: _____   _____

   dough, maiden, batter, whisk, duck   Answer: _____   _____

   chinook, confluence, drizzle, gale, precipitate   Answer: _____   _____

2. Find a common single word that goes with each trio to form a new word or phrase:

blue	motion	drop
cake	worm	off
cottage	down	stand
_____	_____	_____

3. PREVARICATE is to EVADE as TAXONOMY is to:

   a) vary

   b) innovation

   c) modulation

   d) development

   e) classification

4. Which two words are closest in meaning?

   SOPORIFIC, MAUDLIN, SOOTHING, EXHAUSTED, APOLOGETIC

5. Which two words are the most nearly opposite in meaning?

   TRIBULATION, ADMONISH, CONTENTMENT, REPROVE, EXHORT

6. Add one letter to each word to find two areas that are susceptible to flooding.

   MASH   SWAP

7. What is the longest word that can be produced from these ten letters?

   ICAEORTSAB

8. Solve the clues to find five six-letter words. The same three-letter word is represented by 123 in each case.

123 * * * box or container

* 1 2 3 * * Egyptian amulet

* * 1 2 3 * Church of England priests

* * * 1 2 3 surgical instrument

9. Solve the puzzle using one letter:

hrif

ypis

orren

antamoun

10. Solve the puzzle using the same two letters for all the words in each list:

uli _estie_

eacu _appe_

oysho _ephy_

reeto _ippe_

rollo _ithe_

11. Solve the puzzle using the same three letters for all the words in each list:

_i_h_p _d_g_os

_i_s_l _t_v_sm

_i_l_y _c_c_as

  _v_r_ce

12. You have five minutes to read the passage and answer the ten questions below.

Returning to civilian life he took up his quest again, varying a general medical and surgical practice by continued observation and experiment in gland-transplantations upon animals, leaning ever more strongly towards the exclusive use of goats. About this time he heard of the work of Professor Steinach of Vienna in grafting the glands of rats, and producing changes in the character and appearance of the animals by inverting the process of nature and transplanting male glands into females, and vice versa, sometimes with success. He had followed with the greatest interest also the experiments of Dr. Frank Lydston of Chicago, who performed his first human-gland transplantation upon himself, an example of courage that falls not far short of heroism. But Dr. Brinkley was never favorably impressed with the idea of using the glands of a human being for the renovation of the life-force of another human being. He was looking to the young of the animal kingdom to furnish him with the material he proposed to use to improve the functioning of human organs, and more certainly as time passed he drew to the conclusion that in the goat, and in the goat alone, was to be found that gland-tissue which, because of its rapid maturity, potency, and freedom from those diseases to which humanity is liable, was most sure under right conditions of implantation to feed, nourish, grow into and become a part of, human gland-tissue.

[*The Goat-Gland Transplantation* by Sydney B. Flower, 1921]

Answer using a, b, or c:

   a) True (the statement follows logically from the information contained in the passage)

   b) False (the statement is logically false from the information contained in the passage)

   c) Cannot say (cannot determine whether the statement is true or false without additional information)

1. Dr. Brinkley had experimented with gland transplantation upon animals other than goats in the past.

2. Dr. Frank Lydston performed the first human-gland transplantation.

3. Dr. Brinkley considered Professor Steinach a hero.

4. Dr. Brinkley reached the conclusion that the goat was the only animal from which it was suitable to harvest glands capable of becoming a part of human gland-tissue.

5. Dr. Brinkley heard about the work of Professor Steinach of Vienna before his return to civilian life.

6. Dr. Brinkley strongly disapproved of the work of Dr. Frank Lydston.

7. Professor Steinach had some success in transplanting glands between male and female goats.

8. Steinach exclusively transplanted male glands into females.

9. Dr. Brinkley liked Dr. Frank Lydston.

10. Dr. Frank Lydston and Dr. Brinkley had never met in person.

VERBAL FLUENCY

Verbal fluency relies on semantic (meaning) memory and phonemic (word sounds) memory. It is measured by a verbal fluency test which generally involves listing as many different items in a group as possible within a time limit—often one minute.

Neuropsychological research shows that this task activates both frontal and temporal lobe areas of the brain. The frontal lobe is important for the phonemic component and the temporal lobe processes the semantic modifications. Tests on thousands of people, children and adults, have revealed that healthy individuals share several performance characteristics:

1. The rate at which new words are produced declines hyperbolically during the test.

2. Most of us say the more obvious words early on in the test (and repeat them more often) before moving on to less common words.

3. We produce clusters of words, linked by meaning and sound. If the category was "animal," saying "cow" usually triggers a cascade of farm animals—"sheep, pig, goat"—and saying "cat" leads to a cluster of domestic pets—"dog, rabbit, bird, hamster, mouse, gerbil, goldfish."

The diagram is a cluster analysis of animal semantic fluency data from 55 British schoolchildren of ages 7–8. Notice that the animals cluster according to the environmental context in which they are observed—**farm, home, ocean, zoo**. This cluster pattern forms in childhood and stays with us for the rest of our lives. Verbal fluency tests on adults and even zoology PhD students have produced identical schematic results.

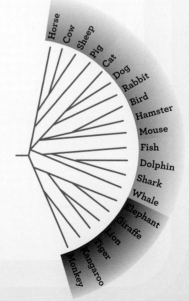

The patterns of recall are so predictable that deviation from these norms is usually a sign of cognitive impairment, caused by brain injury (especially lesions on the frontal lobe) or neurological conditions and disorders. So verbal fluency tests are a useful clinical diagnostic tool and are quite accurate in screening for dementia.

The COWAT (Controlled Oral Word Association Task) is a cognitive test of verbal processing ability used to assess brain impairment. The most common letters chosen are F, A, and S. A score of under 17 indicates concern, although some physicians use 14 as a cutoff.

1. PERFORM YOUR OWN CLUSTER ANALYSIS

Take a group of friends, coworkers, or members of your family and give them one minute to silently write down a vertical list of as many animals as they can. Now compare the results and you will see this clustering at work.

2. ELEPHANTS IN DENMARK

This trick relies on this memory-clustering phenomenon and some mathematical direction to showcase your mind-reading ability.

Read these instructions to your audience, pausing after each one to give them time to make the necessary calculations:

1. Pick a number between 2 and 9. It can be 2 or it can be 9, or any number in between.

2. Multiply your number by 9.

3. Now you have a two-digit number. Add the digits together.

4. Subtract 5.

5. Now find the letter that corresponds with your result. A = 1, B = 2, C = 3, etc.

6. Think of a country that begins with your letter. For example, "C" might make you think of Canada or "F" could be France.

7. Take the second letter in the name of that country and think of an animal.

8. Now close your eyes and visualize your animal while I read your mind.

9. Say, "I DIDN'T KNOW THAT THERE WERE ELEPHANTS IN DENMARK."

THE HUMAN
SPELLCHECKER

If you rely on the spellchecker in your word processing software to spot all your typos and clumsy grammar, and to generally compensate for your sloppiness or fat finger syndrome, you'll have no doubt learned the hard way that there is no substitute for good old-fashioned human spellchecking. It doesn't matter how sophisticated automatic spellchecking becomes—errors of omission, transposition, or substitution, as well as specialist words, are overlooked.

Read any modern novel and the visual barrage of typos suggests that even major publishing houses place too much trust in their digital spellchecker or hire incompetent proofreaders.

Whether you are applying for a job, making a presentation, or writing for a website, the importance of spelling cannot be overestimated. Spelling mistakes destroy credibility and cost you money, not least when your expensive "Nitendo console" or "Tomy Hilfiger" jacket sells for 99 cents on eBay because you didn't bother to check the spelling. Every day hundreds of eBay auctions are created with misspelled titles, and lots of free websites exploit this by finding spelling mistakes so savvy shoppers can grab a bargain and profit from other people's carelessness.

Use these proofreading tips whenever you have finished a piece of work (don't proofread if you plan to rewrite or edit further):

1. Take a break. Set the piece aside for at least an hour, preferably 24 hours.

2. Print a paper copy. People read differently on screen and are more inclined to skim and miss errors.

3. Read out slowly, aloud, and telegraphically—one word at a time and almost robotically, rather than using the natural flowing cadence of speech. This helps you to see what is actually there, rather than what the context and flow might fool you into thinking is there.

4. Read with the expectation that you will find mistakes. You will spot mistakes more easily if you assume they are there. Be happy when you spot a mistake (rather than frustrated that you made it), to motivate you to continue proofreading ever more carefully.

5. Focus on one element of your writing at a time. For example, you might read once for sense, then a second and third time for spelling and punctuation without thinking about the content or story.

6. Watch for contractions and apostrophes. If you don't know the rules, then learn them once and for all RIGHT NOW and you'll never be in doubt again:

   - Apostrophes are NEVER used to form plurals, even when using abbreviations (e.g. the plural of DVD is DVDs).

   - It is, there is, is not, he is, she is, I am—anything where two words are contracted, uses an apostrophe—it's, there's, isn't, he's, she's, I'm.

   - Apostrophes are used in the possessive except with its, your, yours, hers, our, ours, theirs. The apostrophe comes before the s with singular and after the s with plural (the dog's ball = one dog, the dogs' ball = more than one dog).

7. Watch for repetitions (the the, a a), transposed words or letters, and homonyms (words that sound the same but are spelled differently); these won't be detected by a spellchecker: words like from/form, their/there, house/horse.

8. If in doubt, assume you've made a mistake. Make a note and CHECK in a dictionary or grammar book.

9. Create a list of your common mistakes and read it before you begin so your brain is primed to look out for them.

Read the passage (excerpted from Chapter Two of *Wuthering Heights* by Emily Brontë) and see if you can spot fifteen errors.

On opening the little door, two hairy monsters flew at my throat, bearing me down, and extinguishing the light; while a mingled guffaw form Heathcliffe and Hareton put the copestone on my rage and humilation. Fortunately, the beast seemed more bent on stretching there paws, and yawning, and flourishing their tails, then devouring me alive; but they would suffer no resurection, and I was forced to lie till their malignant masters pleased to deliver me: then, hatless and trembling with wrath, I ordered the miscreants to let me out—on their peril to keep me me one minute longer—with several incoherent threats of retaliation that, in their indefinite depth of virulency, smacked of King Lear.

The vehemence of my agitation brought on a copious bleeding at the nose, and still Heathcliff laughed, and still I scalded. I don't know what would have concluded the scene, had their not been one person at hand rather more rational then myself, and more benevolent than my entertainer. This was Zillah, the stout housewife; who at length issued fourth to inquire into the the nature of the uproar. She though that some of them had been lying violent hands on me; and, not daring to attack her master, she turned her vocal artillery against the younger scoundrel.

This internet meme demonstrates how easily we understand meaning in text, despite typos. It helps to explain why so many typos go unnoticed by the casual reader.

Cdnuolt blveiee taht I cluod aulaclty uesdnatnrd waht I was rdanieg. The phaonmneal pweor of the hmuan mnid. Aoccdrnig to rscheearch at Cmabrigde Uinervtisy in Egnlnad, it deosn't mttaer in waht oredr the ltteers in a wrod are, the olny iprmoatnt tihng is taht the frist and lsat ltteer be in the rghit pclae. The rset can be a taotl mses and you can sitll raed it wouthit a porbelm. Tihs is bcuseae the huamn mnid deos not raed ervey lteter by istlef, but the wrod as a wlohe. Amzanig huh? Yaeh and I awlyas tghuhot slpeling was ipmorantt!

> **They Say:**
> **You don't know what you've got till it's gone.**

> **Truth:**
> **You knew exactly what what you had; you just thought you'd never lose it.**

**Many readers are not aware that the
the brain will automatically ignore a second
instance of a short word like "what" when it
it starts a new line.**

Now go back and reread that last last sentence slowly and telegraphically one more time.

Now re-read the sentence before this one. Did you spot that "what" was repeated (what you had) then "the" (the brain) was repeated, then "it" (it starts a new line), and finally, "last" (last sentence)?

VOCABULARY

IN MID-JUNE, 2009, THE COMPANY GLOBAL LANGUAGE MONITOR (GLM) ANNOUNCED ITS BELIEF THAT THE ONE MILLIONTH WORD HAD BEEN ADDED TO THE ENGLISH LANGUAGE (ALTHOUGH OTHER ESTIMATES PUT THIS FIGURE CLOSER TO TWO MILLION AND THAT'S NOT INCLUDING THE 600,000 KNOWN SPECIES OF FUNGUS). THEY ESTIMATE A NEW WORD IS CREATED EVERY 98 MINUTES.

We have so many words from which to choose and yet most adults only use a few thousand in their active daily speech (although nearly everyone knows at least 35,000 words and many people know more than 100,000). But there is a well-established correlation between a wide vocabulary and success.

Champion Scrabble players have some of the highest recognition vocabularies of anyone in the world. Former U.K. Scrabble champion Allan Simmons claims he can recognize around 100,000 of the 160,000 words of nine letters or under included on the Scrabble list.

The best way to expand a large working vocabulary is to grow up in a language-rich environment surrounded by books and with parents who read, read to their children, and encourage them to read. It's never too late to learn. Building your vocabulary can become a quick and easy part of your daily routine once you make the effort to become consciously aware of words you hear and read. A ten-year-old reading for six minutes a day is exposed to about 430,000 words a year. If you become more attentive to the vocabulary and increase your recall by just one percent, that's an extra 4,300 words in your brain tank each year.

Building your vocabulary will allow you to express yourself more clearly and fluently, and the returns (social, psychological, financial) are their own reward. If you learned a new word each day for the next three years, you would have over a thousand new words; if you spent five minutes a day learning five new words, you'd have over 18,000 within a decade.

Reading lots of books is a good way to keep existing vocabulary fresh in your mind, but you have to make a conscious effort if you want to learn new words. Keep a dictionary near to look up unfamiliar vocabulary, otherwise you will ignore the meaning and push on with the story.

Whenever you look up a new word, circle it in your dictionary with a red pen, so next time you open that page you can reread the word and its definition to consolidate it in your memory. Try also to consciously introduce recently learned words into your everyday writing and speech. Even when you hear someone use an unfamiliar word on the TV, reach for that dictionary.

HOW MANY WORDS DO YOU KNOW?

To estimate the size of your own vocabulary, find a medium-size dictionary, one which contains about 100,000 entries or 1,000 pages. Read 30 pages at random and keep a tally of the number of words you recognize AND the number of words you understand (the former will be larger than the latter). Better still, check the definitions of the words you think you know because you may still be wrong! Finally, divide both totals by 30, and multiply by the total number of pages in your dictionary to discover how many words you recognize and know. It will probably be much higher than you think!

WHICH EIGHT OF THESE WORDS DO NOT EXIST?

(Look them all up in the dictionary and expand your vocabulary!)

abacinate	eleemosynary	flunge	lerret	testiculate
argand	enodate	fribble	lucubration	tribution
autolatrist	eructation	fugacious	perchery	utriform
callipygian	estivate	funambulist	quiddity	
delitescent	exultion	jentacular	scrutable	
despumate	fabiform	labrose	spiracle	

WORDSEARCH

The wordsearch puzzle contains 26 unusual words, each of which starts with a different letter of the alphabet.

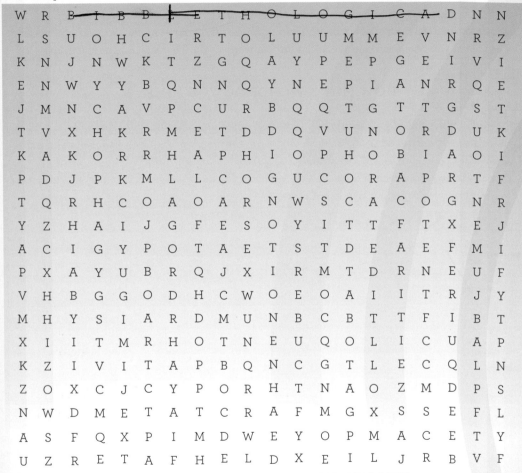

```
W  R  B  I  B  B  L  E  T  H  O  L  O  G  I  C  A  D  N  N
L  S  U  O  H  C  I  R  T  O  L  U  U  M  M  E  V  N  R  Z
K  N  J  N  W  K  T  Z  G  Q  A  Y  P  E  P  G  E  I  V  I
E  N  W  Y  Y  B  Q  N  N  Q  Y  N  E  P  I  A  N  R  Q  E
J  M  N  C  A  V  P  C  U  R  B  Q  Q  T  G  T  T  G  S  T
T  V  X  H  K  R  M  E  T  D  D  Q  V  U  N  O  R  D  U  K
K  A  K  O  R  R  H  A  P  H  I  O  P  H  O  B  I  A  O  I
P  D  J  P  K  M  L  L  C  O  G  U  C  O  R  A  P  R  T  F
T  Q  R  H  C  O  A  O  A  R  N  W  S  C  A  C  O  G  N  R
Y  Z  H  A  I  J  G  F  E  S  O  Y  I  T  T  F  T  X  E  J
A  C  I  G  Y  P  O  T  A  E  T  S  T  D  E  A  E  F  M  I
P  X  A  Y  U  B  R  Q  J  X  I  R  M  T  D  R  N  E  U  F
V  H  B  G  G  O  D  H  C  W  O  E  O  A  I  I  T  R  J  Y
M  H  Y  S  I  A  R  D  M  U  N  B  C  B  T  T  F  I  B  T
X  I  I  T  M  R  H  O  T  N  E  U  Q  O  L  I  C  U  A  P
K  Z  I  V  I  T  A  P  B  Q  N  C  G  T  L  E  C  Q  L  N
Z  O  X  C  J  C  Y  P  O  R  H  T  N  A  O  Z  M  D  P  S
N  W  D  M  E  T  A  T  C  R  A  F  M  G  X  S  S  E  F  L
A  S  F  Q  X  P  I  M  D  W  E  Y  O  P  M  A  C  E  T  Y
U  Z  R  E  T  A  F  H  E  L  D  X  E  I  L  J  R  B  V  F
```

• ASTROBLEME • BIBBLE • CABOTAGE • DIGNOTION • EMACITY
• FARCTATE • GRADGRIND • HAGIOLATRY • IMPIGNORATE • JUMENTOUS
• KAKORRHAPHIOPHOBIA • LETHOLOGICA • MACROSMATIC • NUDIUSTERTIAN
• ONYCHOPHAGY • PAUCILOQUENT • QUIRE • RETROITION • STEATOPYGIC
• TITTYNOPE • ULOTRICHOUS • VENTRIPOTENT • WIDDIFUL • XEROPHAGY
• YARBOROUGH • ZOANTHROPY

WORD DEDUCTION

Match each word with its correct definition. In most cases you should be able to use your existing knowledge of common related words or word fragments to deduce the meanings.

hard scar tissue which grows over injured skin	tardiloquous
process of infection	macrotous
horse-drawn carriage with folding top	unguligrade
acorn-bearing	ranivorous
walking on hoofs	janitrix
winking	habilable
big-eared	widgeon
yellowish	landau
ten-line poem	vaticide
frog-eating	quadrilocular
pastoral or rustic poem	caducity
a straight bundle of straw used for thatching	sanative
birthmark	fabulist
killing of a prophet	octad
having shiny smooth scales	balaniferous
freshwater duck	decastich
slow in speech	xanthic
healing	yelm
to burn	eclogue
to blind using a red-hot metal plate	abacinate
set of eight things	ignify
a female janitor	ganoid
capable of being clothed	nevus
being of a transitory or impermanent nature	keloid
having four compartments	zymosis
one who invents fables	palpebration

SPEED READING

TRAINING YOURSELF TO SPEED READ MAY INVOLVE UNLEARNING SOME OF THE BAD HABITS YOU PICKED UP AS A CHILD. AS CHILDREN WE ARE TAUGHT THE ALPHABET, THEN WE PROGRESS TO WORDS AND PHRASES AND SENTENCES.

With practice our vocabulary grows and our speed and fluency increase but speed reading involves taking your attention away from individual words and phrases to take in bigger phrases, even whole sentences in one sweep of the eye. Anyone can learn to speed read without sacrificing comprehension. In fact, in many cases it increases comprehension.

An average reader reads about 200 words per minute with about 60 percent comprehension; speed reading can boost your speed to over 1,000 words per minute with about 85 percent comprehension. Here's how it works:

1. Before you begin, have a clear purpose for your reading and what information you want to absorb. Reading speed and efficiency are governed by motivation. Speed readers know what they want to achieve from the text. For instance, when reading a novel, you look for story and character development and visualize descriptive passages, while a self-help book contains concepts, advice, and instructions. If you establish what you're looking for, you know where to direct your attention.

2. Read silently. Don't even hear the words in your head, just read the words and let them flow into your thoughts. Subvocalization slows down your reading to a snail's pace because it makes you "play" every single word, like practicing scales on a piano. Speed reading is more like running the back of your thumb along the keyboard to play a glissando of thirty notes in less than a second.

3. You may have to hold the book/screen farther away from your eyes to make a broad sweep with your eyes. Speed readers optimize the reading distance.

Experiment until you find the most effective and comfortable speed reading distance.

4. Skim quickly once, for context, to give you a framework on which to build the rest of your comprehension, then speed read for meaning.

5. Instead of reading individual words or phrases, darting your eyes back to reread certain words, keep your eyes moving forward from left to right at a faster but constant speed. Only move your eyes back when you start a new line.

6. Run your finger along the line to force yourself to maintain a constant speed and to discourage you from "regressing." Eventually you should be able to move your hand away and simply run your eyes left and right along a *narrow band in the center of the line*. While moving down the page, pick up the text on either side of the band with your peripheral vision.

7. Spot places where you can skim and scan. With practice you develop an intuition to recognize filler material, purple prose, repetition, and recapping or heavily descriptive passages that are surplus to requirements (e.g. if you are reading a chapter of a thriller novel simply for plot development, you can skim over that three-paragraph description of a chill, damp, windy night until the story begins to move forward again).

8. Relax. When you are in the zone, speed reading feels smoother and easier than conventional reading and it is less tiring than slavishly paying attention to every single word. Relax your face, extend your gaze, let the words wash over you, and you'll start to soak up blocks and sentences.

RIDDLES

Riddles have been around for thousands of years, appearing in many different cultures. One of the oldest riddles is "The Riddle of the Sphinx" which comes from Greek mythology and has its earliest roots from about 470 BC. "Which creature has one voice and yet becomes four-footed and two-footed and three-footed?" (answer on page 276).

The oldest known riddle is more than a thousand years older and appears on the famous Rhind Mathematical Papyrus, which was taken from the tomb of an ancient Egyptian scribe in the nineteenth century, and today is kept in the British Museum in London. The papyrus contains 84 different mathematical problems including this:

In seven houses there are seven cats. Each cat catches seven mice. Each mouse would have eaten seven ears of corn and each ear of corn, if sown, would have produced seven hekats of grain. How many things are mentioned in total?

The answer is an astounding 19,607. There are seven houses, 49 cats (7 x 7), 343 mice (7 x 7 x 7), 2,401 ears of corn (7 x 7 x 7 x 7), and 16,807 hekats of grain (7 x 7 x 7 x 7 x 7).

7 + 49 + 343 + 2,401 + 16,807 = 19,607

EINSTEIN'S RIDDLE

Albert Einstein wrote this riddle during the nineteenth century. He said that 98 percent of the world population would not be able to solve it (although he may have meant that only 2 percent could solve it in their heads).

1. There are five houses, painted five different colors.

2. In each house lives a person of different nationality.

3. Each person drinks a different kind of beverage, smokes a different brand of cigarette, and keeps a different pet.

1. The British man lives in a red house.

2. The Swede has a dog.

3. The Dane drinks tea.

4. The green house is just left of the white house.

5. The owner of the green house drinks coffee.

6. The Pall Mall smoker keeps birds.

7. The owner of the yellow house smokes Dunhill.

8. The man in the middle house drinks milk.

9. The Norwegian lives in the first house.

10. The man who smokes Blends lives next to the one who keeps cats.

11. The man who keeps horses lives next to the Dunhill smoker.

12. The man who smokes Blue Master drinks beer.

13. The German smokes Prince.

14. The Norwegian lives next to the blue house.

15. The Blend smoker's neighbor drinks water.

WHO OWNS THE FISH?

TWELVE RIDDLES

1. Three wise women are standing in a row facing forward. Peri-banu is at the front, Soraya in the middle, and Zeheratzade at the back. Each woman is wearing either a black or a white hat. They know that at least one hat is black and one hat is white but they don't know the colors of their own hats. Without speaking to each other or anyone else, how can one of the women work out the color of her own hat?

2. Two men catch two fish in two minutes. At this rate, how many men could catch 500 fish in 500 minutes?

3. The more you take, the more you leave behind. What are they?

4. What goes up the chimney down, but can't go down the chimney up?

5. What has a foot but no legs?

6. I have a little house in which I live all alone. It has no doors or windows, and if I want to go out I must break through the wall. What am I?

7. There were five men going to church and it started to rain. The four that ran got wet and the one that kept still stayed dry. Why?

8. I fly but have no wings. I cry but have no eyes. I see the sky get dark and I see when the sun comes up. What am I?

9. Little trotty hetty coat, in a long petticoat, and a red nose—the longer she stands the shorter she grows. What is it?

10. It is in the rock, but not in the stone; It is in the marrow, but not in the bone; It is in the bolster, but not in the bed; It is not in the living, nor yet in the dead. What is it?

11. What walks all day on its head?

12. It's been around for millions of years, but it's no more than a month old. What is it?

DINGBAT PUZZLES ARE VISUAL WORD RIDDLES. THE BEST WAY TO SOLVE THEM IS TO SAY WHAT YOU SEE.

SGEG

7 9 5 3
WHELMING

DDDWESTDDD

1234
U

GOGOGO
GO
GO
GO
GO

ARMS
ARMS
UP
ARMS
ARMS

ALGEBRA AND THE
VANISHING CAMEL

Algebra as we know it today appeared at the end of the sixteenth century with the work of French mathematician François Viète. At its simplest, algebra is doing arithmetical calculations using nonnumerical mathematical symbols, such as x, y, and z.

The word "algebra" comes from the Arabic word *Al-Jabr*, which first appeared in an Arabic treatise written in AD 820 by the Persian mathematician, Muhammad ibn Mūsā al-Khwārizmī, entitled *The Compendious Book on Calculation by Completion and Balancing*. The exact translation of *Al-Jabr* is unclear, but historians think it meant "restoration" or "completion," a reference to the technique of canceling terms on opposite sides of the equal sign in an equation.

Before the sixteenth century, the dominant algebra was the same system that had been developed in Persian Babylonia three thousand years earlier. Archaeologists have recovered clay tablets dating from 1800 to 1600 BC that express fractions, algebra, quadratic, and cubic equations, and even the Pythagorean theorem $a^2 + b^2 = c^2$. However, the algebra was what we now call "rhetorical algebra"—written in full sentences, so for example, x + 1 = 2 would be "The thing plus one equals two."

The next development in algebraic expression was made in the third century AD by the acknowledged father of algebra, Diophantus of Alexandria, although most of his book *Arithmetica* does not survive today. His "Diophantine equations" inspired seventeenth-century French lawyer and amateur mathematician Pierre de Fermat to propose his famous theorem (now known as Fermat's Last Theorem) that no three positive integers a, b, and c can satisfy the equation $a^n + b^n = c^n$ for any integer value of n greater than two. He famously scribbled his conjecture in the margin of his copy of *Arithmetica* with the tantalizing boast that his proof was too big to fit on the page. Mathematicians spent the next 350 years trying to prove it.

SOLVE THESE PUZZLES USING ALGEBRA

🎃	⏰	🎃	🎃	110
⏰	🎃	🍡	🍡	62
🎃	⏰	🎃	⏰	100
80	70	66	56	

🚗	🚗	🎁	🎁	20
🎁	🚗	🎸	🎁	40
🚗	🚗	🚗	🎸	56
19	27	39	31	

For example, if we call the pumpkin x, the alarm clock y and the popsicle z, we know that 3x + y = 110 and that 2x + 2y = 100. These are called simultaneous equations. If 3x + y = 110, then y = (110 - 3x). You can substitute (110 - 3x) for y in the second equation to find the value of x.

2x + 2(110 - 3x) = 100

2x + 220 - 6x = 100

-4x = 100 - 220

-4x = -120

x = 30

Now substitute 30 for x in one of the equations to find the value of y, then you can work out the value of z.

....

THE VANISHING CAMEL

A dying sheikh summoned each of the three princes one at a time. To his eldest son he bequeathed half of his camels, his middle son received one third of his camels, and his youngest son, one ninth of his camels. A servant was sent to count the camels. There were 17. Everyone scratched their heads, since there was no way that 17 animals could be divided according to the sheikh's wishes without chopping one of them into pieces. The sheikh summoned the local mathematician who rode to the palace on his worn-out old camel and immediately proposed a solution. What did he do?

NUMBER SEQUENCES

A number sequence is an ordered list of numbers in which the order is significant. The elements in a sequence form part or all of a countable set, such as the natural numbers. However, a sequence can be finite (e.g. counting from 1 to 20) or infinite (all positive odd integers: 1, 3, 5, 7 . . .).

There are several famous and important sequences in mathematics. The sequence of prime numbers (a natural number greater than 1 that can be divided, without a remainder, only by itself and by 1) which begins 2, 3, 5, 7, 11, 13, 17 . . . is an example of an infinite sequence (Euclid proved this 2,300 years ago). Primes become less frequent as the sequence progresses, so searching for them is a field of mathematics all by itself, and large primes are essential for modern cryptology.

Another famous and beautiful infinite sequence is the Fibonacci Series 0, 1, 1, 2, 3, 5, 8, 13, 21, 34 . . . in which each number is the sum of the two previous numbers. This sequence is found frequently in nature, from the spiral of a seashell, the scales on a pineapple, and the arrangement of petals on a flower to the pattern of florets in the core of a daisy blossom and the shoot growth of plants like the sneezewort.

To solve any polynomial sequence you use the method of "finding the successive difference."

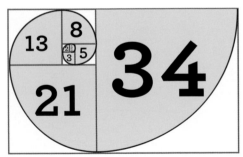
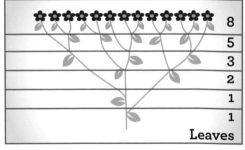

Suppose you have the sequence 3, 6, 11, 18 . . .

Write down the numbers in one row, then below them their differences, and then proceed writing successive differences:

$$3 \quad 6 \quad 11 \quad 18 \quad 27$$
$$3 \quad 5 \quad 7 \quad 9$$
$$2 \quad 2 \quad 2$$

Eventually you will reach a constant row (in this case it's 2 2 2). Now work backward up the rows. You now know that the second row is formed by adding 2 to the previous number, so once you have 11, you can add it to the 27 in the top row to get the next in the sequence = 38.

$$3 \quad 6 \quad 11 \quad 18 \quad 27 \quad 38$$
$$3 \quad 5 \quad 7 \quad 9 \quad 11$$
$$2 \quad 2 \quad 2 \quad 2$$

SEQUENCE PUZZLES

1. In 1202, Italian mathematician Leonardo Fibonacci considered the question: How many pairs of rabbits can be produced from a single pair of newborn rabbits in one year if:

   • rabbits always produce one male and one female offspring

   • rabbits can reproduce once a month

   • each animal takes one month to reach breeding maturity

   • no rabbits die

   Hint: This puzzle can be solved using the Fibonacci Series to work out how many pairs of rabbits would exist at the beginning of each month.

   1 2 3 4 5 6 7 8 9 10 11 12 13

   1 1 2 3

2. What comes next in the sequence?

   a) 1, 4, 9, 16, 25, 36, 49, _____, _____

   b) 0, 1, 3, 6, 10, 15, _____, _____ (clue: •.•.)

   c) 1, 5, 12, 22, 35, _____, _____ (clue: ⬠)

   d) 1, 4, 27, 256, _____, _____

3. What is special about this finite number sequence?

   8, 4, 4, 9, 9, 7, 6, 3, 3, 2, 0

DO IMPOSSIBLE SUMS
IN YOUR HEAD

The key to mental arithmetic is recognizing ways to simplify the sums that you have to make and reducing the number of operations that you have to perform to reach the answer. There are scores of techniques including breaking down, halving, or doubling numbers so you can use your times tables, to Vedic Math, which is an entire system of methods that sometimes seem like magic tricks to the untrained observer. Use these techniques to make mental arithmetic easier.

1. Make a quick estimate so you know approximately where you're heading. For example, multiplying 25 x 52 is approximately 25 x 50 = 12.5 x 100 = 1,250. The exact answer is 1,300, which you could have reached by adding another (2 x 25). Alternatively, you may have noticed that 52 is the same as 13 x 4 (most people know this from playing cards). So the sum is 25 x 4 x 13 = 100 x 13 = 1,300.

2. When adding up a list of numbers, look for groups that make multiples of ten. For instance in this list 7+4+ 21+ 9 + 2+ 8 +36 you can group (2 +8) + (36 + 4) + (21 +9) + 7 = 10 + 40 + 30 + 7 = 87 which is an easier calculation than climbing to the answer by thinking 7, 11, 32, 41, 43, 51, 87.

3. Break down numbers into easier separate calculations.

   For example: 74 - 38 = 74 - 30 - 8 = 44 - 8 = 36.

4. When multiplying two large numbers, split them into factors, perform some of the larger sums that appear in your times tables (which everyone should know) and then multiply by the other factor, rounding up to a multiple of ten, and then subtracting the multiple of the difference. Which sounds more complicated to explain than it is to perform:

   24 x 36 = 2 x (12 x 12) x 3 = 6 x 144 = 900 - 36 = 864

   16 x 14 = 2 x (8 x 7) x 2 = 4 x 56 = 200 + 24 = 224

5. Learn your 13th, 15th, 17th, and 19th times tables. For example, this calculation is easy when you know that 4 x 17 = 68.

   36 x 68 = 3 x (12 x 17) x 4 = 12 x 204 = 2,400 + 48 = 2,448

6. Vedic Math offers an even quicker way to multiply ANY two 2-digit numbers, e.g. 46 x 82

Step 1

Multiply the numbers in the left-hand column (4 x 8 = 32)

$$\underline{4}6$$
$$= 32$$
$$\underline{8}2$$

Step 2

Multiply the diagonals and add the result (4 x 2) + (8 x 6) = 56

$$46$$
$$= 56$$
$$82$$

Step 3

Multiply the numbers in the right-hand column (6 x 2 = 12)

$$4\underline{6}$$
$$= 12$$
$$8\underline{2}$$

Step 4

Place the three results side by side 32 56 12 and if any of the results are two-digit numbers, working from left to right, add the left digit to the adjacent number (32 + 5)(6 + 1)2

Answer = 3,772.

This might seem complicated at first, but you will soon get the hang of it after practicing a few calculations on paper. Take your time. Go slowly to make sure you understand the principle. Check your answers with a calculator. Finally, when you are confident that you've cracked the method, put pen and paper to one side and start doing the four steps in your head. Visualizing the numbers, manipulating them diagonally and vertically, and retaining three results in your head will have a powerful impact on your working memory.

SPOT THE RELATIONSHIP
BETWEEN NUMBERS

It's difficult to imagine life on earth before humans discovered numbers and it is certain that society, both ancient and modern, would scarcely function without them. However, something is even more powerful than the numbers themselves and that is the relationship between them. True power comes from manipulating numbers, combining them, abstracting them, and understanding how other people use them to gain power, make money, or create scientific miracles. This all boils down to an understanding of the relationship between numbers.

For example, do you know why soccer player David Beckham chose the number 23 for the back of his shirt when he joined the professional Spanish soccer club, Real Madrid? A businessman and sports fan couldn't fail to spot that it's the same number that basketball legend Michael Jordan wore and consider that maybe Real Madrid were trying to cash in on a magic number in the sporting world. Marcus Du Sautoy, the Simonyi Professor for the Public Understanding of Science and a Professor of Mathematics at the University of Oxford in England, has made the same observation. In his book *The Number Mysteries*, he observes that 23 is a prime number and then proposes the novel theory that "at the time of Beckham's move, all the Galácticos, the key players for Real Madrid, were playing in prime number shirts: Carlos . . . number 3; Zidane . . . number 5; Raul and Ronaldo . . . 7 and 11." He muses, "perhaps it was inevitable that Beckham got a prime number," and he cites a possible psychological advantage of playing a team of primes, based on his own experience of his Sunday league team being promoted after he persuaded the team to change its uniforms to primes.

These bizarre number relationships surround us; they heave into sight with satisfying regularity once we begin to look out for them. In nature, one of the key relationships between numbers is the syncopated life cycles of animals and their predators. Du Sautoy describes an American species of cicada that hides underground and only surfaces every 17 years, en masse, to breed and lay eggs. Then they all die, the next generation hatch and burrow underground where they remain for another 17 years. Seventeen is a prime number, one that ensures that the breeding cycle of the cicada coincides with the life cycle of its main predator less frequently than if it emerged after an even number of years (*see* puzzle 1 on page 92). He concludes, "as the cicadas discovered, knowing your maths is the key to survival in this world."

What is the relationship between the numbers 8 and 27? At first, you might think, not very much. So let's look at the factors. The former has the factors 1, 2, 4 and 8; the second 1, 3, 9, 27.

Can you see a link yet? Have you noticed that both sets of factors are geometric sequences? So 2 x 2 x 2 = 8 and 3 x 3 x 3 = 27. So 8 and 27 can be represented as 2^3 and 3^3. So both numbers feature in the cube number sequence $u_n = n^3$ which looks like this: 1, 8, 27, 64, 125, 216 . . . (1^3, 2^3, 3^3, 4^3, 5^3, 6^3 . . .).

You can always find interesting and useful relationships between numbers, although prime numbers are the most stubborn of numbers to give up their secrets. This explains why problems like the "abc conjecture" remain some of the most important unsolved challenges in mathematics. Huge cash prizes are available to anyone who can solve them.

The more you tinker around under the hood of mathematics, the more connections you can make, the more beautiful, deep, and ubiquitous these relationships become and the closer you edge toward winning a million dollars!

THE GOLDEN RATIO

Possibly the most fundamental relationship between numbers in nature and design is the golden ratio. Two numbers are in the golden ratio if their ratio is the same as the ratio of their sum to the larger of the two quantities.

The golden ratio (represented by the Greek letter "phi" ϕ) is a special decimal fraction approximately equal to 1.618033. It appears many times in geometry, art, architecture, and nature, from the proportions of the Parthenon (the ancient Greek temple dedicated to Athena in Athens) and the *Mona Lisa,* to the design of this Aston Martin.

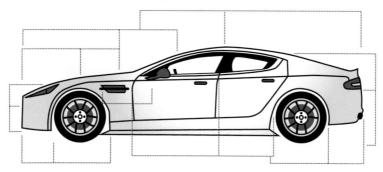

Most amazing of all, the golden ratio is synonymous with the Fibonacci Series: 0, 1, 1, 2, 3, 5, 8, 13, 21, 34, 55, 89, 144 . . . (*see* page 86). The farther along the sequence we go, the closer the ratio between a number and its predecessor approaches 1.618.

In humans, physical attraction is linked to phi. The more closely a face adheres to phi, the more attractive those traits are considered, since they are a potential indicator of reproductive fitness and health. Even our smiles can't escape the beautiful tyranny of the golden ratio. Studies have shown that the most attractive smiles are found in individuals whose central incisors are 1.618 times wider than the lateral incisors, which are 1.618 times wider than canines.

1. Suppose there were three species of subterranean cicadas. The blue cicada has a burrowing/breeding cycle of 7 years; the red cicada 12, and the yellow cicada 13 years. They share the same predator which emerges once every 8 years. All four species burrow underground in the year 1900, up to and including the year 2000:
    a) Which cicada will meet its predator four times?
    b) Which cicada will meet its predator once?
    c) Which cicada will never meet its predator?

2. What is the relationship between these two sequences?
    Hint: There are 25 prime numbers between 1 and 100. Both of these sequences add up to 25.
    4, 4, 2, 2, 3, 2, 2, 3, 2, 1 and 5, 1, 7, 0, 1, 0, 6, 0, 5, 0

1	2	3	4	5	6	7	8	9	10
11	12	13	14	15	16	17	18	19	20
21	22	23	24	25	26	27	28	29	30
31	**32**	**33**	**34**	**35**	**36**	**37**	**38**	**39**	**40**
41	42	43	44	45	46	47	48	49	50
51	**52**	**53**	**54**	**55**	**56**	**57**	**58**	**59**	**60**
61	**62**	**63**	**64**	**65**	**66**	**67**	**68**	**69**	**70**
71	72	73	74	75	76	77	78	79	80
81	82	83	84	85	86	87	88	89	90
91	92	93	94	95	96	97	98	99	100

3. What is the relationship between 1,597 and 2,584?

PRIME NUMBERS AND
THE HUMAN BRAIN

In the previous section you were introduced to some of the curious properties of prime numbers, so now let's examine them in greater depth. A prime is a natural number greater than 1 that can be divided, without a remainder, only by itself and by 1. The sequence of primes begins 2, 3, 5, 7, 11, 13, 17, 19, 23, 29, 31 . . . and is an example of an infinite (though unpredictable) sequence.

Primes are indivisible numbers that are the building blocks of all other numbers. All other whole numbers can be factored down to their prime factors. For example, the building blocks (factors) of 64 are 1, 2, 4, 8, 16, 32, and 64 but the prime number 2 is the foundation of the other numbers: $2^2 = 4$, $2^3 = 8$, $2^4 = 16$, $2^5 = 32$ and $2^6 = 64$. Therefore 64 has just one prime factor (2) because 2 is the only number that you need to build 64.

The factors of 510 are: 1, 2, 3, 5, 6, 10, 15, 17, 30, 34, 51, 85, 102, 170, 255, 510. But they can all be reduced down to the prime factors 2, 3, 5, and 17. Prime numbers truly are, in the words of Marcus Du Sautoy, "the hydrogen and oxygen of the world of mathematics." Prime numbers may even be the means by which we communicate with extraterrestrials. In his science fiction novel, *Contact*, American astronomer, astrophysicist, and cosmologist Carl Sagan explains in some detail how prime numbers could form the basis of a universal language, since primes exist independently of human language and thought.

THE SIEVE OF ERATOSTHENES

The third-century BC Greek mathematician Eratosthenes of Cyrene devised a quick method to find all the prime numbers up to 100. First write down all the numbers from 1 to 100. Cross out 1 (as shown in the example on page 94) because it is not a prime. Since 2 is the first prime, all multiples of 2 can't be prime, so circle them all in purple and move on to the next number, 3. Any multiples of 3 can't be prime, so you can circle them in green this time and move to the next uncircled number 5, etc. using a different color each time. By the time you reach 11, all you are left with are uncircled primes.

This is one of the earliest recorded examples of an algorithm—a step-by-step procedure for solving a problem by applying a specific set of instructions (*see* page 96). It is still the most simple and effective method for locating the smaller primes (those less than, say, a million).

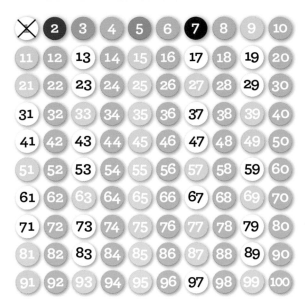

The first 100 numbers are awash with primes. There are 21 primes between 100 and 200, 16 primes between 200 and 300, and only 14 between 700 and 800. As you would expect, the primes get more scarce the farther we count, because there are more factors.

PRIME PATTERNS

Some physicists believe that research into prime numbers will lead to a greater understanding of the complex computational apparatus of the human brain. The distribution of prime numbers is thought to be random, but quantum physics and probability theory are being used to try to discover if there is a hidden pattern among the smaller primes. Alexander Bershadskii from ICAR, Israel, explains the significance in his May 2011 open access article, "Hidden Periodicity and Chaos in the Sequence of Prime Numbers":

"A physicist may ask: Why should one be interested in finding these patterns? The answer is: Comparison. If one can recognize patterns in an apparently random system, then one can compare these patterns with the patterns known for some other system of interest. We have already mentioned the comparison with certain quantum systems. Another intrinsic comparison can be made with the computational properties of brains, where the natural numbers certainly should play a crucial role. The neuron signals are also apparently random.

Can one compare patterns observed in these signals with the patterns in the prime numbers sequence in a constructive way, in order to shed a light on the computational apparatus of the brain?"

1. What are the smallest three prime numbers that can be written as a sum of the squares of two other prime numbers?

2. The first ten prime numbers are 2, 3, 5, 7, 11, 13, 17, 19, 23, 29.

   The prime factors of 30 (the number after 29) are 2, 3, and 5, so 30 is not a prime.

   30 + 1 = 31 which cannot be made by multiplying any of the previous prime numbers together, so it is a prime.

   Euclid used this elegant proof to show something fundamental about the set of prime numbers. What was it?

3. What's so special about the number 15,485,863?

THE AMAZING HALF-DOZEN LEFTOVER TRICK

Ask a friend to pick any prime number bigger than 5 (but not to tell you).

Tell them to:

Square it (multiply the number by itself)

Add 17

Divide by 12

Without knowing which prime number was chosen, you can announce:

There will be a remainder of 6. Or if they punched the numbers into a calculator, the answer will end with ".5"

THE EQUALLY AMAZING TWO DOZEN TRICK

If you square any prime number bigger then 3, then subtract 1, the answer always divides by 24!

Try it with these prime numbers and see: 83, 277, 2,707, 6,053, 17,449.

ALGORITHMS AND
ARTIFICIAL INTELLIGENCE

An algorithm is a step-by-step procedure for solving a problem by applying a specific set of instructions. We program computers using algorithms. We write computer software that gives the computer a series of steps and it completes them with blistering speed. The earliest computers worked on the same principle, except that the mechanism consisted of metal wheels, gears, and cogs, instead of zeros and ones. The operator set up the initial conditions and then the mechanical computer would crunch through a series of predetermined operations to reach the inevitable result.

The earliest known mechanical computer is over 2,000 years old. The Antikythera Mechanism was discovered in 1901 by six sponge divers off the coast of Crete. It was on the ocean floor among the remains of a ship that had sunk in 76 BC. The device was originally constructed using 32 interlocking bronze gears fitted inside a wooden case and is thought to be an astronomical calculator.

The main difference between this extraordinary artifact and modern computers is the speed at which they can perform calculations, but they can only work if we tell them what to do—by giving them algorithms.

COMPUTERS AND THE HUMAN BRAIN

We created computers, so it isn't surprising that their operation is governed by our metacognition (understanding of thinking), logic, and mathematics, but recent research has revealed that there is a link between how a computer "learns" using recurrent neural networks (RNNs) and algorithms, and how our brains function while we sleep.

One of the earliest RNNs, a Boltzmann machine, was invented in 1985 by AI pioneers, Geoffrey Hinton and Terry Sejnowski. It is "stochastic," which means it introduces *random variations* into the network. A Boltzmann machine starts with a random distribution of "weight" within its network. It is then "trained" by being fed data, one layer at a time; weights are then tweaked to reinforce the observed response inside the network. This observation is made by comparing the firing pattern of the nodes within the network with the random baseline pattern when the machine is not being fed data. Over time, meaningful relationships between nodes are gradually established and reinforced by this weight tweaking.

Ten years after he cocreated the Boltzmann machine, Hinton proposed a theory that sleep "serves the same function as the baseline component of the algorithm, the rate of neural activity in the absence of input" (*Quanta Magazine*, Natalie Wolchover). The brain relies on sleep to figure out which neural connections need to be reinforced, which is why sleep is essential for memory consolidation. "You're figuring out how correlated would these neurons be if the system were running by itself. And then if the neurons are more correlated than that, increase the weight between them. And if they're less correlated than that, decrease the weight between them."

ALGORITHMIC MAGIC TRICK

This trick works well with two or three people at the same time. It relies on the golden ratio (*see* page 91) and a simple algorithm.

1. Give your subject a calculator and a pen and paper and ask them to write down two whole numbers between 1 and 50 (but not tell you).

2. Ask them to add the two numbers.

3. They now have three numbers. Ask them to add the two larger numbers.

4. Repeat at least another eight times (add the largest two numbers each time).

5. Ask them to tell you the highest number and then tell them to add the two largest numbers one final time.

6. While they are doing this, you can predict what their final number is by performing this simple algorithm: MULTIPLY THE NUMBER THEY TOLD YOU BY 1.61803398 (this is the golden ratio) and then round up or down to the nearest whole number.

For example if they chose 13 and 45, steps would appear like this:

13 + 45 = 58

45 + 58 = 103

58 + 103 = 161

103 + 161 = 264

161 + 264 = 425

264 + 425 = 689

425 + 689 = 1,114

689 + 1,114 = 1,803

1,114 + 1,803 = 2,917

1,803 + 2,917 = **4,720** (this is the number they give you)

2,917 + 4,720 = **7,637** (while they work this out, you multiply 4,720 by 1.61803398 = 7,637.1203 = **7,637** to the nearest whole number)

HOW TO CALCULATE THE SQUARE
OF SEVEN AND A HALF IN YOUR HEAD

Here's the algorithm: $n^2 - (n - 0.5)^2 + (n - 0.25)$

That looks complicated but all it means is to find 7.5 squared, subtract the half to get 7, square this (to get 49), then add 7.25 = 56.25

This works for ANY number that ends in a half so:

to find 9.5 squared, subtract the half to get 9, square this (to get 81), then add 9.25 = 90.25

to find 23.5 squared, subtract the half to get 23, square this (to get 529), then add 23.25 = 552.25

VISUAL DISCRIMINATION

VISUAL DISCRIMINATION IS THE ABILITY TO DISTINGUISH THE DIFFERENCES AND SIMILARITIES IN SHAPES, FORMS, COLORS, SIZES, POSITIONS, AND ORIENTATIONS.

We constantly use our sight to compare the features of different items and to tell items apart. Without this ability we wouldn't be able to read, write, recognize our friends, cook a meal, drive a car, or even brush our teeth. Individuals can develop this skill, but most of us already enjoy a high level of visual discrimination that we take for granted.

The most important brain area involved in this ability is the occipital lobe, at the back of the skull. Face recognition is a specific aspect of visual discrimination associated with a part of the temporal lobe and occipital lobe called the fusiform gyrus. Facial recognition disorders such as acquired prosopagnosia (also known as face blindness) are often the result of occipito-temporal lobe damage.

The eponymous "Man Who Mistook His Wife for a Hat" in Oliver Sacks' famous case study of brain function problems, suffered from a visual discrimination disorder called agnosia. He was a highly erudite and talented musician who not only failed to see faces but "saw faces when there were no faces to see" and "when in the street he might pat the heads of water hydrants and parking meters, taking these to be the heads of children." He relied on individual details to recognize people, such as an item of clothing, the sound of their voice, the color of their nail polish, or a distinctive moustache. Sacks describes how at the end of the consultation the man "reached out his hand and took hold of his wife's head, tried to lift it off, to put it on. He had apparently mistaken his wife for a hat! His wife looked as if she was used to such things."

1. SPOT THE DIFFERENCES PUZZLE

Find ten differences between the two beach scenes.

2. SHAPE MATCHING

Which red and yellow shapes match exactly
(apart from having been flipped, rotated, or both)?

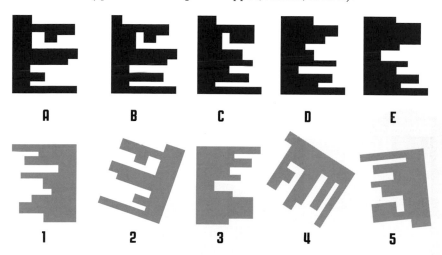

3. CRIME SCENE

Five fingerprints discovered at a crime scene were tested against ten fingerprints on the police database. How many of the lifted prints can you match with the database?

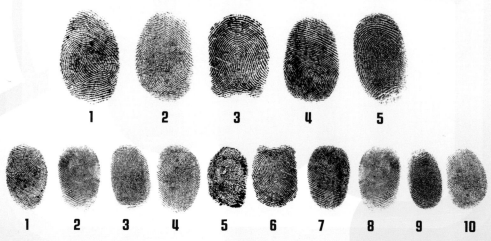

CONTRAST DISCRIMINATION

This is one aspect of our visual discrimination that is ripe for duping; designers of illusions often exploit contrast to fool the viewer's perception.

In 1935, Gestalt psychologist Kurt Koffka described this simultaneous contrast illusion (now known as the Koffka Ring Illusion). A gray ring on a light and dark background appears uniform, but when the halves are slid apart vertically, the two halves of the ring appear to be different shades of gray. If the rings are intertwined, the effect is even more startling.

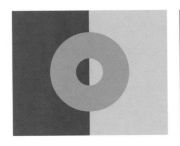   

1. Are the three center squares the same or different colors?

2. Which red circle is the bigger?

THE CHARPENTIER SIZE—WEIGHT ILLUSION

Prepare two boxes, one large and one small. Tape a filled one-liter plastic bottle to the bottom of each box so it can't roll around. Close the box lids and place the boxes on the floor. Ask a volunteer to lift each box one at a time and decide which is the heavier.

Which box do you think they will choose? Maybe the bigger one, because it looks heavier? Actually, the opposite is true. Repeated tests have shown that subjects report the smaller box to be the heavier.

The Charpentier Illusion was first published in 1891 by French physician Augustin Charpentier but we still don't fully understand why it works. Charpentier discovered that if you place identical weights inside closed boxes of differing sizes and then lift the boxes, the smaller box will always feel heavier than the bigger one.

Until recently, the traditional explanation was that when you pick up the bigger box, you overcompensate for its size and put too much effort into lifting. This makes the larger box appear lighter than it really is, so you judge the smaller box to be heavier.

However, in 2000 this theory was disproved by Professor Randy Flanagan and his student, Mike Bletzner, at Queen's University, Ontario, Canada. They allowed subjects to alternately lift both boxes so that they could correctly judge the force required in each case. Even after they had become accustomed to using the correct amount of lifting force and were TOLD that both boxes weighed the same, subjects still judged the smaller weighted box to be heavier. In a related experiment, subjects reported the same thing even when the smaller box was made lighter.

The illusion is one of visual perception rather than leverage, or people using a different stance to lift the bigger box. This has been proved because the illusion also works with boxes that differ only in their construction material (rather than size). Metal containers feel lighter than wooden containers of the same size and mass; darker objects feel lighter than brighter objects of the same size and mass.

VISUAL MEMORY

Visual memory is a vitally important perceptual and learning skill. It is the ability to store visual sensations and perceptions when the stimuli that prompted them have been removed. Research suggests that in sighted people, 80 percent of learning relies on the eyes; visual memory and the ability to form and retain mental images are key components of learning.

Information remains in our visual memory for a very short time, approximately several hundred milliseconds, shorter than auditory memory which lasts for a few seconds and can be retained indefinitely with repetition (e.g. when someone tells us a phone number, we can repeat it to ourselves until we find pen and paper to write it down).

When we perform a visual memory test like the one on the next page, most of us do not rely on short-term photographic recall alone; we have to think about what we are seeing, pay attention, and internally verbalize to interpret and store the visual data (e.g. I can see two oranges, a mug, a blue pen, a book). Very few people can close their eyes and scan the visual image in their minds as if it were still there. However, the ability to recall images in great detail for several minutes is more common in childhood. Between two and ten percent of children have this skill but it seems to diminish after the age of six, probably because language and auditory memory become dominant.

Some individuals, such as the British autistic savant Stephen Wiltshire, have eidetic memory and can recall visual information apparently indefinitely, and in minute and accurate detail. Wiltshire draws detailed pen and ink drawings of cityscapes from memory. He drew a 33-foot-long panorama of Manhattan after a short helicopter ride, although even he appears to "think" about what he views, rather than just blink his eyes and take a mental photograph. He says, "When I am drawing I am thinking about the information and the details so I can memorize it and then draw it back." He is passionate about cities, so he is emotionally engaged and highly motivated to remember what he sees, which is another important memory component.

Study the picture for one minute. Look at it carefully and try to remember as many details as possible. After the minute is up, turn the page and answer the questions.

1. How many pairs of shoes are there?

2. What colors are the towels?

3. What is directly below the black sunglasses?

4. What is inside the basket?

5. What colors are the two telephones?

6. On the top row, which direction does the hook of the coat hanger point, left or right?

7. On which horizontal row is the globe?

8. Which continent is visible on the globe, America or Africa?

9. At the top left is a pile of how many pairs of jeans?

10. What is below the red shirt?

11. Do the blue stripes on the blue shirt go from top left to bottom right or from top right to bottom left?

12. Which two objects below are NOT in the picture?

13. What color is the lightbulb, yellow or white?

14. What color is the little label inside the waistband of the blue jeans?

15. How many piles of newspapers are there?

16. What color is the sand in the egg timer?

17. What are the headphones resting on?

18. What color is the hairbrush?

19. The single olive-green sneaker fits which foot, left or right?

20. What color is the lace on this shoe?

FIGURE GROUND

Figure ground is the perceptual skill that enables us to pick out objects from their background or surrounding images. We recognize shapes and can distinguish them because of their form or silhouette, even when presented with a visually complex scene. Form, silhouette, or shape are naturally perceived as figure (object), while the surrounding area is perceived as ground (surroundings/background).

"Hidden picture" puzzles and specific types of visual illusions work by creating an ambiguous relationship between figure and ground, so that one image hides within another, or figure and ground merge or swap places.

One of the most famous figure-ground illusions is the so-called "Boring figure" which is named after the man who brought it to public attention, the experimental psychologist Edwin Boring, who was born in 1886 in Philadelphia. The image was drawn by cartoonist W. E. Hill and is entitled *My Wife and My Mother-in-Law*. The image can be viewed either as a beautiful young woman or an old lady wearing a head scarf (the chin and left ear of the young woman are the nose and left eye of the old lady respectively).

Another famous figure-ground illusion is Rubin's vase, created around 1915 by the Danish psychologist Edgar Rubin. Rubin explains: "When two fields have a common border, and one is seen as figure and the other as ground, the immediate perceptual experience is characterized by a shaping effect which emerges from the common border of the fields and which operates only on one field or operates more strongly on one than on the other."

Figure ground features as one of the six principles of Gestalt—a theory of visual perception developed by German psychologists in the 1920s. Gestalt means "unified whole" and works on the basis that people tend to organize visual stimuli into groups, every stimulus is perceived in its simplest form, and the whole is greater than the sum of its parts. The Gestalt principle of area states that the smaller of two overlapping figures is perceived as figure, while the larger is regarded as ground.

Another artist who played with figure and ground was the sixteenth-century Italian painter Giuseppe Arcimboldo, who painted portrait heads made out of fruit, vegetables, flowers, and a variety of other objects.

During the twentieth century, Dutch graphic artist M. C. Escher produced many woodcuts, lithographs, and mezzotints depicting positive-negative geometric shapes (*Day and Night*, 1938) or flocks of tessellated birds transforming into fish.

The dream architecture of Surrealists such as Salvador Dalí also included illusions which manipulate the figure-ground relationship. *The Invisible Man* (1929), the first painting in which Dalí used double images; *Apparition of Face and Fruit Dish on a Beach* (1938); and *Slave Market with the Disappearing Bust of Voltaire* (1940) are prime examples of this technique.

Recently even the notoriously ambiguous *Mona Lisa* has come under renewed scrutiny after artist Ron Piccirillo found the heads of a lion, an ape, and a buffalo in the background after turning the painting on its side. His discovery and references in da Vinci's journals have convinced Piccirillo that the painting is a depiction of envy.

Contemporary branding design often exploits the figure-ground relationship. For example, the corporate logo of FedEx has a white arrow hidden within the orange "Ex"; a negative space in the middle of the Formula One logo creates the "1," of which the viewer only becomes aware when it shifts in perception from ground to figure (it's also an example of visual closure—*see* page 111).

Figure-ground manipulation isn't just restricted to the art world. Camouflage is visually disruptive because it breaks up contour and silhouette, so figure and ground blend together. There are examples throughout the animal kingdom of species that have evolved to resemble their surroundings, and military camouflage exploits the same principle of disrupting the relationship between figure and ground.

How many of the objects below can you find hidden in the picture?

1. The first rectangle contains a six-sided hexagon. Which of the figures that follow also contain a six-sided figure?

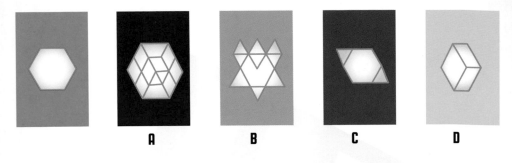

2. Can you spot these shapes within the pattern?

VISUAL CLOSURE

Visual closure is the ability to visualize a complete whole from incomplete information or a partial picture. It is the visual equivalent of the inductive reasoning discussed on page 36. This skill enables us to quickly form a "Gestalt" understanding of objects and the visual environment even when details are missing. It is a foundation skill for fluency and speed in reading and spelling. When we first learn to read, our eyes fix on one word at a time, but as we become faster and more proficient, they fix less often so we only perceive a part of a word and our brain fills in the rest.

Visual closure is one of the six principles of Gestalt (*see* page 108). It enables you to read these words, even though parts of the letters have been erased:

You can also recognize this animal and figure out that this picture fragment is from a car: And if you are very skilled, you might even recognize it as a Porsche.

Closure also makes us perceive shapes in negative space, like the cube, triangle, and 3-D sphere:

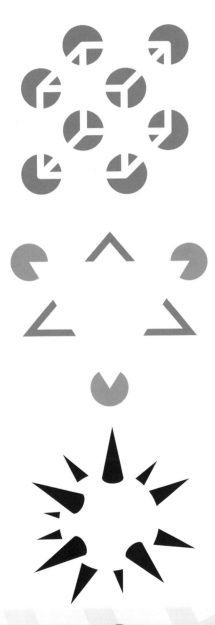

CAN YOU NAME THESE FAMOUS LANDMARKS?

NEAR–FAR
FOCUS SHIFTS

In people with normal healthy eyesight, about 70 percent of eye focussing is performed by the cornea, the transparent front part of the eye that covers the iris and pupil. Behind the cornea is a layer of aqueous fluid and then a second lens system. The ciliary muscles in the eye change the shape of the crystalline lens by stretching it at the edges, to focus light rays onto the retina, the light-sensitive region at the back of the eye.

The ciliary muscles are relaxed when we gaze into the distance, but they have to work hard to achieve near focus. The efficiency of a person's near and far focus depends on the strength and flexibility of the eye muscles. People can experience eye focussing problems for a variety of reasons, but eye strain and tense, rigid ciliary muscles make it harder for them to change the lens to the required shape, so vision becomes blurred. Other factors that affect the eye muscle are loss of flexibility due to aging (a condition called presbyopia, which also involves a loss of elasticity of the crystalline lens, causing the need for bifocals and/or reading glasses), poor diet, lack of exercise, smoking, and alcohol abuse.

Extended periods of close-focus work, such as reading, working on a computer, or texting, can also cause eye muscle tension. You may have noticed how looking at a computer screen or cell phone for an extended period can make your far focus blurred when you take a break and look out of the window. This is because your eye muscles become strained and cannot perform near–far focus shift quickly enough. When doing near-focus work it is important to take regular breaks and to shift your focus into the distance. Your eye muscles relax when you look at something far away (which is one of the reasons why staring at the horizon or at a landscape is so refreshing).

Another sign of eye strain is over-focussing for close work (accommodative spasm); your eyes feel jittery and uncomfortable when you focus on fine print or work in dim light. Fortunately, you can improve the relaxation and flexibility of your eye muscles with this simple exercise to help you perform near–far focus shifts more easily. If you have eye strain and your vision is blurred on close-up reading, far-focus reading, or both, practice this exercise daily to improve your vision and to relax your eyes.

1	2	3	4	5
6	7	8	9	10
11	12	13	14	15
16	**17**	**18**	**19**	**20**
21	22	23	24	25
26	**27**	**28**	**29**	**30**

1. Hang a page-a-month wall calendar on the wall and sit down facing the wall about three yards away from it.

2. Hold this book about 6 inches/15 cm from your eyes and focus on the number 1. If it is too blurry, move the book farther away to help you to focus.

3. Once the 1 on the page is sharply in focus, shift your attention to the wall calendar and focus on the 1 on the calendar. Keep concentrating until the number is sharply in focus.

4. Now move your eyes back to the page and focus on the number 2. When it is sharply in focus, switch your attention to the number 2 on the wall calendar.

5. Repeat this process with every number of the month.

6. If you completed the task with ease, try again, only this time hold the book a little closer to your face so that your eyes have to work harder for near focus. With daily practice you should be able to perform the exercise while holding the book 3½–4 inches/8–10 cm away from your eyes and still maintain efficient near–far focus.

ENJOYABLE AMBIGUITY, PARADOXES, AND
OPTICAL ILLUSIONS

The romantic poet John Keats only once mentioned one of his core ideas about creativity, which he called "negative capability." In a letter to his brother dated Sunday, December 21, 1817, Keats wrote, "at once it struck me, what quality went to form a Man of Achievement especially in literature & which Shakespeare possessed so enormously—I mean Negative Capability, that is when man is capable of being in uncertainties, Mysteries, doubts without any irritable reaching after fact & reason."

According to Dr. David Rock, author of *Your Brain at Work: Strategies for Overcoming Distraction, Regaining Focus, and Working Smarter All Day Long*, "the brain is primed to experience at least a mild threat from most forms of uncertainty." Success and creativity require discipline, structure, dedication, and a clear vision, but the quality that ties these attributes together is the courage to tolerate uncertainty. Great leaders have this and so do great artists and sportspeople.

The need for certainty and control is detrimental to our creativity, as David Bayles and Ted Orland explain in their book *Art & Fear: Observations on the Perils (and Rewards) of Artmaking*: "People who need certainty in their lives are less likely to make art that is risky, subversive, complicated, iffy, suggestive, or spontaneous. What's really needed is . . . an overriding willingness to embrace mistakes and surprises . . . and tolerance for uncertainty is the prerequisite for succeeding."

It is curious that so many of us seek the safety of certainty and yet we are thrilled and intrigued by optical illusions. We are delighted by the bafflement, the paradox of knowing that our senses are being fooled, that our perceptions are vulnerable and fragile. Expand your creativity and well-being by embracing uncertainty. Don't rush to solve a problem because, to quote the author Alexander Cheung, "it is in ambiguity that dreams are hatched, hopes are nurtured, and possibilities run wild."

Here are some optical illusions. Remember the wonder you experience from viewing them to remind you that uncertainty can be healthy and exhilarating; it doesn't have to be met with fear and a furrowed brow.

STRAIGHT LINES?

ACCENTUATE THE POSITIVE

1. Look at the yellow dot for 15 seconds

2. Now look here

Optical illusion cube

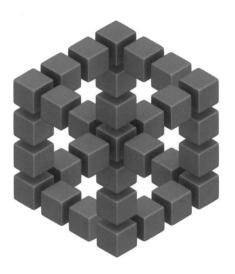

These concentric circles
resemble one single spiral.

The Penrose triangle

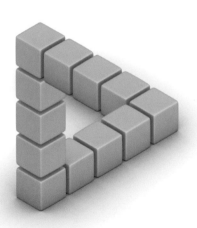

Stare at the white dot and
the picture will start to move.

BIG PICTURE THINKING

Big picture thinkers are imaginative, strategic, and visionary but they can be disorganized, impulsive, easily bored, and lack attention to detail. At the other end of the spectrum, the detail-conscious people work on the logistics, the nuts and bolts, the finer details that the big picture people overlook. In any organization there should be a healthy mix of both kinds of people.

Of course, most of us lie somewhere along the spectrum rather than at the edges, but we all have a preference or strength for big picture or details. However, the big picture people tend to be the leaders, the CEOs, the generators of ideas, the paradigm shifters. They create something that makes everyone else scratch their heads and say, "Why didn't I think of that?" They can usually employ teams of detail obsessives to make their vision a reality so they don't really need to sweat the small stuff. But if you're a detail monkey and you want to broaden your horizons, these strategies will help you.

To become a big picture thinker, you just have to copy what big picture thinkers do, and no one saw a bigger picture than Steve Jobs.

He created a company that was totally design driven and valued beauty and human intuition above spreadsheets and quarterly reports. He didn't just think globally but even bigger! One of his famous aspirations was "I want to put a ding in the universe." The attention to detail of Apple design is also legendary, but it is all driven by the untiring quest for simplicity and purity. Jobs knew what people wanted. He never got so distracted by details that he forgot that customers are emotional beings. He had vaulting ambition, intuition, a desire for beauty, and a relentless focus on the emotional experience of real people. You may not share Jobs' ambition but the other three motivations are what make us human and life worth living.

When you watch a movie in which a corporate slave throws his papers in the air and escapes from his cubicle, it's because he or she has suddenly seen the bigger picture—people, beauty, and intuition. In *The Matrix*, the exact same motivations lead Neo out of the office and down the rabbit hole where he literally sees the bigger picture.

When you look at it like that, who wouldn't want to ignore the details and become a big thinker?

BECOMING A BIG THINKER

1. Imagine the possibilities. This requires courage and some may say a big ego, but the first step to allowing yourself to think big is honesty. Be honest with yourself about what you really want and your perspective will change.

2. Follow your intuition. This doesn't mean you won't make mistakes. In fact, it will mean making more mistakes, but it will indicate that you are traveling somewhere rather than standing still. Attention to detail can also be synonymous with sticking to the comfort of what we know, getting distracted by the little stuff, instead of having the courage to take bigger risks.

3. Allow yourself to become emotionally attached to the bigger picture. This invites the possibility of getting emotionally hurt. No one ever got hurt by something they didn't care about, but nothing has ever been achieved without individuals who were prepared to lay themselves on the line and to encourage the passion and commitment that creates this vulnerability.

4. Start right away doing whatever you think you need to do to make the bigger picture a reality. This involves action rather than thinking, talking, or dreaming.

5. Now you can be strategic. Now you can bring focussed, detailed strategy into play because it is a tool to serve the big picture rather than an emotional blinker or something you have to do because it comes with your pay level.

6. Always make your attention to detail serve the bigger goal.

KILL THE ANTS

The acronym ANTs stands for Automatic Negative Thoughts, which are a major, controllable factor in our daily experience. Learning to recognize and combat them affects our brains at a deep chemical, endocrinal level.

A recent study coauthored by Drs. Andrea J. Levinson and Zafiris J. Daskalakis of Canada's Centre for Addiction and Mental Health (CAMH) has found that people with major depressive disorders have altered functions of the neurotransmitter GABA (gamma-aminobutyric acid). In the study, people with the most treatment-resistant forms of illness had the greatest reductions of GABA levels in the brain.

Scientists agree that our brains and bodies are controlled by neurotransmitters which communicate by releasing chemicals. Our every thought and emotion involves the release of chemicals. Dr. Levinson says that "GABA provides the necessary inhibitory effect that we need in order to block out excessive brain activity that in depression may lead to excessive negative thinking."

It is well known that the stress hormone cortisol affects learning and memory, lowers immune function and bone density, increases blood pressure and cholesterol, and, at increased levels, can ultimately lead to heart disease. Cortisol is released in response to fear or stress by the adrenal glands as part of the fight-or-flight mechanism and after its release it remains elevated for several hours.

The pituitary gland is an endocrine (hormone-producing) gland. It is about the size of a pea and is located at the base of the brain, behind the bridge of your nose. Among the many hormones it releases (including growth hormone and thyroid-stimulating hormone), the gland produces the important Adrenocorticotrophic Hormone (ACTH) which regulates levels of cortisol.

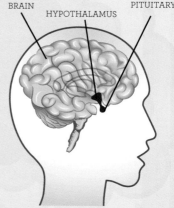

BRAIN   HYPOTHALAMUS   PITUITARY

So your thoughts and emotions directly affect the chemical activity in your brain. Your thoughts do matter. Clearly an imbalance in brain chemistry cannot be cured simply by positive thinking, but it is worth noting that although you can't think and feel your way out of major depressive disorders, you do have some control over the chemical reactions that are happening in your brain.

RECOGNIZE NEGATIVE THOUGHTS

1. **Hyperbole:** In negative situations, whenever you use expressions like "I never," "I always," or "that's typical" you are overgeneralizing and exaggerating the negative. Switch this around and make it a rule that you will only use hyperbole when something GOOD happens. This will reinforce a belief that good things regularly happen to you (which is true, but we are programmed to remember and pay more attention to threats and negative experiences—it's called negativity bias—a trait that kept our ancestors from being eaten by predators, but not so useful to modern humans who make far fewer daily life-and-death decisions).

2. **Prediction:** We ridicule those who claim to be able to predict the future, especially if they are making money from it, but we think nothing of making negative predictions about our own lives. Since no one can predict the future, it makes no sense to base our present decisions on this and even less sense to choose negative predictions over positive ones.

3. **Projection:** This is just as flawed as prediction, but happens in real time. We think we know what other people are thinking, so we act accordingly. We think a person hates us, so we avoid them; we assume someone looks down on us so we become haughty or defensive. Again, it is impossible to know another person's thoughts so it makes no sense to choose negative ones over positive.

These three ANTs—hyperbole, prediction, and projection—wreak havoc with our pituitary glands. Many people avoid "positive thinking" because it appears to be such a simplistic and reductive approach to complex human behavior and, above all, because it seems phony. Yet those same people allow an equally phony negative belief system to dominate their lives. So make the ANTs work for you. You probably can't stop yourself from hyperbolic thinking, prediction, and projection, but you can change the operands from negative to positive.

TRUST YOUR INTUITION

In a 2006 article in *Seed* magazine called "Who Wants to be a Cognitive Neuroscience Millionaire?", Ogi Ogas, a final year PhD student at Boston University's doctoral program in cognitive neuroscience, explains how his understanding of the human brain helped him to win $500,000 on the *Who Wants to be a Millionaire?* game show. He explicitly links intuition with memory and begins his analysis by stating, "Folk wisdom holds that on standardized tests you should go with your first impulse. Research tends to support this idea: A first impulse is more often correct than a second, revised decision."

Visual closure is the ability to visualize a complete whole from incomplete information or a partial picture (*see* page 111). A similar process, called priming, occurs with memory which Ogi Ogas says was his first technique: "The priming of a memory occurs because of the peculiar 'connectionist' neural dynamics of our cortex, where memories are distributed across many regions and neurons. If we can recall any fragment of a pattern, our brains tend to automatically fill in the rest." He used priming to answer the $16,000 question: "This past spring, which country first published inflammatory cartoons of the prophet Muhammad?" He didn't know the answer, but he remembered having a conversation with his friend Gena about it, so he chatted with the host Meredith Vieira about this conversation and tried to recall where and when it took place and whatever details he could remember. Suddenly he pictured Gena rolling his eyes and saying, "What else would you expect from Denmark?"

However, he says that he used "pure intuition" to correctly answer the $250,000 question: "The department store Sears got its start by selling what specific product in its first catalog?" Once again, he didn't know the answer but the word "watches" popped into his head before the answers were displayed and he also thought of railroads. When he got home he looked up the details and discovered that railroad station agent Richard Sears had sold watches to other station agents along the Minneapolis and St. Louis Railway for a year before meeting up with Alvah C. Roebuck. At some point in the past he must have been exposed to this information and his intuition retrieved part of that memory. His intuition didn't just come out of the ether; it was the result of buried memories.

Here are ten general knowledge questions. If you don't know the answers, that's a bonus. Write down the thoughts that spring to mind, like Ogi Ogas's "watches." Tune into all the "I-was-going-to-say-that" thoughts and make a note of them. Then see where these key words lead you as you dredge your memory. Finally, check the answers on page 277 and look up some additional details on Wikipedia and see if you can find a connection between your intuition and the actual facts. There will be some instances that prove that your intuition was actually linked to a distant memory.

1. What does HTML stand for?

2. Which nation first gave women the right to vote?

3. Who was the ancient Greek goddess of agriculture?

4. Who was La Divina?

5. Who is America's most published playwright?

6. The Chinese called this vegetable "mad apple," believing it to cause insanity.

7. Who painted *Las Meninas*?

8. What two cities were linked by the Orient Express?

9. What is philematology?

10. What was used to erase lead pencil marks before rubber came into use?

CROSSING THE MIDLINE

Your vertical midline is an imaginary line drawn from the top of your head, along the bridge of your nose, through your navel, and ending between your legs. Crossing the midline—moving a part of the body so that it operates on the other side of the line—is a vitally important skill for brain development and motor coordination in babies and young children. In fact, it is one of the developmental goals that pediatricians look for at a baby's six-month checkup.

Crossing the midline is necessary for bilateral coordination ("ability to use both sides of the body at the same time") and dominance in one hand, which is important for fine motor skills such as writing. Typically, children with low muscle tone lack the necessary core stability to twist their bodies to cross the midline, so both bilateral coordination and hand dominance will be delayed along with other cognitive skills such as reading (which is a crossing the midline activity). Children who have difficulty crossing the midline may appear ambidextrous, which should be a cause for concern, not a sign that the child is going to be a Major League Soccer player.

CORPUS CALLOSUM

The right side of the brain controls the left side of the body and the left side of the brain controls the right side of the body. The two hemispheres are connected by the corpus callosum, the largest white matter structure in the brain.

Crossing the midline needs both sides to be working together and increases the communication between the two hemispheres. Even in adulthood, physical activities that cross the midline give your brain a complete workout and improve coordination, balance, reasoning skills, mathematical ability, and creativity.

BOUNCE, CLAP, CROSS

Sit in a chair with your feet flat on the ground, your back straight (rather than slumped), and your knees facing forward (rather than splayed out wide). Hold a ball in your right hand. To a count of four, bounce it onto the floor between your legs (1), catch it with your left hand (2), pass the ball to your right hand (3), and then bend your elbow so that both hands come to rest at shoulder height (4), ready to begin the sequence again. Repeat for three minutes. For a greater challenge you can increase the speed, but make sure you don't lose the rhythm.

HEEL TAP

Stand with your legs shoulder width apart with your arms by your sides. To a count of eight:

1. With your weight on your left leg, bend your right knee and bring your right heel across the midline until you can touch it with your left hand (keep your left hand on your left side, rather than move it right to meet your foot).

2. Return your right foot to its starting position.

3. With your weight on your right leg, bend your left knee and bring your left heel across the midline until you can touch it with your right hand (keep your right hand on your right side, rather than move it left to meet your foot).

4. Return your left foot to its starting position.

5. Repeat steps 1–4, only this time move each leg behind the other leg.

ELBOW TAP

Stand with your legs shoulder width apart with your arms by your sides. To a count of four, bend and touch right elbow to left knee as you raise your leg, stand, and then touch left elbow to right knee.

GRAPEVINE WALKING

Stand facing forward with your legs together and arms by your sides.

1. Take five steps to the right (step your left leg in front of your right leg, then move your right leg to the right, while continuing to face forward).

2   Take five steps to the left (step your right leg in front of your left leg, then move your left leg to the left, while continuing to face forward).

3. Repeat steps 1–2, moving your leading foot behind the standing leg.

REVERSE
BRAINSTORMING

Sometimes we have to stand on our head to change our perspective and solve a problem. Reverse brainstorming is just like regular brainstorming only instead of trying to find a solution to a problem, the aim is to find all the ways that you could *cause* the problem or make it worse.

Instead of asking "How can I succeed in this endeavor," you explore ways that you can really mess it up and then take those suggestions and reverse them again to reach a solution.

This process will highlight assumptions and weaknesses and may be a revelation, since you may discover that some of the strategies that you thought were helping to solve the problem might actually be contributing to it.

QUESTION: HOW CAN WE ATTRACT MORE CUSTOMERS TO SPEND MONEY ON OUR ONLINE STORE?

Reverse the question: How can we ensure that **fewer** customers spend money on our online store?

Brainstorm for as many ideas as possible ...

- Make sure meta description is full of irrelevant and misleading details, or have hundreds of them with spammy repeats and put them in the wrong location
- Remove cross-linking between pages on the website
- Lower our search engine ranking
- Increase our prices
- Make the website hard to navigate and boring to look at
- Reduce quality of goods
- Display poor customer feedback prominently on the home page
- Never update the website
- Have lots of broken links
- Have poor spelling and grammar
- Copy and paste sales material from other websites

- Break off trading links with other websites
- Link with websites that have nothing to do with ours
- Avoid social media

Now reverse again . . .

- Check meta tags are accurate; stick to one keyword phrase per page; name each page; read an article about effective Google searches for tips on how to optimize our website
- Find out whether meta tags are even important any more
- Improve our search engine ranking
- Check prices regularly to ensure that they are competitive
- Make the website content easy to navigate and visually stunning
- Increase quality of goods; establish an atmosphere of trust, teamwork, and cooperation with suppliers; iron out any misunderstandings; ensure quality tracking is accurate
- Display glowing customer feedback prominently on the home page; deal with dissatisfied customers quickly and effectively to maintain good word-of-mouth reputation
- Constantly update the website
- Regularly check that links are active and relevant; use hyperlink names rather than "click here"; build/add a handful of rich anchor text links each month
- Hire a proofreader?
- Make sure copy is original and customer-focussed
- Increase trading links with other websites; establish linking agreements so links, deep links, and framing are appropriate
- Build up our profiles; create powerful profiles on Facebook, Twitter, and Google Plus

REVERSE BRAIN DUMPS

When you are searching for inspiration, open up a Word document and write down everything that comes to mind about the topic. Don't self-censor. Approach it with an open mind and a spirit of nonjudgment. Include questions that need answering, emotional responses (likes and dislikes, hopes and fears, etc.), and let your intuition prime your memory to produce deep associations. Now look at what you've created and reverse it—reverse inquiries and questions, write down the antonyms to everything you've come up with, and see where they take you.

ROUTINE BREAKING

It is well established that novelty is good for the brain and body, increases your alertness, attention, and creativity, and makes your brain form new neural connections. The best way to keep your brain youthful is to present it with new stimulation, to break your routines, and give your brain what it craves the most: a break from the norm.

Have you noticed how exhausting foreign vacations are? Aside from the traveling, change in climate, increase in physical activity, and overindulgence in food and alcohol, one of the main reasons is that your brain is working much harder; it is bombarded with new experiences, novel sights, sounds, smells, tastes, textures, colors, the challenges of a foreign language, unfamiliar customs, and social observances. All this rich new input is, however, very good for your brain and your creative juices.

New experiences encourage the growth of dendrites, the branched projections which receive electrochemical messages from other neurons. The more your dendrites develop and branch out, the greater the surface area available for receiving information, so the more complex the electrochemical stimulation received from other neural cells.

You don't have to go on vacation to mix things up and break your routine. Here are some routine-breaking suggestions to fertilize your dendrites:

1. Take a shower with your eyes closed. Your other senses will become heightened, the smells of the shower gel and shampoo, the tingle of the water on your skin, the steam in your nostrils, the water in your ears and sloshing around your toes. Your spatial awareness will also be challenged as you fumble for objects.

2. Use your nondominant hand or foot to perform everyday tasks like brushing your teeth, scooping an omelet out of the pan, opening a door, using keys, washing, holding a knife and fork, drinking, walking the dog, etc.

3. Step outside your comfort zone. Challenge yourself to do one thing a week that scares you (without intentionally exposing yourself to physical danger).

4. Choose some music you think you will really hate and really pay attention to the musical structures, the tropes, and the clichés, but also try to bridge the gap between you and the music to allow the possibility that you could enjoy it; after all, somebody bothered to create it and it's been released, so someone must think it's worth a listen.

5. The next time you go to a coffee shop or a restaurant, choose something on the menu that you would normally overlook.

6. Take risks. Those who risk nothing, gain nothing.

7. Ask someone who you know has a different taste in literature to recommend one of their favorite books. Read it. No matter that you like spy thrillers and your friend just loves chick lit. Give it a chance. At the very least, it gives you another point of common connection with your buddy.

8. Start saying yes and no more often. Say yes to the stuff that you know you ought to say yes to but are too frightened to explore; say no more often to social engagements and commitments that are overextending you and which you are only doing out of a sense of duty.

9. Talk to people you wouldn't normally talk to.

10. Every week perform one spontaneous and no-strings-attached act of kindness.

2#
IMPROVE
YOUR MEMORY

HOW THE BRAIN
REMEMBERS

WHO DOESN'T WISH THEY HAD A BETTER MEMORY? BUT FEW OF US HAVE THE FIRST CLUE HOW OUR MEMORIES WORK. SOME PEOPLE SHRUG OFF MEMORY LAPSES, BELIEVING THAT THEY HAVE ALWAYS BEEN FORGETFUL, OR VIEWING THEM AS AN INEVITABLE CONSEQUENCE OF ADVANCING YEARS. NEITHER NEED APPLY TO YOU.

When an individual pops up on television making claims of photographic (eidetic) memory, we blindly admire their miraculous mind powers. However, the good news is that genuine eidetic memory—the ability to recall events, images, or other data with almost perfect precision—is very rare. It's more common in early childhood, but the majority of the extraordinary memory feats displayed by adults are the result of sophisticated memory techniques collectively referred to as mnemonics. Anyone can learn these systems with practice, regardless of their intelligence.

We can all transform our memory powers and it starts by learning how the brain remembers. In the past, memory was compared to a filing cabinet; next, our memories were increasingly likened to a hard drive, which is a terrible comparison because computers store information randomly. Today neuroscientists believe that memory is much more tangled and complex, involving the interaction of many different sensory and memory systems across the entire brain.

The memory-forming process begins with perception. We see, hear, feel, touch, and smell, and the resulting electrochemical impulses travel to a part of the brain called the hippocampus (the name comes from the ancient Greek for horse—*hippos*—and sea monster—*kampos*—as its appearance is similar to a seahorse). This filters out and simplifies the data and integrates all the sensory information into one combined package. The hippocampus and the frontal cortex of the brain are involved in deciding what information is worth remembering.

STUDY THE PICTURE FOR TWO MINUTES. LOOK AT IT CAREFULLY AND TRY TO REMEMBER AS MANY DETAILS AS POSSIBLE. AFTER THE TIME IS UP, TURN THE PAGE AND ANSWER THE QUESTIONS.

1. What color is the balloon?

2. How many butterflies are there?

3. What is directly to the left of the handprint?

4. What animal was asleep on the armchair?

5. What object is directly below the hat?

6. Are the stripes on the cushion vertical or horizontal?

7. Does the stalk of the leaf point to the right or left?

8. What object is in the top right-hand corner?

9. Is the envelope open or closed?

10. What does the Polaroid photo show?

11. How many colors does the knitted hat have?

12. Is the apple closest to the hat or the shell?

13. Which three objects are not in the picture: rope, pencils, sock, key, lollipop, bell, sunglasses, beans, bow tie?

14. Name three metal objects.

15. How many hats are there?

16. What color of paint is on the paintbrush?

17. Which two objects are NOT in the picture?

18. How many pairs of shoes are there?

19. What sport could you play with the ball?

20. What flower was on the bottom line?

Now check your answers by looking at page 135, then *see* page 278 for your assessment.

Your brain has about 100 billion cells called neurons which receive and transmit electro-chemical signals. Neurons communicate with each other in response to the stimuli that your senses receive, and memories are laid down as these connections are reinforced by repetition, in much the same way that cross-country skiers create grooves in the snow, which make a route easier to traverse.

Recent research into gamma waves at the Kavli Institute for Systems Neuroscience and Centre for the Biology of Memory at the Norwegian University of Science and Technology (NTNU) has shown that brain cells also use a switching system to literally tune into the wavelength of other neurons; they can choose which of the thousands of inputs to focus on, by tuning into different gamma wavelengths, like turning the dial on a radio.

Study this picture for one minute. Pay particular attention to the food items and try to remember as many details about them as possible. After the minute is up, turn the page, keep reading, and then answer the two questions.

The more you learn, the more of these connections are created between neurons. These fluid connections are changing and developing all the time. Connections which are used very little will disintegrate while those that are reinforced grow stronger, which is why we learn by practice and forget or lose specialized skills through disuse. For instance, it is widely acknowledged that during infanthood there is a critical period for the acquisition of certain skills, such as native language. A young child has heightened sensitivity to learning languages but after the age of about five, native-like fluency becomes progressively challenging because the brain becomes more specialized, and any unused linguistic neural pathways are appropriated for other salient brain functions.

To commit something to memory you must first pay attention. The sensory information enters your short-term memory. It can keep between four and seven items for about 30 seconds (this increases if you use a technique such as chunking—*see* page 207—to break down a set, such as twelve numbers chunked into three groups of four). You can also increase this time by repeating words to yourself, effectively resubmitting the information to your short-term memory.

Important information that you (and/or your subconscious) deem worthy of remembering, passes from your short-term memory into your long-term memory through repetition, emotional engagement, and your existing network of memory associations (since the more you know about a subject, the easier it is to make meaningful and memorable associations and neural connections).

In the previous exercise you may have noticed that you were only able to retain certain details if you made a specific point of noticing them, while other information was available to you with some prompting, although you may not have recalled it if you had merely listed everything. Notice, too, that third-party suggestion can alter your memories (did questions 12 and 17 implant the false memory of an apple?).

So, here are your two questions:

1. Write down all the food items that you can remember.

2. Write down all the nonfood items that you can remember.

Unsurprisingly, we remember information better when we pay special attention to it. This is blindingly obvious, but it also highlights that sometimes we pay attention to the wrong things and then think that we have a bad memory when we can't recall the desired information. You were instructed to focus on the food items; since you had limited time it was inevitable that your recall of the other items was more limited. You no doubt counted the slices of bread, noticed that there were four apples, one of which had been eaten; you counted three eggs and four bread rolls. Maybe you even had time to observe how the apples were arranged—was it A or B? Go back and check!

A   B

So you've learned the importance of focus, but now you're feeling cheated. So here are five more questions.

1. What color is the memory stick?

2. What color is the rubber band on the rolled-up wad of bills?

3. What color is the single rose?

4. What color is the iron?

5. What color is the telephone?

Sorry, you're not getting rewarded that easily. That was another opportunity to ram home the message that attention is everything. If you had been asked to focus on the colors red and black, these five answers would be so easy you'd be complaining.

The best way to improve recall is to increase attention at the memory-forming stage. Most memory recall problems are actually caused by a failure to store information properly in the first place. Most of the strategies in this book enhance this memory-forming stage.

So memory creation requires attention, but memory *retrieval* can be conscious or involuntary (for example, a piece of music or a smell can make you recall an incident from years ago). The stronger your network of associations, the easier your recall will be, even if you have to approach a memory from an oblique angle (a technique called memory priming, which involves brainstorming your memory for everything you know on a subject to supply the answer that eludes you—*see* page 175).

Another way to categorize long-term memory is the distinction between declarative and nondeclarative (procedural) memory. Declarative memory (*see* page 173) is information we consciously store, such as facts and events, and we tend to describe and think about them using words; procedural memory (*see* page 177) involves actions—often but not exclusively physical— that we perform without having any conscious awareness of how we learned them or any need to consciously recall them: These include walking, talking, riding a bicycle, taking a shower, catching a ball. These long-term memories automatically snap into action whenever we need them.

Another important feature of memory is that it is fluid. Memories are continually being modified to inform our present circumstances. Every time we access a memory, we reinforce but also subtly change it, depending on our current interpretation. Recent research by Northwestern Medicine, published in the *Journal of Neuroscience* in August 2012, indicates that recalling a memory can make it less accurate. Lead researcher of the study, Donna Bridge, explains: "A memory is not simply an image produced by time traveling back to the original event—it can be an image that is somewhat distorted because of the prior times you remembered it". In fact, your memory can grow less precise with each recall by reinforcing earlier recall errors, so that it can end up totally false. This helps to explain why revisiting a cherished place from our past sometimes fails to live up to expectations because we have idealized it by repeated recall.

GRID MEMORY EXERCISE

This exercise extends over three days. Turn over now to receive your instructions.

DAY 1:

Spend two minutes studying the 25 objects on the previous page. Do not read any farther until you have done this.

WELCOME BACK

In the Northwestern Medicine study in Chicago, subjects had to memorize the location of a group of objects and then place them in a grid, from memory, three times over the next three days. The study found that inaccuracies in recall from the second day negatively affected recall on the third day. This is why it is important when learning, to return regularly to the source material rather than entrench inaccurate memories (if you have ever had to learn lines for a play, you will be familiar with how easy it is to learn—and how hard it is to unlearn—faulty approximations and wrong words).

Now draw a 5 x 6 grid on another piece of paper. Referring to the words only, try to place each item on your blank grid. Do not check your answers.

apple, croissant, laptop, shirt, green iron, starfish, hand with note, chick, nut, chair, crossed stack of bills, red balloon, red iron, stereo, side view notes, notepad, cat, shoes, telephone, guinea pig, calculator, cup and saucer, laptop, sunglasses, green balloon

DAY 2:

Do not look at the images or your grid from Day 1. Referring to the words only, try to place each item on another blank grid. Do not check your answers.

DAY 3:

Do not look at the images or your grids from Day 1 or 2. Referring to the words only, try to place each item on another blank grid.

Now check your answers from all three days and you'll be able to observe and track the compounded recall errors you have made throughout the exercise.

MYTHS ABOUT MEMORY

It's curious that there are so many persistent myths about memory, despite the fact that we all use and experience our own memories every day. Here are 12 common misconceptions:

MYTH 1—AMNESIACS FORGET WHO THEY ARE

By far the most common type of amnesia is anterograde amnesia, the inability to form new memories; retrograde amnesia, the loss of past memories and identity, is much rarer. Despite this, retrograde amnesiacs are overrepresented in movies—probably because they make a better plot.

MYTH 2—MEMORY IS A THING

Many people view memory as an innate quality located in a specific part of the brain, or as separate items stored ready for retrieval. Although certain parts of the brain play important roles in memory function, memory is a holistic multifaceted process rather than a physical place; it is an activity and a skill that can be developed with practice and using strategies. Also, no memories exist in isolation; they exist in a matrix of associations.

MYTH 3—SOME PEOPLE REMEMBER BEING BORN

It is highly unlikely that an adult can recall episodic memories from the first year of life, mainly because the hippocampus is too immature to form and store long-lasting memories.

MYTH 4—HYPNOSIS CAN HELP WITNESSES OF CRIMES TO RECALL MORE ACCURATE DETAILS

Hypnosis can lead to more recall but not always greater accuracy; sometimes it can reinforce inaccurate memories and create false ones. In fact, it is easy to create false memories even without hypnosis, as several "familial informant false narrative procedure" studies have shown. Parents are encouraged to mislead their grown-up children by introducing a false memory into a childhood reminiscing exercise. Afterward, up to 30 percent of the students recall the false event as if it had really happened.

FALSE MEMORY EXERCISE

One of the most interesting things about memory is how easily it can be distorted. This exercise demonstrates how simple it is to implant a false memory.

Ask a friend to perform a short memory test with you. Prepare them for the test by saying the following sentence:

"I am going to say a list of words that I want you to try to remember. Pay attention to me carefully while I read out this list. Make a mental note of them and try to remember them. Are you ready? The list begins now."

Read out this list of 15 words, allowing about a second for each word.

Cotton candy, sugar, bitter, love, taste, bite, honey, nice, tooth, pastry, chocolate, heart, cake, eat, pie

Now say: *"OK, that's the list. Now spend a few moments with your thoughts while you try to remember as many items on the list as you can."*

Hand them pen and paper and get them to write down as many of the words as they can.

Now say: *"I'd like you to tell me whether these four words were on the list. The first word is taste. Write down yes, no, or not sure. Was taste on the list? The second word is roof. Was that one of the words on my list? Write down yes, no, or not sure. The third word is brief. Write down yes, no, or not sure. Did brief appear on my list? The fourth word is sweet. Did sweet appear on my list? Write down yes, no, or not sure. OK, the memory test is over. Now tell me: What did you write for sweet?"*

Most people who take this memory test are convinced that "sweet" is on the list. However, most of the words are related to sweet. In this instance the false memory was created by association and the power of suggestion.

STUDY THIS PICTURE FOR ONE MINUTE. AFTER THE MINUTE IS UP, TURN THE PAGE, STUDY THE SECOND PICTURE, AND ANSWER THE QUESTION.

TEN ITEMS ARE MISSING FROM THIS PICTURE.
HOW MANY OF THEM CAN YOU WRITE DOWN?

MYTH 5—OLDER PEOPLE HAVE POOR MEMORIES

It is well established that mental exercises during childhood and late adulthood contribute to a slower mental decline in old age, but a team at Tübingen University in Germany has proposed a theory that healthy old people don't suffer mental decline at all: They just know so much that their brains take longer to process all the information, in the same way that a computer's hard drive slows down when it's full. It's never too late to develop your memory skills.

MYTH 6—A STRONG MEMORY IS A SIGN OF INTELLIGENCE

Visual working memory capacity has been correlated with academic success and fluid intelligence (problem solving), but having a wide general knowledge, winning quizzes, and peppering your conversation with pithy quotations is no indicator of a high IQ, although it often passes for such. Real intelligence is demonstrated by a person's ability to assimilate new information and to think creatively. However, that is not to say that people who demonstrate extraordinary memory skills lack intelligence, because it takes intelligence and discipline to develop any skill to a high level. If you develop your memory skills, you will be able to outperform a high-IQ person who lacks a systematic approach to memorizing and retrieving information.

MYTH 7—FORGETTING OCCURS GRADUALLY

Actually, most forgetting occurs immediately after an event. Most of what we forget, we never remembered in the first place, or stored in a haphazard way, making retrieval difficult.

MYTH 8—CONFIDENT RECOLLECTIONS ARE ACCURATE RECOLLECTIONS

Confidence is not an indicator of objectivity nor accuracy of recollection. Our memories are altered by many factors, especially information we receive after the event. Much research has been done on the "misinformation effect" which happens when our episodic memory becomes distorted by postevent information. In one famous study, subjects were shown photos of a college student in a bookstore with different objects; when they were made to read a misleading passage of text after viewing the images, their recall of the objects was adversely affected.

MYTH 9—DEVELOPING MEMORY SKILLS IS EASY

Anyone can improve their memory, but many of the techniques take practice, just like any other skill. You can learn a mnemonic to memorize the colors of the spectrum but remembering takes effort to learn and apply memory techniques, rather than tricks. Anything worth doing requires attention and mental effort.

MYTH 10—MEMORY IS LIKE A VIDEO RECORDER

A video recording is an objective and accurate record of visual data, whereas memory is fluid, active, and subjective; memories change every time we access them, which is good for those who want to heal themselves by reframing painful memories, but bad news for the justice system, because the memories of eyewitnesses are notoriously subjective and fickle. We see and remember what our emotions, prejudices, and belief systems want us to remember.

MYTH 11—MEMORY IS PRIMARILY VISUAL

Memory begins with perception through the five senses, but images stored in the long-term visual memory are reinforced and given meaning by their connection with other stored knowledge, which is often semantic. Researchers at MIT and Harvard demonstrated this with experiments in which participants were shown a stream of 3,000 images of different scenes, such as golf courses, amusement parks, and ocean waves; then they were shown 200 pairs of images, each featuring one previously seen and one new image, and had to pick out the former. Recall was most accurate where the new and old images featured different scenes (e.g. golf course/airport rather than airport/airport), suggesting that during the memorization process, the visual images had been categorized and meaning had been attached to them using a non-visual format.

MYTH 12—TAKING A PHOTOGRAPH AIDS MEMORY

Actually the opposite is true. A study led by Linda Henkel, a psychology professor at Fairfield University in Connecticut, found that people remember 10 percent fewer objects and 12 percent fewer details than people who just observe them. She explains, "When you press click on that button for the camera, you're sending a signal to your brain saying, 'I've just outsourced this, the camera is going to remember this for me.'" This is further proof that attention is a key component of memory.

PARTY PEOPLE MEMORY TEST

You have thrown a party and these are the first nine people to arrive. They are very pleased to see you. To help you remember who came to your party, use a real camera or your cell phone to photograph them, either one by one or in small groups—they have held a pose for you. You have just 60 seconds to do this, under 7 seconds for each guest.

CAN YOU PICK OUT YOUR NINE GUESTS FROM THIS IDENTITY PARADE?

NOW TRY THE SAME EXERCISE WITH THIS NEW GROUP OF FRIENDS, ONLY THIS TIME SPEND YOUR 60 SECONDS JUST LOOKING AT THE PEOPLE.

CAN YOU PICK OUT YOUR NINE GUESTS FROM THIS IDENTITY
PARADE? YOU SHOULD FIND IT EASIER THIS TIME.

YOU REMEMBER MORE
THAN YOU THINK

In 1946, the American pediatrician Dr. Benjamin Spock published his book *Baby and Child Care*, which went on to become one of the biggest bestsellers of all time. For 50 years its sales were second only to the Bible. Spock encouraged parents to be more flexible and affectionate toward their children and to trust their own parental instincts. His critics blamed him for creating a new permissiveness, a "Spock generation" of pampered and indulged beatniks who sought instant gratification. However, the book's opening sentence and core message, "You know more than you think you do," is very relevant to the study of memory.

We do not remember facts in isolation; everything is connected and context is very important. Here are five images of a reasonably well-known country.

Stripped of context and rotated 180 degrees, the first image is fiendishly elusive for obvious reasons. If you are very familiar with the shape of the country, you might be able to recognize it from the second image without the added context supplied in the third image (that it's an island). Now you simply have to trawl your memory for islands. The fourth image tells you that it is off the coast of Africa (if you know that Mozambique is in Africa). For many people the fifth image supplies enough information to correctly name the island nation. The more context that is supplied, the easier it is to recall the desired information from your memory. The shape becomes familiar when we are supplied with context.

However, if you are still struggling, it is also the name of a 2005 computer-animated comedy movie produced by DreamWorks Animation featuring Marty the zebra (Chris Rock), Alex the lion (Ben Stiller), Melman the giraffe (David Schwimmer), and Gloria the hippopotamus (Jada Pinkett Smith). You see? You remember more than you think. If you are still clueless, then take comfort from the fact that you probably recognize the word "Madagascar" even if you didn't know where it is. Failing that, stored in your memory is, at the very least, the knowledge that "Madagascar" is a country/island/place/movie/name/word.

For decades, cognitive psychologists have believed that although the short-term memory contains fewer items than long-term memory, it is more detailed than the information contained in the long-term memory, which is more generalized and fuzzy. However, recent research by Timothy F. Brady, a cognitive neuroscientist at the Massachusetts Institute of Technology, indicates that long-term memory is capable of retaining much finer visual detail than once thought. Observers were shown 2,500 pictures of real world objects for 3 seconds each over a period of five hours. Later that day they were shown pairs of similar items and asked to choose which of the items they had already seen. Not only were they more than 90 percent correct at identifying familiar items, but they were able to notice subtle differences between two superficially similar objects, such as bells with different handles or differently shaped pieces of fruit.

Here are five images of Madagascar. Only one of them is correct. Can you remember which it is?

See? You do remember more than you think.

SET A TIMER AND ALLOW YOURSELF 90 SECONDS TO
OBSERVE THESE OBJECTS. THEN TURN THE PAGE AND
FOLLOW THE INSTRUCTIONS.

HERE ARE 20 PAIRS OF OBJECTS. CHOOSE WHICH ITEM FROM EACH PAIR APPEARS ON THE PREVIOUS PAGE.

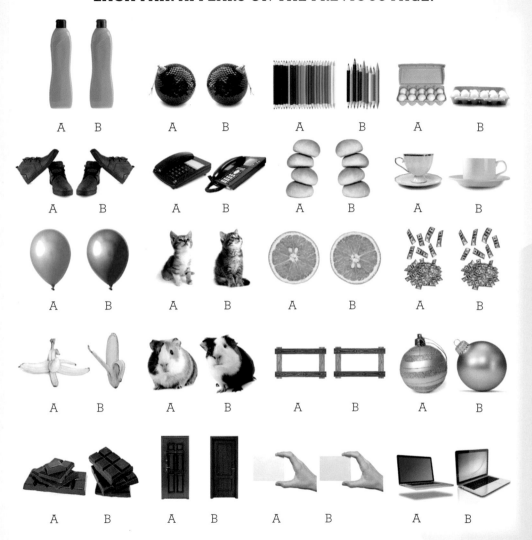

Now check your answers and you may be pleasantly suprised.
Most people will get at least 14 correct.

MEMORY ABILITY IS DEVELOPED,
NOT INNATE

A HUNDRED YEARS AGO IT WAS WIDELY BELIEVED THAT EXPERTS WERE BLESSED WITH AN INNATE AND SUPERIOR ABILITY TO STORE INFORMATION IN THEIR MEMORY.

However, recent research has shown that experts develop memory skills that are limited to their specific area of expertise and that their memories are comparable to those of the general public when the same information is presented in an unfamiliar way.

For example, chess grandmasters can recognize a huge number of chess positions and develop optimal moves from them; they can look at a board containing 20 or more chess pieces and remember the positions of each piece. However, if these pieces are randomly arranged rather than replicating actual game play, chess experts fare no better than anyone else. This was demonstrated by a famous study by William Chase and Herbert Simon called "Perception in Chess" which was published in *Cognitive Psychology* in 1973.

This shows that chess experts do not use eidetic (photographic) memory, but instead recall a collection of meaningful associations between the pieces.

Professional mnemonists, like eight-time World Memory Champion Dominic O'Brien, make their living by memorizing vast amounts of data such as decks of cards, lists of numbers, or unfamiliar names. In common with chess experts, they have spent many years of intense preparation developing memory techniques for specific memory tasks. In May 2002, Dominic O'Brien entered the *Guinness Book of Records* for memorizing a random sequence of 2,808 playing cards (54 packs) after looking at each card only once. He then recited them in order and made only eight errors, four of which he corrected. But he, like everyone else in the mnemonist community, has developed a personal system (The Mnemonic Dominic System) and has spent years practicing to reach an international level of performance. If you passionately want to improve your memory, then your innate memory ability is far less important than your willingness to learn and practice the techniques that will show dramatic results.

HOW AND WHY
DO WE FORGET?

To many people, forgetting is an inconvenience with entirely negative consequences, but actually, sifting, refining, and forgetting experiences are important components of the memory process, and forgetting is part of a healthy mind. There are four main reasons why we forget information: Storage failure, retrieval failure, interference, and motivation.

STORAGE FAILURE

We often mistakenly talk about having forgotten something when we simply failed to commit it to long-term memory in the first place. Most forgetting takes place soon after we learn something. Our brains decide what information is useful for our day-to-day life, and extraneous data is rejected.

In a famous experiment by research psychologists Raymond Nickerson and Marilyn Adams in 1979, subjects had to pick out a genuine 1-cent coin from 14 inaccurate ones. Fewer than half of the test subjects could identify the correct penny. How could such a seemingly familiar object, handled every day by millions of people, be so hard to spot? The reason is that memory is regulated on a need-to-know basis. All that daily life needs is recognizing a penny by its size, shape, color, and a few salient details, such as Lincoln's head. For most people, any deeper knowledge is not needed beyond this basic functional information, so it isn't remembered.

Try this experiment now. Think about your front door key. How much detail can you remember? Shape, size, and color most likely, enough so you can tell it apart from any other keys on your key ring. But what about the writing? You can probably guess the brand name, but fetch it now and take a look at the other side; there may be a whole load of numbers and writing you've never even noticed before, let alone remembered.

RETRIEVAL FAILURE

"We really construct memories rather than record them," explains Elizabeth Loftus, Professor of Psychology at the University of Washington. "We store bits and pieces of information, and when it comes time to retrieve we take bits and pieces of our experience from different times and we integrate it." Retrieval failure is one of the most common causes of forgetting. The information is in your long-term memory (and you may even know that you know it), but you can't access it. One explanation is "decay theory": That just as we construct memories, we reinforce them by revisiting them; if memories are not revisited, they gradually fade away. However, this clearly doesn't apply to all long-term memories, since we can all recall events, faces, and places that we haven't visited or thought about for decades.

INTERFERENCE

The "interference theory" of memory suggests that memories compete and interfere with each other in two basic ways: Proactively (an old memory makes recall of a new memory more difficult) and retroactively (when new information disrupts your ability to recall older information). Much research has been done on the effect of interference on the learning of lists; unsurprisingly, as the number of lists increases, so does the interference. In one such experiment, subjects had to learn a list of ten paired adjectives. Two days later they were able to recall close to 70 percent of the items. However, subjects who were also asked to learn a new list the day after the first recalled only 40 percent, and those who had learned a third list had only 25 percent recall.

MOTIVATION

Sometimes we either suppress (consciously) or repress (subconsciously) memories, often unpleasant and even traumatic events. Psychologists disagree about the mechanism involved in repression, since a major component of memory retention is revisiting and rehearsal of memories, so it may simply be that by avoiding thinking of unpleasant events our memories of them are weakened.

Humans tend to have a greater recall of unpleasant memories compared with positive ones. This psychological phenomenon is called negativity bias. While it is an important survival skill for avoiding danger and minimizing the repetition of negative experiences, research has shown that negative experiences have a greater impact on people than positive or neutral ones. Professor Teresa Amabile is Edsel Bryant Ford Professor of Business Administration in the Entrepreneurial Management Unit at Harvard Business School. Her research into the psychology of everyday worklife has found that professionals viewed negative setbacks twice as strongly as positive achievements in a working day. For this reason, consciously trying to act and think positively is an important tool, because we have to overcompensate for negativity bias.

TAKING CARE OF YOUR HEALTH IS THE
BEST MEMORY BOOST

Memory techniques can produce substantial cognitive improvements, but by far the best way to boost your memory is to improve your health. From exercise to sleep and nutrition, here are some of nature's ways to improve your memory.

SLEEP

Your brain relies on sleep to figure out which neural connections need to be reinforced. It can't do this effectively while you are awake, which is why sleep is essential for memory consolidation and learning new information. Research has shown that depriving students of sleep after they had learned a new skill significantly decreased their memory of that skill up to three days later. Some areas of memory are affected more than others. Procedural memory (which involves motor and perceptual skills—*see* page 177) is more affected by sleep than declarative memory (learning of facts—*see* page 173).

STRESS

Stress interferes with neurotransmitter function and can even decrease the size of the prefrontal cortex and the hippocampus. Neurotoxins such as drugs and alcohol also place considerable stress on your body and nervous system; heavy alcohol use has also been linked to a reduction in the size of the hippocampus. However, moderate drinking appears to be better for your memory than total abstinence.

EXERCISE

Taking moderate exercise at least three times a week increases blood flow and oxygenation of the brain, which improves neural function, including memory. Studies have shown that the speed of declarative memory tasks, such as learning vocabulary words, was increased by 20 percent when performed after an intense workout.

DENTAL HYGIENE

Flossing before bed can boost your memory. When bad bacteria collect between your teeth, they enter the bloodstream and cause inflammation throughout the body, including the brain.

MEMORY FOODS

A healthy diet is vital for good brain function. Don't skip breakfast or cut out food groups. A study at Tufts University found that cutting out carbohydrates impaired performance on memory-based tasks.

Whole grains: Cereal grains that contain germ, endosperm, and bran (such as rolled oats, brown rice, rye bread) provide vitamins B6, B12, and B9, and provide slow-release energy, to ensure stable blood sugar levels for optimal memory function.

Nuts and seeds: These are a powerhouse for the memory and many of them help maintain healthy levels of the calming neurotransmitter serotonin and the mood stabilizing hormones epinephrine, norepinephrine, and dopamine; they also increase oxygen flow to the brain. Many (especially pecans) are a good source of zinc, used in the hippocampus to process memory, provide omega-6 and omega-3 fatty acids, and protect the brain against motor neuron degeneration.

Berries and green vegetables: Dark berries such as blueberries, blackcurrants, and blackberries, are the best memory fruits; they provide vitamin C and protect the brain from oxidative stress; strawberries contain more vitamin C than oranges and reduce the risk of age-related brain decline; pomegranates and dark leafy green vegetables (spinach, broccoli, kale) contain high levels of folic acid and may promote healthy beta-amyloid function to reduce the risk of Alzheimer's disease.

Avocados: The term "superfood" is much overused, but avocados deserve the accolade; they are rich in monounsaturated fat, which aids blood flow, they lower blood pressure, and stimulate the central nervous system.

Fish: Oily fish (salmon, mackerel, tuna) are rich in omega-3 fatty acids, which are very important for the function of neurons.

Sage: This herb has been used as a memory tonic for thousands of years. Many studies have focussed on the essential oil but adding fresh sage to your diet may also promote memory.

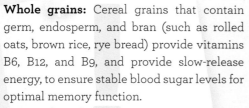

You can learn heaps of mnemonics and read as many books on the subject as you like, but all that memory-busting work will be wasted unless you fuel your brain and body with the correct nutrients. Here are two practical and tasty ways to help develop optimal brain health.

MEMORY SMOOTHIE

This delicious drink will help to stabilize blood sugar, increase blood flow to the brain, and supply you with phytonutrients, folates, and beta-carotene.

½ cup unsweetened carrot juice

⅔ cup fresh blueberries

½ cup peeled and grated raw beets

¼ cup chopped avocado

heaping ½ cup toasted almonds or walnuts

3 normal size ice cubes

½ teaspoon fresh lime juice

1 thin slice fresh ginger

Place all the ingredients in a blender and blend until the texture is smooth and velvety.

POWER SEED AND NUT GRANOLA BARS

2 cups rolled oats

½ cup (1 stick) butter

3 tablespoons flax seeds

¼ cup pecans

3 tablespoons almonds

3 tablespoons shelled sunflower seeds

⅓ cup brown sugar

3 tablespoons corn syrup or honey

1. Preheat the oven to 350°F.
    Place all ingredients in a food processor and pulse until fully mixed. Don't overdo it: You don't want the oats to completely lose their integrity.

2. Spoon the mixture into a lightly greased baking pan, measuring about 8 inches square, and then press the mixture flat.

3. Bake in the preheated oven until golden brown (about 20–30 minutes).

SHORT-TERM MEMORY

SHORT-TERM MEMORY, ALSO KNOWN AS ACTIVE OR PRIMARY MEMORY, INVOLVES TEMPORARY STORAGE OF INFORMATION WHICH DECAYS VERY QUICKLY.

Most of us can reliably store between four and seven items in our short-term memory for between 15 and 30 seconds. Short-term memory is often referred to as working memory, but actually they are different. The short-term memory only stores information, while, as the name suggests, working memory involves mental organization or manipulation of the information, as happens when you perform mental calculations or play tic-tac-toe or chess in your head (depending on your working memory ability).

Your five main senses—sight, hearing, taste, smell, touch—receive sensory information which is briefly stored in your short-term memory, as a mixture of auditory, visual, and semantic information (since we might see an object and then repeat—rehearse—the word in our heads, to store the word in our auditory memory). For more information about the part of the short-term memory we call sensory memory, *see* page 165.

Only information that is rehearsed and encoded passes from the short-term memory into the long-term memory. If you receive a piece of information and someone immediately distracts you and prevents you from rehearsing it, it will quickly fade from your short-term memory. Much research has been done into the size, duration, and effect of interference on short-term memory.

Psychologist George Miller of Princeton University's Department of Psychology was the first person to measure the capacity of the short-term memory. In 1956 he published his seminal paper, "The Magical Number Seven, Plus or Minus Two: Some Limits on Our Capacity for Processing Information," in *Psychological Review*. The paper introduced the "magic number seven (plus or minus two)", which became widely cited as the number of objects a person can hold in their short-term memory without using rehearsal or special memory techniques. Other studies have shown that people find it easier to remember numbers than letters.

THE BROWN–PETERSON TASK

In 1959, Lloyd and Margaret Peterson conducted an experiment with 24 psychology students at Indiana University to measure the duration of the short-term memory when rehearsal is prevented. The students heard a meaningless consonant trigram, e.g. TDH, then they had to immediately count backward verbally in threes or fours from a specified random number for 3, 6, 9, 12, 15, or 18 seconds. The counting was designed to prevent them from rehearsing the trigram in their memories. Participants were able to recall 80 percent of the trigrams after 3 seconds of counting but this fell to less than 10 percent after 18 seconds of counting.

A second experiment was conducted by John Brown with 48 Indiana University psychology students. The control group of 24 students performed the Peterson experiment but the other 24 participants were allowed to repeat the trigram aloud until they were given the number and had to start counting backward from it. The rehearsal interval was varied, and the study concluded that a longer rehearsal period resulted in greater recall.

You can conduct your own Brown–Peterson Task on a willing volunteer. Here are 48 consonant trigrams.

NRP	SGH	SGN	LWH	DTP	RPJ	CLT	ZHW
DTQ	MPX	BKR	ZKC	KBP	XRN	FPS	NWL
PCW	PYK	MCW	MZQ	LJB	JWF	PBZ	YBV
WNG	LRC	BCX	BQM	KSF	LCV	LPD	BQT
PRK	YCV	TBX	DMB	JYW	KFL	XNZ	MDT
WSD	YFP	HCX	DPW	CNJ	YSP	NQW	MDP

If you make up your own trigrams, be sure to avoid memorable acronyms such as MGM or KFC.

Repeat eight times with six different counting times—3, 6, 9, 12, 15, and 18 seconds—and record the number of letters correctly recalled each time. That should keep you busy!

SENSORY MEMORY

YOUR SHORT-TERM MEMORY IS CONTINUALLY BOMBARDED WITH SENSORY INPUT FROM YOUR FIVE MAIN SENSES—SIGHT, HEARING, TASTE, SMELL, AND TOUCH. EACH SENSE HAS A CORRESPONDING SHORT-TERM MEMORY STORE, BUT THE MOST COMMONLY STUDIED ARE SIGHT (ICONIC), HEARING (ECHOIC), AND TOUCH (HAPTIC).

ICONIC MEMORY

This visual sense memory is very brief: less than 100 milliseconds. If you wave a sparkler in the dark, iconic memory allows you to perceive continuity of movement, so the sparkler will appear to draw lines and shapes, because you visually remember its trajectory. Here's another example of iconic memory:

1. Look at the yellow dot for 15 seconds   2. Now look here

Iconic memory is important for visual continuity but its rapid rate of decay accounts for a much-studied psychological phenomenon called "change blindness." This is the failure to notice a change (even significant differences) in a visual stimulus. Our ability to retain visual information in one glance to the next is actually remarkably limited.

LOOK AT THESE TWO PHOTOGRAPHS. HOW QUICKLY CAN YOU SPOT A SINGLE MAJOR DIFFERENCE?

ECHOIC MEMORY

Scientists disagree about how long this auditory memory lasts: anywhere from one to ten seconds. It is easier for us to remember the sounds that have linguistic meaning for us, such as letters, words, and numbers, because these sounds are already stored in our long-term memory. Adults and children with learning disabilities often have shorter echoic memories, so they have to work harder to understand the spoken word, which is why additional visual input can be useful. Visual stimuli can be scanned by the eye again and again while the brain makes sense of the information, whereas auditory information is usually only supplied once. We all have a preference for either visual, auditory, or kinesthetic learning because we often have one dominant type of memory (iconic, echoic, or haptic) and corresponding learning style (take the test on pages 191–196 to find yours).

ECHOIC MEMORY GAME

Give each player a pen and paper. Here are ten lists of one-syllable words. The first list has just four objects and the last has 13. Read the first list aloud evenly and clearly (it should take about two seconds). As soon as you have finished speaking, players attempt to quickly write down all the objects. Now read the next list at the same pace as the first (it should take about two and a half seconds) and once again, players may start writing as soon as you have finished speaking. By the time you reach the tenth list (which should take about seven seconds) most players will be struggling. The person who correctly writes down the most objects is the winner.

cat, bulb, fish, sky
roof, claw, lamp, cup, bed
pin, tree, hat, spade, coat, gun
heart, spoon, tent, cake, horse, wall, spot
shelf, hedge, mouth, chair, bread, girl, box, pig
ear, class, bird, train, bag, rent, salt, wind, comb
hand, rat, soil, door, night, pen, fox, dirt, egg, hawk
moon, wax, nest, wand, sheep, sword, silk, queen, sand, badge, zoo
throne, meal, base, mint, art, ghost, plate, quilt, edge, match, home, rest
tongue, mind, frog, noise, rice, pest, glove, song, rail, vase, dime, bell, shade

Now, as a brief demonstration of the power of "chunking" (*see* page 207), read out these two lists of 12 words (with the rhythm "dum-di-dum-di-dum-di-dum, dum-dum-dum-dum-dum") and see their recall dramatically improve. (You can also repeat some of the longer lists above and chunk them in the same way.)

ghost, hawk, hand, rent, wind, sheep, spade
bread, home, frog, cake, shelf

----

heart, song, hat, door, tree, sword, ear
sky, glove, hedge, pest, cup

HAPTIC MEMORY

This sensory memory is the information that is briefly retained after a tactile stimulus has been supplied. We have haptic sensory receptors all over our bodies that can detect different types of tactile stimuli, such as pressure, pain, and itching. This information is transmitted through the spinal cord to the primary somatosensory area in the human cortex, which is located in the postcentral gyrus of the parietal lobe of the brain.

Developments in haptic technology have snowballed since the beginning of the twenty-first century so now we are accustomed to receiving haptic feedback from a wide range of everyday consumer devices such as vibrating cell phones, game controllers, and joysticks.

As well as protecting us from danger, information derived from haptic memory enables us to predict how much force to use for everyday tasks, such as grasping and lifting. However, we also use a lot of visual clues, which can sometimes mislead. If identical weights are placed inside two boxes of differing sizes, the smaller box will feel heavier than the bigger one. This is called the Charpentier Illusion, named after the nineteenth-century French physician Augustin Charpentier. The same effect also occurs with construction materials: Metal containers and darker objects feel lighter than wooden boxes and brighter objects of the same size and mass. Scientists disagree on the reason why this happens, but it is likely that one factor is a temporary conflict between the visual and haptic memory systems.

TWO SUITCASES TRICK

We have all felt foolish after using too little or too much force to lift a suitcase. You can actually study this phenomenon yourself. Take two identical suitcases. Fill the first so that it is heavy and leave the other one empty. Now ask an unsuspecting victim to help you carry them. Give them the heavy suitcase, so they form a haptic memory of the force required; then a bit later get them to pick up the empty one.

It's really hard to play this trick on yourself because even if you get someone to shuffle the suitcases behind your back, when you pick them up, you will find that your body is primed for both possible outcomes.

LONG-TERM MEMORY

ONCE A MEMORY HAS PASSED FROM THE SHORT-TERM MEMORY BUFFER INTO THE LONG-TERM MEMORY, THE MORE IT IS SUBSEQUENTLY REVISITED AND REHEARSED, THE STRONGER IT BECOMES.

Once implanted, a long-term memory can last forever, but the data isn't fixed in the memory like an insect in amber. Each time a memory is revisited it is altered. This description is the standard Atkinson–Shiffrin Memory Model (formulated in the 1960s by Richard C. Atkinson and Richard Shiffrin) but there are alternative memory models like the Baddeley–Hitch (formulated in the 1970s by Alan Baddeley and Graham Hitch), which presents an alternative version of the short-term memory in which a central executive controls input from several slave systems such as the sensory memories.

Pick one of the four images on the next page. Spend three minutes observing the details, then close the book and draw the most accurate reproduction you can from memory using colored pencils. Now compare your drawing with the photo and spend another three minutes observing the same photo. Then close the book and draw the object a second time. Repeat this process as many times as you like and you should eventually create a detailed representation in your long-term memory.

Notice that this task doesn't just rely on your visual memory. For instance, if you have chosen the striped candies or the boots, you will almost certainly have consciously counted the five white stripes or the four white lace eyelets. Even people who are judged to have a photographic memory (eidetic memory, *see* page 181) often appear to "think" and make mental notes about what they view, rather than just blink their eyes and take a mental photograph. The autistic savant Stephen Wiltshire, who draws detailed pen and ink drawings of cityscapes from memory, admits, "When I am drawing I am thinking about the information and the details so I can memorize it and then draw it back."

TOPOGRAPHICAL
MEMORY

TOPOGRAPHICAL MEMORY INVOLVES THE ABILITY TO ORIENT OURSELVES IN SPACE, RECOGNIZE FAMILIAR PLACES, OR REMEMBER AND REPEAT A JOURNEY WE HAVE TAKEN.

It draws upon procedural memory because sometimes it involves a series of steps (turn right, walk forward three blocks, turn left at the church...) but it also requires the ability to imagine and recall places you have visited in no particular order (e.g. if you wanted to recall the three nearest gas stations to your home, you could mentally jump from one location to the other without making the whole journey).

In his book *The Brain's Sense of Movement,* Professor Alain Berthoz, an expert in the physiology of perception and action, says, "The ability to find one's way home or to memorize a route is not unique to humans; crabs return to the sea, bees to the hive, and desert ants to their nest using the sun to find their way. Each species has devised individual solutions to the same problem." The topographical memory feats of animals like the salmon (which battles hundreds of miles upstream heading home to breed) or the elephant (which develops a mental map of lifesaving water holes within vast areas of territory, passed down through successive generations) is also well known.

Scientists have spent decades attempting to understand the complex relationship between our vestibular apparatus (the nonauditory portion of the inner ear) and topographical memory. The vestibular system detects and tracks our movements, especially the neck, head, and eyes, and sends information about how fast we are moving to the brain, like a tachometer. The topographical memory tells us which route to follow, but our spatial orientation system also uses the vestibular information to work out the distance traveled.

All these systems work together to enable us to perform a complex operation such as walking from bed to bathroom in total darkness in the middle of the night. Alain Berthoz describes experiments that have led to "a fundamental concept: That vestibular memory is memory of movement, not of position... so the brain memorizes movement, not just places."

RABBIT MAZE

Here is a very simple demonstration of topographical memory in action. It would be impossible to complete this maze with your eyes closed, but thanks to your topographical memory, if someone else guided you to the carrot, you could find your way back to your starting position.

Close your eyes. Get a friend to place the book on the table in front of you (either sideways, upside down, or the right way up) and then get them to place the index finger of your dominant hand on the page so that it's touching one of the rabbits. When you are ready, your friend must guide your finger firmly along the maze until it reaches the carrot that is farthest away. Make sure your fingertip stays in contact with the page during the journey. Now, keeping your eyes closed, move your finger across the page in a straight line and stop where you think your carrot hunt began. You should be able to do this with considerable accuracy, using your topographical memory.

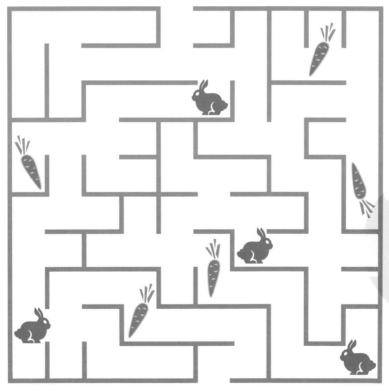

DECLARATIVE MEMORY

DECLARATIVE MEMORY IS A FORM OF LONG-TERM MEMORY THAT IS ASSOCIATED WITH REMEMBERING FACTS AND KNOWLEDGE. IT CAN BE DIVIDED INTO TWO TYPES: EPISODIC MEMORY AND SEMANTIC MEMORY.

EPISODIC MEMORY

This is the memory of all the autobiographical events in your life: The places you have visited, the parties you have been to, the good and bad things that have happened to you, and all the other contextual data associated with these events, like the time and place, the emotions and physical feelings you experienced, who you were with, what you were wearing.

These memories are highly subjective and can also affect future behavior. For example, if you have a strong episodic memory of being stung by a bee when you were six years old and found it painful and frightening, you may develop a fear of bees and wasps in adult life and try to avoid them. Episodic memory is often represented by visual imagery, but sounds and smells can also be strong triggers for long-forgotten memories (or more accurately, memories we haven't consciously recalled for a long time). We can all be transported back to the places and emotions of childhood by a memorable smell—melting blacktop on a hot day, the sound of an ice-cream truck, the antiseptic whiff of a hospital ward.

The recall of episodic memories often stirs up emotions because when an event occurs, emotion increases the likelihood that it will be recorded as a long-term memory. The fact that an event has been retained in your episodic memory in the first place is a strong indicator that it elicited powerful emotions while, or immediately after, it occurred.

HOW GOOD IS YOUR EPISODIC MEMORY?

There's little you can do to improve your episodic memory, but you can compensate by keeping a daily diary and rereading the previous day's entry each morning. As the following questions demonstrate, some episodic memories are easier to recall than others:

1. What did you have for breakfast this morning?

2. What did you have for breakfast yesterday?

3. What did you have for lunch the day before yesterday?

4. What did you have for breakfast on this day two years ago?

5. How did you celebrate your last birthday?

6. When and where was the last occasion that you injured yourself badly enough to require medical attention?

7. When was the last time you ate chocolate?

8. Why, when, and where was the last time you cried?

9. When and where was the last time and place that you drank a cup of coffee?

10. Can you remember an occasion as a child when you felt really proud?

SEMANTIC MEMORY

This is a more structured collection of facts, meanings, knowledge, and ideas, abstract and concrete, that you have learned that are part of the pool of human knowledge, independent of your own autobiographical relationship with this data.

For example, your semantic memory of a table might include its appearance, associated vocabulary (e.g. trestle, dining room, furniture), function, construction materials, context (you'd expect to see one on the floor, but not up a tree). Much of semantic memory is abstract: If someone told you to draw a table, you could create a generic representation that most people in the world would recognize as a table because semantic knowledge is shared. You could also write the word "table" and communicate the same concept to anyone who shares the same semantic memory of this word.

We learn by experience so our semantic memories are often derived from our episodic memories. Past events in our lives can reinforce semantic memory, but gradually the episodic component becomes less important so eventually we can remember semantic information independently of when, where, and how we first learned it.

The answers to these five questions all require semantic memory. As you can see, we share a common pool of knowledge, but other semantic information is more specialized:

1. Name this object.

2. What color is it?

3. Pick two words that apply to this object:
   a) food
   b) furniture
   c) animal
   d) organic

4. Name the natural organic compound that gives this object its color.

5. True or false? This object contains the phytochemicals quercetin, phloridzin, and chlorogenic acid.

You can improve your semantic memory retention with the study skills on pages 245–267, but you can also improve your recall by using your intuition (which actually means paying attention to associated fragments that pop up from your semantic memory, with support from your episodic memory).

For an example of this, see page 123 about Ogi Ogas, a final-year PhD student at Boston University's doctoral programme in cognitive neuroscience, who won $500,000 on the *Who Wants to be a Millionaire?* game show by using the technique of trusting his intuition.

Here are ten general knowledge questions. If you don't know the answers, all the better; this will give you the opportunity to jump-start your semantic memory by accessing your episodic memory and brainstorming with associated semantic memory fragments to reach plausible answers.

While answering these questions, scribble down words and ideas associated with the topic as they occur to you. Don't disregard anything, however trivial. After you've looked up the answers on page 278, search Wikipedia for more information to see how some of your associated memory fragments could have led you to the answers.

1. Which sign of the zodiac is a person whose birthday is on October 18?

2. In which Asian country does the president live in The Blue House?

3. Whose parents were Andrew Bond and Monique Delacroix and how did they die?

4. Which is the largest joint in the body?

5. What was Elton John's birth name?

6. What is measured on the Beaufort scale?

7. Name the three flavors that make up a block of Neapolitan ice cream.

8. What does the "DC" stand for in DC Comics?

9. How is Mrs. O'Leary's cow said to have caused the great Chicago fire of 1871?

10. What type of nut is usually used to flavor macaroons?

PROCEDURAL MEMORY

This is a form of long-term memory of actions which, once acquired with practice, can subsequently be performed without any conscious process of recall (colloquially and rather misleadingly referred to as doing something "without thinking" or "with your eyes shut").

Procedural memory might include riding a bike, tying shoelaces, reading, juggling, driving a car—any skill that you once had to consciously learn but which you subsequently perform without the need for conscious control.

The acquisition phase of the skill requires practice, but this does not mean just repetition. Basic skill acquisition is achieved by making subtle changes and modifying behavior with each successive repetition, learning from feedback from previous performance to improve and refine present performance.

Literacy expert Dr. Dee Tadlock has developed the patented Read Right® program to support children who are struggling readers. Her procedural memory model uses a four-step predictive strategy along with a conscious awareness of the end result (rather than relying on a detailed understanding of a skill's components). The four steps are:

1) attempt;

2) fail;

3) analyze the result;

4) decide how to change the next attempt to achieve success.

You can use this method to acquire any skill. People who repeat the same task over and over again and fail to improve, miss out on the most important but also the most mentally and emotionally challenging steps—3 and 4. Albert Einstein famously said, "Insanity is doing the same thing over and over again and expecting different results," but he could equally have substituted the words "failure" or "mediocrity."

Repeating the same mistakes can build up bad habits and muscle memories of failure, which can be very difficult to unlearn later. Mindless repetition or rote learning can be an effective (though boring) strategy when approaching semantic memory tasks (*see* page 174), such as learning your multiplication tables or a list of French vocabulary, but it should be avoided at all costs when learning new skills and procedures, otherwise you will become an expert at repeating your mistakes.

In the early 1990s, Dr. K. Anders Ericsson, a psychology professor at Florida State University, introduced the idea that it takes 10,000 hours of practice to become world class at a particular skill (20 hours for 50 weeks a year for ten years, preferably by the age of 20). This figure was then popularized by Malcolm Gladwell as the "10,000-Hour Rule" in his best-selling book *Outliers,* which examines the factors that lead to high levels of success. However, as Geoff Colvin explains in his book, *Talent Is Overrated: What Really Separates World-Class Performers from Everybody Else,* the real issue is that irrespective of how many hours you put in, whether you want to improve or become world class, you have to engage in the right sort of "deliberate practice" (*see* page 197) which uses a model similar to Dr. Tadlock's.

CHOKING AND BEING CLUTCH

At times of extreme stress, experts who have spent years honing their skills can suddenly experience a form of analysis paralysis commonly known as "choking." Some of the most famous moments in sporting history have resulted from an individual or an entire team getting the chokes. One explanation for why this occurs is "explicit monitoring theory," which suggests that the performer suddenly becomes self-consciously aware of the step-by-step components of the skill, disrupting the procedural memory so that it momentarily ceases to be automatic.

The antithesis of choking is when expert performers are "in the zone," when procedural memory is uninhibited allowing optimal performance.

There is also a third variation which we call being "clutch": Coming up with a big play when your team needs you, such as when an underdog rises to the occasion and beats a superior individual or team. The player with "clutch" achieves this by actually increasing his or her conscious awareness of the procedural performance. The same mechanism that causes an expert to choke can actually improve the performance of the relative novice.

EMOTION AND MEMORY

The most vivid events in episodic memory tend to be emotional. We recall events that have an emotional component with more clarity and detail than neutral events. For our Neolithic ancestors this would have been important for social bonding but it would also have been an important survival skill.

Individuals learned about the dangers of their environment through trial and error; there would have been a selective advantage for those who remembered emotional events, and an even greater advantage for those who remembered negative emotional events, as this could help them to avoid or escape similar dangers the next time they occurred. Modern humans retain this "negativity bias"—they have a greater recall of unpleasant memories compared with positive ones.

J. A. Easterbrook's Cue Utilization Theory (University of New Brunswick, Canada, 1959) proposes that when we experience an emotional event, high arousal leads to a narrowed focus-increased attention on the emotional component (the cues) and the causes of those emotions with a corresponding decrease in attention from other nonemotional parts of the stimulus. The emotional parts of the stimulus are encoded, while the other nonemotional details are neglected. This demonstrates once again that attention plays a key role in encoding, retention, and future recall.

This effect is responsible for a phenomenon called "weapon focus effect" in which witnesses to a violent crime can remember and describe the weapon in great detail, but have poor recall of the other details such as the attacker's clothing.

BULLET TIME

When people are placed in heightened emotional states, especially when they experience emergencies, such as a car crash, they frequently report the sensation of time slowing down. Scientists used to think that this was caused by the body producing epinephrine, making the brain think more quickly and providing a boost of energy to either run away from danger or fight. But recent experiments have shown this is not the case: It's a trick of memory.

Scientists at Baylor College of Medicine in Houston measured this apparent time-slowing effect by getting volunteers to jump backward and fall 48 feet into a safety net. During their descent the volunteers reached 70 mph (with no safety ropes), and even though it was completely safe, this terrifying experience produced the requisite fear.

As they fell, each subject was required to read out numbers that flashed onto a little video monitor that was strapped to their wrist. The rate at which the numbers flashed on and off the screen was calibrated so that it was a little too fast to be perceived under normal circumstances, but although subjects reported a perceived slowing of time, their ability to read the flashing numbers was not improved; their perception speeds did not increase.

SO WHAT REALLY HAPPENS IN YOUR BRAIN DURING AN EMERGENCY?

Deep in the brain's medial temporal lobe is an almond-shaped set of neurons called the amygdala which processes memory and emotional reactions. During times of heightened emotion, the amygdala becomes more active and encodes more memories per second than normal, and these memories are also stronger because of the emotional component.

The more memories you have of an event, the longer it appears to take. This also explains why childhood summers appear in retrospect to have been long and sunny: We lay down more memories as children because we are exposed to so many new stimuli and have a heightened emotional response to them; in adulthood we become more world-weary and less attentive to our surroundings.

On the next right-hand page there is a photo of an assailant holding a weapon. Turn the page, stare directly at the assailant, and call firmly three times, "Police, drop your weapon!" Then close your eyes immediately, turn back to this page, open your eyes again, and answer the questions below.

see explanation on page 278

3. How many ears did she have?

2. Write down everything that you can remember about the assailant's physical appearance: clothes, jewelry, makeup, etc.

1. Did you get a good look at the weapon? Write down a description of the gun: colors, shape, etc.

EIDETIC MEMORY

COMMONLY REFERRED TO AS "PHOTOGRAPHIC MEMORY," EIDETIC MEMORY IS THE RARE ABILITY TO MEMORIZE SIGHTS, SOUNDS, AND OTHER OBJECTS WITH A VERY HIGH LEVEL OF DETAIL.

Visual and auditory memory are vitally important perceptual and learning skills. In sighted people, 80 percent of learning relies on the eyes while auditory memory is a key component of language acquisition and comprehension. Between two and ten percent of children appear to have visual eidetic abilities, but these diminish after the age of six as language and auditory memory become dominant.

Genuine eidetic ability in adulthood is very rare and is usually accompanied by significant cognitive deficits. The majority of true eidetic memorizers are developmentally delayed, as epitomized by the character Raymond Babbitt in the movie *Rain Man*. The real-life inspiration for this character was Kim Peek, an American savant, who was not autistic but was born without a corpus callosum, the band of white matter that connects the two hemispheres of the brain. Consequently, he could read quickly with high recall by scanning the left page with his left eye, and the right page with his right eye.

By contrast, most professional memorizers use techniques that they have spent many years practicing, although their memory feats appear so incomprehensible to the casual observer that they can easily be mistaken for eidetic memorizers.

The Russian composer and pianist Sergei Rachmaninov is said to have been able to perfectly recall any musical score after sight-reading it twice. He was unable to perform the same feat with a page of written text, however, so clearly it was a learned and specialized skill (albeit amazing), akin to that of the chess grandmasters who can recognize a huge number of viable chess positions, but fare no better than novice players when viewing a random configuration of pieces.

Mozart is probably the most well-known auditory eidetic. It is said that he could play a piece of music after listening to it only once, or conceive note-perfect symphonies in his head. However, Mozart was not born with the former skill and the latter is a myth, since his heavily annotated manuscripts show that he continually revised and reworked his compositions. Mozart's genius was largely the product of being intensively drilled from the age of three by a domineering father who was a famous composer and expert teacher.

Young Mozart was composing by the age of five, but many of his early compositions were heavily corrected by his father. Geoff Colvin points out in his book *Talent is Overrated* that "Wolfgang's first four piano concertos, composed when he was eleven, actually contain no original music by him. He put them together out of works by other composers." That is not to deny that he grew into one of the greatest composers who ever lived, but this was the result of "years of extremely hard, expert training."

AUTISTIC SAVANTS

Autistic savants who perform complex mental calculations have developed a highly specialized working memory, which allows them to "simply" perform a mental algorithm, unhindered by the distraction of normal social interaction. The right brain compensates for the left brain (*see* page 239), or maybe even has the luxury of being able to use all that left hemisphere brain space that isn't being gobbled up by language. Research has shown that savant abilities decrease as communication skills improve, so it seems that true eidetic ability can only be achieved by sacrificing areas of the brain that would normally be appropriated for resource-hungry socialization skills and other executive brain functions.

MUSICAL MEMORY

MUSICAL MEMORY IS THE ABILITY TO REMEMBER MUSIC-RELATED INFORMATION, INCLUDING NOTES, TONES, MUSICAL SEQUENCES (MELODIES, AND PITCHES. IT IS PRIMARILY NONVERBAL AND ENCODED DIFFERENTLY FROM LANGUAGE, ALTHOUGH IT IS PART OF AUDITORY MEMORY AND THE PHONOLOGICAL LOOP (WORKING MEMORY FOR MAINLY VERBAL INFORMATION).

Both the left and right sides of the brain are involved in processing music (in common with most brain tasks), but studies of patients with brain damage have led scientists to theorize that the left side of the brain is primarily responsible for long-term musical memory, while the right hemisphere is responsible for mediating access to this memory.

Memory expert Hervé Platel was one of the first scientists to explore the distinction between "musical semantic memory" and "verbal semantic memory," since "practically nothing is known about the functional anatomy of long-term memory for music."

He defines the former as "memory for 'well-known' melodies without any knowledge of the spatial or temporal circumstances of learning." He took PET scans of the brains of 11 subjects while they performed musical semantic memory and verbal semantic memory tasks, and discovered that different parts of the brain are activated for each kind of memory, although they share "a common network throughout the left-sided temporal neocortex."

Other research has looked at the relationship between musical and episodic memory. It has long been known that music can trigger memories, often emotional, but a recent study has shown where in the brain this occurs. Petr Janata, a cognitive neuroscientist at the University of California, Davis, scanned the brains of 13 volunteers while they were exposed to 30 different songs from the popular music chart, corresponding to the dates during which they were aged between 8 and 18. Subjects had to indicate when a piece of music triggered an autobiographical (episodic) memory.

Janata observed that the strongest episodic memories were accompanied by the most emotional responses, while the brain scans showed increased activity in the medial prefrontal cortex at these moments.

This study helps to explain why music can reach deep into the memories of patients with dementia. "What's striking is that the prefrontal cortex is among the last [of the brain regions] to atrophy," Janata notes. Patients who appear inert, depressed, and unresponsive can briefly reacquire their identities and become animated when played music from their earlier life. After the music stops, the positive effects continue: Despite previously having been incapable of answering even the simplest questions, now briefly restored for a few minutes, they can talk, engage with others, and even sing.

HOW TO MEMORIZE A PIECE OF MUSIC

If you play an instrument you will know how elusive your musical memory can be. You think you know a piece inside out, then you take a music exam or perform on stage and suddenly your memory doesn't seem so solid. Worse still, performance anxiety threatens to make your mind go completely blank.

What can you do to commit a piece to memory, and then ensure that your memory doesn't choke when you have to play in public?

In later chapters we will discuss how people remember objects in a spatial relationship (*see* page 213) and use landmarks to remember objects outdoors (*see* page 215).

Well, the same happens with playing an instrument. If you have learned to perform a piece in one location, your memories become associated with and, to a certain extent, dependent on that place. You can tune out your surroundings because they are familiar, but when you move to another location, with different sight lines and a different acoustic environment, your music memory has to compete with all these added stimuli and the task becomes much harder.

So, if possible, before a performance or exam, try to replicate those conditions, so your brain doesn't have to take up processing space to block out new stimuli.

FOLLOW THESE TIPS WHEN PRACTICING

1. Analyze the structure of the piece. Not only will this improve your interpretation of the music but it will provide a mental scaffold on which to build your musical memory. Suzuki piano teacher Jenny Macmillan says, "Researchers agree that it is essential to support memory of the sounds, movements, and sight with analysis of the forms and harmonies of the music. In this way, material to be remembered is related to other relevant information."

2. Listen to other performances so that long before you can play the piece yourself, you can hum or sing it, or hear the music in your head.

3. Break the piece down into small phrases and practice those. (Use slow-motion practice to improve your retention as well as intonation—*see* page 203).

4. Start memorizing early in the learning process so that you memorize sections, as this will help improve your ability to interpret the music.

5. When you make a mistake, try to fix it from memory, rather than looking at the score. This helps to reinforce retrieval pathways in the brain. Only then, check the score to make sure you're correct.

6. Don't always start at the beginning, because you will end up familiar with the beginning and less familiar with the end. Start in different places, so you don't become overreliant on continuity and momentum to play the piece.

7. Practice frequently and in different locations, for the reasons already discussed.

8. Rehearse in your mind. Performance psychologist Dr. Noa Kageyama says, "In one study, participants who mentally practiced a five-finger sequence on an imaginary piano for two hours a day had the same neurological changes (and reduction in mistakes) as the participants who physically practiced the same passage on an actual piano." Mental rehearsal activates the same neural pathways as physical practice.

9. Concentrate on the beauty and musicality of the piece rather than the technical details. Make interpretation and expressive musicality your goal, so that any technical attention is a means to this end, rather than a sterile, mechanistic end in itself. Canadian child prodigy Jan Lisiecki was performing in concert halls around the world by the time he was 14. According to violinist and conductor Pinchas Zukerman, "talent of that magnitude comes at least two or three generations apart." Jan says, "I just want to always express how beautiful the music is, how beautifully the composer wrote the music, and not how beautifully I can play it or how fast I can play it, I mean, it's all interpretation but I feel that the interpretation is actually to make the music more beautiful."

HYPERTHYMESIA

A relative of eidetic memory is an extremely rare phenomenon called hyperthymesia, a highly superior episodic memory. Fewer than 30 documented cases of hyperthymesia have been confirmed in peer-reviewed articles. The first reported case was Jill Rosenberg (known in case literature as AJ) in 2006, who can recall details from every day of her life from when she was 14 years old, including events that she read or watched in the media: "Starting on February 5, 1980, I remember everything. That was a Tuesday." She has also suffered from depression because among all the memories which spring unbidden into her consciousness, she is plagued by bad ones: "It's like an endless, chaotic film that can completely overpower me. And there's no stop button."

She has also kept a diary obsessively since she was ten and she compulsively hoards objects and personal memorabilia, which help her to organize and make sense of all the information. It is unclear whether her obsessive traits are causal or consequential or a mixture of both, but she doesn't have to make a special effort to remember the events of her life; instead she lacks the ability to forget them.

DO YOU HAVE A PHOTOGRAPHIC MEMORY?

Probably not, but take this test and see. Focus on the white dot on the first image for ten seconds, then quickly shift your focus to the white dot on the second image.

Everyone keeps a residual image of the first photo for a fraction of a second, enabling them to glimpse the full color image for a fleeting moment when they look at the second photo. However, if you have an eidetic visual memory, you will see a full color image for much longer, maybe even several seconds.

RECOGNITION VS. RECALL

WHICH TESTS DO YOU PREFER: MULTIPLE CHOICE OR THOSE WHERE YOU HAVE TO THINK UP THE ANSWERS ALL BY YOURSELF?

Most people prefer the former because the skill required for multiple choice questions is *recognition,* which is generally easier than *recall,* unless you lose confidence and get led astray by the wrong answers.

When pricing products, supermarkets are very conscious of the distinction between recognition and recall. The price of an item is clearly a salient factor in whether a shopper makes a purchase. Consumer research shows that people have a price range for how much they are prepared to pay. If an item is near the bottom of this price range, it is considered good value and if it is near the top it is considered expensive, which is where other factors come into play such as branding, quality, freshness, etc. When asked to name the price of a particular item, however, many people have difficulty remembering what they paid the last time, although they can recognize whether the price has gone up or down.

Shoppers who remember specific prices and use them to guide purchasing decisions are classified as "price aware"; shoppers who cannot remember specific prices and base their decisions on price differentials are classified as "price conscious." Your memory has a significant impact on your shopping experience and purchasing behavior, and store promotions target "price aware" and "price conscious" shoppers using different strategies.

Here are five items and their prices. Study them for ten seconds and then turn the page.

| 50¢ | $1.15 | 65¢ | $1.00 | $2.00 |

YOUR LOCAL SUPERMARKET HAS A BOGO PROMOTION ON RED APPLES

A single red apple costs $1 but the "buy one, get one free" offer means you can pick up two apples for 50 cents each.

1. Can you remember the original price of a red apple on the previous page?

2. If not, do you have a rough idea what the price was (write down a range)?

3. What percentage of the second red apple is "free"?

Now read on to discover whether you snapped up a bargain.

BOGO

The ever-popular BOGO (buy one, get one free) targets both the price-aware and the price-conscious consumer, by exploiting not only sloppy math skills but also their poor memories.

The bigger the price differential, the higher the margin on a familiar and simple offer like this one. Most people are aware that the BOGO usually involves raising the nominal price of the first item so that the second item is not completely free. In fact it isn't even close to free and in many cases it isn't even half price.

You paid $1 for a red apple in the BOGO promotion. Ordinarily the price of the apple was 65¢, but with the BOGO, each apple cost you 50¢, a saving of 15¢ per apple at the old price.

Still think you know how much of the second apple was free?

At these new prices the second apple isn't free; it isn't even half price. You have paid an extra 35¢ (about 54 percent) so only 46 percent of the second apple is free. Or put another way, that's about this much:

WHAT KIND OF
LEARNER ARE YOU?

ALTHOUGH IT IS POSSIBLE TO LEARN
THROUGH A COMBINATION OF STYLES,
LEARNERS ARE PREDOMINANTLY EITHER
VISUAL, AUDITORY, OR KINESTHETIC.

This quiz will test which one applies to you. Once you know your learning strengths and weaknesses you can ensure that you choose learning strategies that play to your strengths.

Read all 60 questions and make a note every time you answer "yes" to a question. Only answer "yes" if you strongly identify with the statement and feel that it applies to you. If you are ambivalent or disagree with the statement, move on to the next question. Make a note of how many yes answers you give for each section. If one section stands out for you with a lot of yes answers, then that is your predominant learning style. If your answers are evenly spread between two or more sections, then you are a mixture (e.g. auditory-visual).

VISUAL

1. I have neat, legible handwriting.

2. I am really good at spelling; I also believe that good spelling is very important.

3. I prefer video conferencing to a telephone conversation. I like to be able to see the face of the other person so I can better judge what they are saying and feeling.

4. I remember faces but forget names.

5. I find PowerPoint presentations and diagrams very useful.

6. I like to sit at the front of the classroom so I don't get distracted by others.

7. I learn best on my own from books, rather than in a group.

8. When someone asks me to buy a few things from the supermarket, I prefer to write a list than keep them in my head.

9. When faced with a challenging unfamiliar task, I will look online for information or read a book to teach myself. I usually read instructions before attempting any task.

10. I often write things down and take detailed notes.

11. I spend time preparing and reading up on a subject rather than following my gut instinct or jumping right in.

12. If I had to learn lines for a play, I would study the script and practice the thoughts and words in my head, rather than out loud.

13. I get easily distracted by background noise and have difficulty concentrating when several people are talking.

14. I notice the visual similarities and differences between things that other people miss.

15. I'm a fast reader.

16. When I do a crossword, I like to see the clue and see the squares and letters for myself rather than listen to someone else read them out.

17. I am very good at imagining scenes in my head.

18. Unless someone expresses emotion with their face, I tend to overlook how they might really be feeling.

19. I learn well when someone demonstrates a physical task or solves a problem by performing the activity themselves while I watch (and maybe take notes).

20. I don't like listening to too much explanation or verbal lecturing; I could learn the same information more quickly on my own by reading a book.

AUDITORY

1. I understand and remember things better when I or someone else says them out loud.

2. I enjoy learning foreign languages and find them quite easy.

3. I can easily articulate my ideas because I'm a good talker.

4. When I meet someone for the second time, I usually have no trouble remembering their name.

5. While someone is explaining something to me, I might look away from them or close my eyes so I can concentrate better.

6. I prefer telephone conversations to video conferencing. I find the visual information distracting.

7. I pick up subtle clues by listening to other people's choice of words and tone of voice rather than the expression on their face.

8. I often talk to myself while I work.

9. Faced with an unfamiliar task, I'm happy to ask someone to explain it to me.

10. I'm not a fast reader. Sometimes I move my lips while I read.

11. I'm good at remembering spoken lists, such as when it's my turn to buy a round at the bar.

12. I'm a good listener.

13. I can understand verbal instructions easily and rarely have to ask for a question to be repeated.

14. I talk to myself to verbalize things I want to remember.

15. I'm good at telling stories and jokes.

16. I learn best by talking and bouncing my ideas off other people and I enjoy studying with a partner or in a group because I can ask questions, discuss, and hear information and ideas.

17. If I had to learn lines for a play, I would record myself saying them and then listen to the recording.

18. I'm quite articulate and not afraid to talk out loud in class.

19. I would prefer to give an oral presentation than produce a written report.

20. I'm very musical.

KINESTHETIC

1. People say I have illegible handwriting and my spelling's none too impressive either.

2. I will often jump right into doing something without asking how to do it, because there's no better way to learn than by just getting into it.

3. I enjoy playing sports.

4. I can do a lot of things, but they can be difficult to explain in words.

5. When I meet someone for the second time, I might have trouble remembering their name but I have a clear memory of what happened the last time we were together.

6. I enjoy doing practical puzzles that I can solve with my hands.

7. I tend to doodle while I'm on the phone.

8. I find taking long tests or writing essays boring. I often become restless and want to do something physical instead.

9. Faced with a challenging task, I just kind of figure it out as I go along by trying things out. I'll usually only read the instructions as a last resort.

10. My favorite kind of films are action movies. My worst kind of film involves people sitting around a table talking to each other and nothing's happening.

11. I like "getting my hands dirty" and need to be physically active.

12. I tend to follow my gut instinct.

13. If something was bothering me, I'd be more likely to go for a run or go to the gym than sit at home thinking it through.

14. I get really bored and confused when someone tries to explain something by giving me lots of instructions.

15. I don't like sitting down for too long. It makes me feel jittery.

16. I love making and building things or taking them apart.

17. I prefer to try something out, rather than have someone else show me.

18. I use my hands a lot and move my body when I am explaining something, or I might draw a diagram instead.

19. Other people say I'm hyperactive.

20. I understand things best when I can touch or do them.

Here are ten ways to maximize your learning by targeting your learning style. If you are a mixture of styles, use the suggestions from two or more relevant sections.

VISUAL LEARNERS

You learn best by seeing, and it is easiest for you to remember the things you've seen, so adapt your studying to suit your visual learning style:

1. Find a quiet place to study alone, and make your study area visually appealing.

2. Write down lots of notes and make lists to help you organize your thoughts and ideas.

3. Reread your notes immediately after a class because seeing the written words will reinforce your memory retention more than with other types of learners.

4. Use maps, charts, diagrams, mind maps, and outlines—anything that represents information visually. Just writing something down and making an outline will help you to learn.

5. Watch videos and documentaries about the subject you are studying.

6. Highlight keywords and ideas using different highlighter pens to structure information visually.

7. Use flashcards.

194

8. You need time to think the materials through before understanding, so allow yourself this reading and thinking time to help you process the information.

9. Sit at the front of the class so that you can clearly see the teacher's facial expressions and body language because you are sensitive to visual cues.

10. When you hear a new word, write it down so that you have a strong visual representation of the sound, then look it up in the dictionary.

AUDITORY LEARNERS

You learn best by listening, and it is easiest for you to remember the things you've heard, so adapt your studying to suit your auditory learning style:

1. Study with a friend or study group so that you can talk out loud and hear the information. The more times you can hear the information, the easier it will be to understand and encode in your strong auditory memory.

2. Record lectures so that you can sit and listen without taking notes; listen back to them later and then make notes.

3. Recite information out loud that you want to understand or remember, even when you are studying alone.

4. When solving a problem, talk through various options to yourself.

5. Listen to audio tapes and documentaries about the subject you are studying.

6. Sit to the side or near the back of the class so you can concentrate on listening rather than staring at the teacher's face and trying to look attentive.

7. Use rhymes and mnemonics to help you remember lists and recite them out loud.

8. Reinforce your comprehension and memory by explaining concepts to your study partner and getting them to verbally quiz you.

9. If you are having trouble recalling information, close your eyes to block out visual distractions and try to hear the answer. Talk to yourself to prime your memory by association.

10. When writing a first draft, type or write the words and thoughts that you hear in your head without worrying about spelling and grammar; just get the words down on paper and then go back and fix the other details.

KINESTHETIC LEARNERS

You learn best by touching and manipulating objects and involving your body, and it is easiest for you to remember the things you've experienced physically, so adapt your studying to suit your kinesthetic learning style:

1. Take a walk or pace around the room while you read aloud from a book or notecards, or go for a run while listening to the information on an MP3 player.

2. Involve your body in the learning task. If you are reading information on a screen, mouse-click on the words to give a physical feedback to your reading.

3. Knead a stress ball in your hand, chew gum, or doodle ideas and thoughts while you are learning.

4. Use flashcards, because you can touch them, move them, shuffle them, and interact with them physically.

5. If you can't experience something physically, try to imagine yourself physically climbing into a problem to grasp what makes it work.

6. Study in short blocks of time and when you start to get jittery, take a quick break and do something physical, like walking outside for a few minutes.

7. Try to make everything you learn as concrete as possible and relate the information to your everyday life. For example, if you were working on Pythagoras's theorem, build a right-angled triangle with some wooden sticks or straws and manipulate this object with your hands in real time and space to deepen your understanding.

8. Where possible, type rather than write, because it gives more concrete and immediate feedback for the kinesthetic learner and keeps you physically engaged in the process.

9. Vary your activities and don't force yourself to spend too long on one task. You study just as hard as visual and auditory learners, but you benefit from mixing things up a bit more than they do.

10. Wherever possible, use physical objects to support your learning.

TALENT IS OVERRATED, DELIBERATE PRACTICE
BRINGS SUCCESS

In 2007, psychologists K. Anders Ericsson, Michael J. Prietula, and Edward T. Cokely published the article "The Making of an Expert" in the *Harvard Business Review*, making a provocative and challenging assertion for anyone seeking greatness. They declared: "New research shows that outstanding performance is the product of years of deliberate practice and coaching, not of any innate talent or skill."

The article cites the case of two Hungarian educators, László and Klara Polgár, who 40 years ago deliberately set out to show that geniuses are made, not born, and to challenge the popular assumption that women couldn't excel at chess, then a predominantly male-dominated activity. They systematically trained their three daughters intensively in chess from an early age; all three went on to gain top ten ranking in the world among female chess players. Judit, the youngest, achieved the title of grand master at the age of 15 years and 4 months, the youngest person of either gender to do so until then. She has since defeated ten current or former world champions.

So what exactly is "deliberate practice" and what else do you need to engage in it?

1. You must invest time. Ericsson says, "Our research shows that even the most gifted performers need a minimum of ten years (or 10,000 hours) of intense training before they win international competitions."

2. Geoff Colvin gives a comprehensive description of deliberate practice in his book, *Talent is Overrated: What Really Separates World-Class Performers from Everybody Else*: "It is activity designed specifically to improve performance... it can be repeated a lot; feedback on results is continuously available; it is highly demanding mentally ... and it isn't much fun."

3. Practicing must be supervised by an expert teacher, who is "capable of giving constructive, even painful, feedback" and can help devise strategies for improvement.

4. The student must be highly motivated and actively seek out this feedback.

5. When the student's future development eventually exceeds the teacher's level of expertise, the student must find a more expert teacher.

NINE SECRETS OF DELIBERATE PRACTICE

1. Find an expert coach. You need constant feedback from experts whom you trust and respect, otherwise you cannot recognize your mistakes or devise a strategy for improvement.

2. Don't practice the things you are already good at. It may be more fun and less work, but if you want to turn a hobby into real expertise, you must concentrate most of your effort on developing your weak points.

3. To work on your weaknesses you must first admit to yourself that you are worse than you want to be and then you have to believe you CAN and WILL improve—otherwise you will lack motivation during the mentally and/or physically demanding process of deliberate practice.

4. You have to love something to excel at it but this doesn't mean that you will enjoy yourself all the time. If you want to love doing something all the time, just treat it as a hobby but don't complain when you don't improve.

5. A study of London taxi drivers—who train for two years to memorize the routes through the city streets to acquire "The Knowledge"—showed brain growth in the area of the brain which processes spatial awareness. Accept that your brain and episodic memory is like a muscle and needs training to develop.

6. Without daily physical training, no amount of positive thinking, vision, "clutch" (see page 178), or desire to be the best will enable a regular person to sprint 330 feet in under ten seconds. In a very real way, the same applies to the brain's cognitive control and executive functions.

7. Living in a cave does not make you a geologist.

8. Deliberate practice requires—but is also a key component of—self-regulation. Before practice you should set clear goals for the session that also focus on the process of reaching that goal. During the session, you focus on the important self-regulatory skill of self-observation: "For example, ordinary endurance runners in a race tend to think about anything other than what they're doing; it's painful... Elite runners, by contrast, focus intensely on themselves." After the practice session comes the all-important self-regulatory feedback and evaluation. Without this continual metacognition, the practice is incomplete.

9. Live by Thomas Edison's famous observation that "vision without execution is hallucination" and Sam Mendes's 25th Rule for Directors: "Never, ever, ever forget how lucky you are to do something that you love."

LIVELY REPETITION VS.
ROTE LEARNING

THERE'S A LONG-RUNNING DEBATE ABOUT THE ROLE OF REPETITION IN LEARNING. CERTAIN TYPES OF REPETITION SUCH AS "ROTE" LEARNING ARE OFTEN HAILED BY EDUCATIONAL TRADITIONALISTS AS THE WAY TO RAISE FALLING STANDARDS AND GET BACK TO BASICS; PROGRESSIVE EDUCATORS VIEW THEM AS THE ANTITHESIS OF CREATIVE AND ENGAGING EDUCATION. BUT WHO IS RIGHT?

The answer is they are both right (and both wrong). There's nothing wrong with lively repetition (LR) so long as you don't base an entire educational system on it. Don't be afraid to use it; you won't turn your brain to jelly.

It also depends on the context in which rote learning is used and how "fun" you think learning and memorizing should be. Rote learning can be an effective way to memorize certain types of information and activate specific types of memory but it is very damaging when applied to the wrong kind of memory task.

Opponents of rote learning instinctively believe that the only effective learning is fun learning, and that the carrot is always better than the stick. Opponents of learning "parrot fashion" argue that it's boring and paternalistic and that it stifles critical thinking. However, as the previous section has demonstrated, learning and development aren't always fun. In fact, self-development can be highly demanding and downright unpleasant (ask any Olympic champion). Besides, numerous studies into learning and motivation have shown that people aren't always motivated by what we think they are.

In 1968, American psychologist and business management guru, Frederick Herzberg, published a famous article, "One More Time: How Do You Motivate Employees?" in the *Harvard Business Review,* in which he challenged nine myths about motivation. He argued that shorter working hours, spiraling wages, and fringe benefits did not increase motivation in the long run. That sounds like a gift to thrifty or unscrupulous employers.

So what does motivate them? (Don't be unduly influenced by Dr. Herzberg's PhD in electric shock therapy.)

In fact, it turns out that the main motivators are, in descending order of importance: A sense of achievement, recognition, the work itself, increasing responsibility, and opportunity for advancement and growth.

So where does rote learning fit into all this? The main issue appears to be compliance. Rote learning is most effective when the learner is engaged and motivated to perform, rather than have it imposed from above. As modern motivational expert Daniel H. Pink says in his best-seller, *Drive: The Surprising Truth About What Motivates Us,* "Living a satisfying life requires more than simply meeting the demands of those in control. Yet in our offices and our classrooms we have way too much compliance and way too little engagement."

So when an educator sets up a rote learning group session, he or she should give the students a sense of ownership and devise ways of demonstrating to them that the rote memory task is not an exercise in mute submission, but a useful memory tool when used for the appropriate memory tasks. Maybe it's time to rebrand rote learning and rename it "lively repetition."

LEARNING SOMETHING BY LIVELY REPETITION

In her book, *Battle Hymn of the Tiger Mother*, Amy Chua insists: "Tenacious practice, practice, practice is crucial for excellence; rote repetition is underrated in America."

First, let's be clear that lively repetition (LR) is not the same as the "deliberate practice" of the previous chapter. It should never be used for episodic memory tasks (learning a skill) or for tasks which require critical thinking. These demand entirely different tools.

Furthermore, it is important to stress once again that the motivation for LR should be intrinsic, not, as Amy Chua argues, extrinsic which, as many educators and psychologists agree, comes at too great an emotional and intellectual cost. It can be a great way to get people to do boring tasks, but it stifles creative thinking and, in the long run, reduces self-esteem.

WHEN YOU WANT TO LEARN SOMETHING BY LR

1. LR should only be used for quick, routine memorizing of lists of information, such as the periodic table, multiplication tables, mathematical formulas, anatomy in medicine, etc.

2. Don't be boring. Lively repetition should be fun and feel good. Don't dismiss a useful tool just because it's become synonymous with the teaching styles of authoritarian regimes and sharp-elbowed parents.

3. Learning something by heart can provide the most important motivator on Herzberg's list: a sense of achievement. When you've memorized something completely you'll feel an endorphin-releasing sense of accomplishment.

4. Use chunking (*see* page 207) and rhythm to break the text into memorable packets of auditory information. The brain thrives on rhythm and repetition for these kinds of tasks, because the longer the information can be kept in your short-term memory, the more effectively it can be transferred to your long-term memory.

5. Search for a song and if you can't find one, make one up. There are five-year-olds who can name all fifty U.S. states—the YouTube channel "Acroanna" features one of them—a smiling five-year-old named Annie singing a mnemonic song. For a more geographical approach, other songs teach the states going up and down the country from west to east.

6. Recite or sing out loud. There's a good reason for this: it rehearses the information in your auditory short-term memory, and ... *the longer the information can be kept in your short-term memory, the more effectively it can be transferred to your long-term memory.*

7. Use your body (especially if you're a kinesthetic learner—*see* page 193). Devise a dance or hand-clapping sequence, anything that makes you move your body as you sing or recite your text.

8. Complete this sentence without looking back:

THE LONGER THE INFORMATION CAN BE KEPT IN YOUR

. . . .

THE MORE EFFECTIVELY IT CAN BE TRANSFERRED TO YOUR

. . . .

MUSCLE MEMORY AND
MINDFUL PRACTICE

Muscle memory is the ability for muscles to remember a sequence of movements; it is part of your procedural memory (*see* page 177) but it also takes place in your muscles (it's not all in the brain). When you catch a ball or even open a door, you depend on muscle memory.

Apart from repetition, two other techniques that sportspeople, martial artists, and dancers use to boost muscle memory of a physical routine are slow motion and exaggeration, which come together under the umbrella of "mindful practice." This is distinct from deliberate practice (*see* page 197) because it is process-oriented rather than goal-oriented. Despite appearances, slow, mindful movement is a powerful and dynamic way to teach mind and body to learn new skills and to develop coordination. Repetition is an important component—routines must be practiced over and over again—but attention, awareness, and ease of movement are paramount.

MARTIAL ARTS

Martial artists use slow, gentle, and sometimes exaggerated movements to learn and practice correct form and technique. Many people struggle to understand how slow motion blocking, punching, and kicking can be applicable to a real fight. Danny Larusso, the bullied teen in the movie *The Karate Kid,* shares these misgivings. His sensei, Mr. Miyagi, makes him clean and polish cars and paint fences day after day, with the iconic instruction "Wax on, wax off." Only later does Danny realize that these slow and exaggerated movements have trained his muscle memory for high-speed combat.

MOUNTAIN BIKING

Mountain bikers use an important technique called pumping to increase speed by directing forward, upward, and downward momentum, gain traction, and control the height on jumps. Professional mountain biker, BMX rider, and coach Tom Dowie explains how he teaches his students to learn the crucial pumping technique: "I always say it's better to overexaggerate the movement at first to find the feeling yourself and to train your body to the muscle memory of the movement. Try and feel the movement more than think it as you're applying it, it's trusting your brain's already processed it and letting your body go with it."

GOLF

The pioneering American professional golfer Ben Hogan practically invented practice golf and famously spent years researching and experimenting with different methods of swing. Slow motion practice was crucial to making his swing one of the greatest in the history of the game. Slow motion allowed him to recognize his weaknesses and correct them, often in the middle of a tournament. Sometimes he would get up in the night to practice in slow motion in a mirror, to pinpoint the issues that had hindered him during that day's play, so that he could be match-ready the following morning.

WOODSHEDDING

Many music teachers advocate slow practice to develop physical skill and concentration. Playing a piece slowly allows musicians to focus with greater detail on the notes, fingering, intonation, articulation, tone, rhythm, and dynamics, and to notice how small changes can affect the outcome. Violinist and Philadelphia Orchestra concertmaster David Kim explains how he uses mindful super-slow woodshedding (a musician's term meaning private practice): "When you're trying to teach a young person a new language, you repeat a certain word seven times... when I find a difficult spot ... I'll literally kind of woodshed really slowly, I try to do note by note... I'll do the shifts back and forth, minimum seven times, even if they are going well." This detailed slow motion work gives him a powerful feeling of solidity and assurance when he is performing on stage.

THE FELDENKRAIS METHOD

The Feldenkrais Method, used by actors, dancers, and therapists, is a dynamic system that increases self-awareness by breaking movements down into their smallest parts and looking at them in relation to gravity. Its originator, Israeli physicist Moshé Feldenkrais, "devised a series of quiet, exploratory exercises that allow the brain to learn new skills, to evoke new neuromuscular patterns of organic movement and thought. The exercises are slow, gentle, and controlled." This deepens the awareness of how you use your body and increases efficiency. It teaches the brain to create effective movement; it teaches the body to serve the brain's intentions. In fact, a key question in Feldenkrais is "What will best serve my intentions?"

Slow, mindful movement increases attention and awareness, which are major preconditions for brain neuroplasticity to occur. Movements should not be repeated by rote; they organically serve intention. Michael Merzenich, a leading neuroscientist in the field of brain neuroplasticity and a supporter of Feldenkrais, stresses, "One of the lessons of this research is that stereotypy is the enemy. And that you really want to exercise the brain with a variety of movements, a variety of actions. A variety of challenges."

TAKE AN EXTENDED COFFEE BREAK

Try this with a cup of coffee. Take *four minutes* to reach for a drink, bring the cup to your lips, take a sip, and return the cup to the table. It's fascinating and you will learn surprising details about the quality and efficiency of your body movements.

It's actually quite hard to do. At first, most people go too fast. You need to allow about 45 seconds to reach for the cup, another 45 seconds to bring the cup to your lips, 45 seconds to drink, 45 seconds to return the cup to the table, and 45 seconds to return to your starting position. That still leaves another 15 seconds to fill. So slow down even more!

You've been using a cup without dribbling or scalding yourself for years now, so you probably think there's nothing more to learn. Yet, if you slow the whole process down you will be viewing something you take for granted with new eyes; not only will it make you realize what amazing coordination is required for the simplest of tasks, but you will notice areas where you could make the movement more efficient. For instance, you might find that you grip the handle too tightly or that you hold tension in your jaw. You might discover that you stick your tongue out or crane your neck forward unnecessarily in anticipation of the cup reaching your lips.

WEBER'S LAW

One of the psychophysical mechanisms that supports slow motion and mindful practice is Weber's law, which states that "The change in a stimulus that will be just noticeable is a constant ratio of the original stimulus."

Imagine you were carrying a pile of five books and someone placed another book on top of the pile—you would notice it. But if you were carrying a huge box containing a hundred books, you wouldn't notice the weight of one extra book.

The same principle applies to movement. Slowing down a movement and extending its range (exaggeration) allows you to notice more subtle variations in that movement, making it easier for you to apply the correct form and technique, achieve maximum efficiency, and nail every single little detail.

MUSCLE MEMORY ISN'T JUST IN THE BRAIN

Brain neuroplasticity and the developing of skills shows up as increased brain mass in specific memory areas; the same is true of muscle memory, which results in physical and chemical changes in the muscle. It's well known in sports science that athletes can quickly regain lost muscle mass, strength, flexibility, and coordination when they return to training after a long period of inactivity, because strength training permanently increases the number of cell nuclei within the muscle fibers. This is why sports, especially strength training, at an early age can have lasting benefits in adulthood.

TEN TIPS FOR SLOW MOTION PRACTICE

Slow motion practice can improve any skill that involves physical movement, whether it's your golf swing or getting out of a chair efficiently without putting too much stress on your back, neck, and knees.

1. Focus on the present moment; concentrate on the process rather than a goal.

2. Be aware of your breathing. Breathe in through your nose and out through your mouth. Don't hold your breath. Observe how you combine the breath with the movement. Slow motion movement will reveal any areas where they are in conflict.

3. Imagine joints and bones moving, rather than muscles contracting, relaxing, and doing work.

4. Try to make the movements effortless. This will help the movement to flow but it will also highlight the places where you are using too much effort.

5. Break down big tasks into smaller and smaller ones so that you can examine and perform the tiniest possible components.

6. When you identify an area of weakness, try to perform the action well at least seven times before moving on to the next component.

7. Complete the whole movement. Slow motion allows you to see where you are cutting movement short and not using the full range of your body's capabilities, or curtailing a physical action.

8. Make slow, mindful practice a habit because you will gain maximum benefit if you use it regularly in a structured and consistent way.

9. If it is safe to do so, perform the slow motion activity at least once with your eyes shut.

10. Slow motion practice doesn't have to be real; you can visualize. Mental imagery has a huge impact on sports, and professional sportspeople now habitually use slow motion visualization to focus on technique.

CHUNKING
AND PATTERNS

MOST OF US CAN RELIABLY STORE BETWEEN FOUR AND SEVEN ITEMS IN OUR WORKING MEMORY. IF YOU THINK THAT'S POOR, YOU'D BE RIGHT, AT LEAST COMPARED TO AN ANIMAL WITH WHICH WE SHARE 98.8 PERCENT OF OUR DNA—THE CHIMPANZEE.

At the Primate Research Institute of Kyoto University, Professor Tetsuro Matsuzawa has spent years conducting cognitive tests on Ai, a 36-year-old chimpanzee, and her 13-year-old son, Ayumu, to discover that chimps have extraordinary memories. Matsuzawa says, "They can grasp things at a glance. As a human, you can do things to improve your memory, but you will never be a match for Ayumu." The chimpanzees can locate in sequence the numerals 1 to 9 spread randomly across a computer screen and then covered by white squares, after originally seeing them for only a fraction of a second.

However, something special separates us from chimps, remarkable though they are. Our delight in pattern recognition allows us to boost our working memory by consciously splitting up information into more memorable chunks. Furthermore, according to neuroscientist Daniel Bor, a research fellow at the University of Sussex in England and author of *The Ravenous Brain: How the New Science of Consciousness Explains Our Insatiable Search for Meaning*, the human desire to find patterns is the very source of human creativity.

Find patterns and use chunking when you need to remember a group of numbers or letters or even a group of objects. You do this already with telephone numbers and when reciting the alphabet. Try to link the material to something in your previous experience that forms a memorable pattern. When someone gives you a twelve-digit number to memorize, use chunking to split it into three groups of four. The number 159407201969 is much easier to remember as 1594 0720 1969 and even easier still if you spot that 0720 1969 (July 20, 1969) was the date that Neil Armstrong stepped onto the surface of the moon.

CAN YOU SPOT THE RELATIONSHIP BETWEEN THE SYMBOLS AND THE NUMBERS?

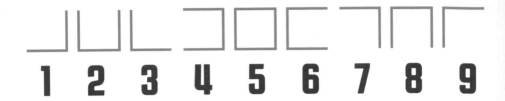

USE CHUNKING TO CRACK THE CODE:

267	3	5	*GREEN*
5	67	48	*RED*
49	9	2	*ORANGE*
-	- -	-	*BLUE*
	- -	- - -	*WHITE*
- -	-	-	*YELLOW*

HOW CAN THIS MYTHICAL BEAST HELP YOU REMEMBER THESE SIX ANIMALS?

SEQUENCES

HERE IS A DELICIOUS BOX OF 24 CHOCOLATES,
WHICH YOU ARE GOING TO LEARN,
IN THE CORRECT ORDER, WITHIN
THE NEXT SEVEN MINUTES.

On page 210 an empty tray needs filling. Take a quick look. Scary isn't it? Twenty-four little cubicles that you are going to fill up in the correct order without making any errors.

First, let's try your customary method. Give yourself a minute to stare blankly at the top two rows while your anxiety levels slowly rise! Then turn the page and see how you get on.

WELL, HERE'S THE EMPTY TRAY. YOU HAVE TWO MINUTES TO FILL IT UP.

Now, one of two things will have happened. Either you will have remembered the positions of a few standout pralines (like the blue shiny one, or the striped one) and then tried to fit the others around them, or you will have become so confused by the new configuration that it will have interfered with your fragile memory, leaving you totally confused.

However, don't despair. The reason you struggled is that these abstract symbols don't hold any meaning for you, apart from looking good enough to eat. If they were letters or numbers, you'd be able to say them out loud, using chunking (*see page 207*) to keep them in your auditory memory long enough to fill the blank boxes. But how do you remember 24 fairly similar abstract items? In four minutes. Yes, four (you've used three already). So what's the solution? Create a story.

This is just one example and it won't be entirely suitable for you because it hasn't come from your head and it isn't your personal set of visual associations, so you may want to write your own. (Incidentally, when you've mastered this technique, you'll be able to reduce seven minutes to two.)

The story is inspired by shapes and other visual details. Read the story three times (if you're an auditory learner, read it aloud each time) and then turn the page. Now use the story to recall the correct order of the chocolates and you should be able to remember many more chocolates than you did before.

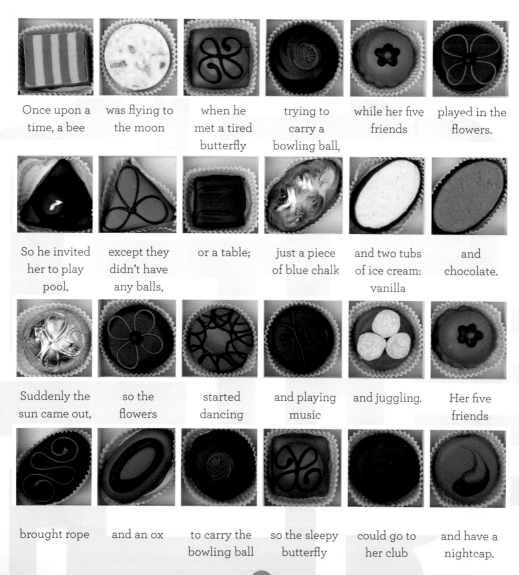

Once upon a time, a bee	was flying to the moon	when he met a tired butterfly	trying to carry a bowling ball,	while her five friends	played in the flowers.
So he invited her to play pool,	except they didn't have any balls,	or a table;	just a piece of blue chalk	and two tubs of ice cream: vanilla	and chocolate.
Suddenly the sun came out,	so the flowers	started dancing	and playing music	and juggling.	Her five friends
brought rope	and an ox	to carry the bowling ball	so the sleepy butterfly	could go to her club	and have a nightcap.

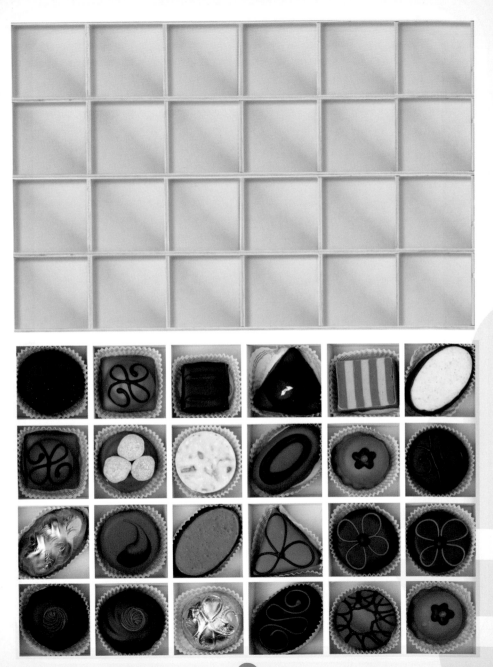

OBJECT RECALL

How good are you at remembering objects? Here's a visual memory test similar to the one on page 145. Spend one minute looking at the picture below, then turn the page and answer questions 1 and 2.

How did you get on? Did you find it harder to figure out what objects were missing because they had been jumbled around? This is because we don't remember objects in isolation but in patterns and groups, in relationship to each other.

Most people find it easier to remember the missing knife, green boot, and candle than the scissors and newspaper, because the first three are all part of a set. However, you probably wouldn't have noticed there was an orange missing unless you had taken the trouble to count them. So grouping and patterns help us to remember objects, but when we look at a group of objects, our ability to "subitize" (know immediately how many items there are at a glance) is quite low, about four, unless the items are arranged in familiar shapes.

1. How many objects have been removed?

2. Name the missing objects.

Now turn back to the previous page.

Now study this picture for two minutes. Then turn the page and answer questions 3 and 4.

How did you get on this time? There were eight items missing (rather than six) and yet you were probably able to recall all of them because they were all fruit or berries. Once you recognized that a whole category of items had vanished, you could use your semantic memory of fruit and berries to prompt you. Instead of trying to remember what was missing, you could come at the problem from the other side, running through the fruit and berry items in your semantic memory to check if they had been in the picture.

CATEGORIZE AND LOOK FOR PATTERNS

To memorize a group of objects, look for patterns and semantic relationships between them, because you can't always rely on the spatial arrangement to help you, since that is subject to change, whereas semantic patterns rarely change.

THE PARTHENON OBJECT EXPERIMENT

This phenomenon of grouping objects together spatially also works outdoors on a grand scale. A team led by Timothy McNamara, Professor of Psychology at Vanderbilt University, conducted a study to demonstrate how orientation of the viewer and the surrounding area impacts memory for object locations.

The study took place in Centennial Park in Nashville, Tennessee, where stands a full-scale replica of the Parthenon, the ancient temple on the Athenian Acropolis in Greece. Participants were blindfolded and taken to the park. Their blindfolds were then removed and they were led to one of two paths along which they walked and had to memorize eight objects located along their route. The first path was a rectangle whose sides matched the orientation of the Parthenon; the other path was at 45 degrees to it. The objects were located at the intersections of the two paths. The participants who had walked on the first path had significantly better recall of the relative location of the objects than those who had walked on the misaligned path. They had used the largest object in the vicinity—the Parthenon—for spatial orientation as a frame of reference for the other eight objects.

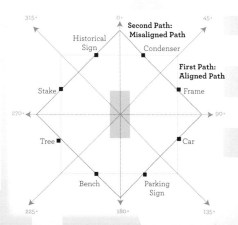

3. How many objects have been removed?

4. Name the missing objects.

Now turn back to the previous page.

HOW DOES CULTURE SHAPE MEMORY?

Write down the first five things that you can remember about your last birthday party.

What did you include in your list? The color of the cake, the gifts you received, the food you ate, or was it the people who were there? According to a recent U.S. study, this depends on your culture. Americans tend to focus on visual details—such as the color of the decorations or the type of frosting on the cake. East Asians in the study would have better remembered interpersonal details—who cut the cake or the people present.

Angela Gutchess, assistant professor of psychology at Brandeis University, and her team performed a series of memory tests on 65 students from the United States and East Asian countries, including China, Japan, and Korea.

Both groups of students scored similarly on general memory tests but the Americans were better at object recall.

"Your culture influences what you perceive to be important around you," explains Angela Gutchess. "If your culture values social interactions, you will remember those interactions better than a culture that values individual perceptions. Culture really shapes your memory."

MEMORY HOOK
NUMBER SHAPE

A hook is a mental coat hook on which you hang the information you want to commit to memory. It's an effective way to remember a group of items such as a shopping list and in a specific order.

First you must associate each number with one memorable object that closely resembles the written form. Converting abstract data into pictures makes them easier to remember. Here are some examples, but feel free to devise your own:

1 = candle   **2** = swan   **3** = heart   **4** = sail of a yacht   **5** = hook

6 = elephant's trunk   **7** = ax   **8** = hourglass   **9** = balloon on a string   **10** = doughnut

| 1 | 2 | 3 | 4 | 5 | 6 | 7 | 8 | 9 | 10 |

Now take your shopping list and associate a number image with each item to form a memorable tableau, the crazier the better.

1. **Bread:** Candle sandwich—imagine biting into it
2. **Cheese:** Swan swimming in a lake of melted cheese
3. **Baked beans:** Baked bean can being carried by a butler on a red velvet heart cushion
4. **Peanut butter:** Yacht sail smeared with peanut butter
5. **Apples:** Big green apple with a hook in it
6. **Olive oil:** Elephant in a health spa having a hot oil massage
7. **Carrots:** Paula Dean chopping carrots with an ax
8. **Chips:** Potato chips flowing like sand through a giant hourglass
9. **Ice cream:** Child carrying a balloon and an ice cream
10. **Dishwasher tablets:** A dishwasher filled with doughnuts

To recall the items, just think of each number image one at a time (candle, swan, heart, etc.) and the associated item on your shopping list (bread, cheese, baked beans) will spring back into your mind!

TOP TEN STARTING MLB PITCHERS EVER

1. Walter Johnson	6. Greg Maddux
2. Nolan Ryan	7. Bob Feller
3. Roger Clemens	8. Tom Seaver
4. Cy Young	9. Christy Mathewson
5. Warren Spahn	10. Sandy Koufax

You can memorize this list by associating a number image with each pitcher to form a memorable tableau. If you can visualize the faces of these men or you know something about them, you'll have an easier task because you only have to associate the face or another piece of your knowledge with the number shape (e.g. Walter Johnson holding a candle, Nolan Ryan riding a swan, Roger Clemens making a heart sign with his hands, etc.).

However, if you aren't a sports fan and these guys are just names to you, then you'll also need to devise a familiar image to help you recall the name or part of the name:

1. **Walter Johnson: Walter** White (from *Breaking Bad*) gives a **candle** to Magic **Johnson**

2. **Nolan Ryan: Batman** (directed by Christopher **Nolan**) rescues **Ryan** Seacrest who is being attacked by a **swan**

3. **Roger Clemens:** A jolly-**roger** flag-waving pirate sends a **heart**-shaped Valentine's card to **Clem** (the peaceful Loose-Skinned Demon from *Buffy the Vampire Slayer*)

ONCE UPON A HOOK

Imagine you had to memorize the 13 original colonies, in the order in which they joined the Union. This storytelling game is a great way to have fun and learn a list at the same time.

Take turns to tell a silly story, which links the items together and shoehorns your number images in the most implausible way for maximum comic effect. You might begin, "Once upon a hook, Richard Branson (**Virgin**ia) balancing a **candle** on his head was having a tea party (Boston, **Massachusetts**) with Marcel Proust (**Swan's** Way) when he sat on a huge granite teapot (Granite State, **New Hampshire**) and had a **heart** attack…" If your partner doesn't understand any of the linking references, s/he challenges and you must explain yourself. This helps you to build up multiple associations, which will embed the items and their order firmly in your memories.

MEMORY HOOK
NUMBER RHYME

This is very similar to the number shape system but instead you associate each number with one memorable object that rhymes with the spoken form. This method uses both the visual and the auditory memory and is an effective way to remember a group of items.

Begin by pairing each number with a rhyming memorable object. Here are some examples, but feel free to devise your own (use the first word that springs into your mind).

1 = wand   **2** = shoe   **3** = tree   **4** = door   **5** = hive

6 = sticks   **7** = heaven   **8** = crate   **9** = wine   **10** = hen

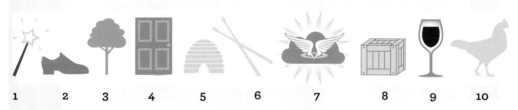

1   2   3   4   5   6   7   8   9   10

Now take your shopping list and associate a number image with each item to form a memorable tableau, the crazier the better.

1. **Bread:** Loaf of bread with a wand sticking out of it
2. **Cheese:** Smelly shoe stinks of cheese, with flies and smoke coming out of it
3. **Baked beans:** Tree with baked bean cans growing on it
4. **Peanut butter:** Door with peanut butter smeared on the handle
5. **Apples:** Apple stuffed into the entrance of a beehive, angry bees
6. **Olive oil:** Dipping sticks into olive oil and eating them like bread sticks
7. **Carrots:** A carrot sitting on a cloud
8. **Chips:** A huge crate filled with potato chips
9. **Ice cream:** Ice cream floating in a glass of wine
10. **Dishwasher tablets:** A hen sitting inside the dishwasher

To recall the items, just think of each number image in turn (wand, shoe, tree, etc.) and the associated item on your shopping list (bread, cheese, baked beans) will spring back into your mind!

THE RANKING OF POKER HANDS

1. Royal flush	2. Straight flush	3. Four of a kind	4. Full house	5. Flush
6. Straight	7. Three of a kind	8. Two pairs	9. One pair	10. High card

You can memorize this list by associating a number rhyme image with each hand to form a memorable tableau.

1. **Royal flush:** King Henry VIII flushing a wand down the toilet
2. **Straight flush:** Country star George Strait flushing his shoe down the toilet
3. **Four of a kind:** A square garden with a tree planted at each corner
4. **Full house:** A house filled with doors
5. **Flush:** Flushing a hive down the toilet
6. **Straight:** George Strait with some sticks
7. **Three of a kind:** Three clouds forming a triangle
8. **Two pairs:** A crate with two pears in it
9. **One pair:** A pear sitting in a wine glass
10. **High card:** A hen doing the high jump

Notice how you can use George Strait twice, and do lots of toilet flushing without confusion because the number rhyme image takes care of the order of the items in the list, and the other details help you remember the details of the list. The "four of a kind" and "three of a kind" required some additional mental imagery to help you remember the numbers within the item by forming a shape with your number rhyme images.

NOW USE THIS MEMORY TECHNIQUE TO MEMORIZE THIS LIST:

1. Iceland	2. Norway	3. Denmark	4. Finland	5. Austria
6. Switzerland	7. New Zealand	8. Sweden	9. Singapore	10. Canada

Do you know what this list represents? (*see* page 279 for answer).

MEMORY HOOK
ALPHABET

This is similar to the number shape and number rhyme systems on the earlier pages, only this system involves the entire alphabet, allowing you to remember longer lists.

First you must associate each letter of the alphabet with an object. There are two ways to do this, either by sounds or by using concrete words.

Here is an example of each kind of alphabet, but feel free to devise your own (use the first word that springs into your mind):

Sound	Concrete		Concrete
A = hay	A = apple	N = hen	N = ninja
B = bee	B = ball	O = hoe	O = orange
C = sea	C = cat	P = pea	P = panda
D = deer	D = duck	Q = cue	Q = queen
E = knee	E = elephant	R = oar	R = rat
F = effort	F = frog	S = ass	S = sugar
G = jeans	G = grapes	T = tea	T = tent
H = age	H = hen	U = ewe	U = umbrella
I = eye	I = igloo	V = veal	V = violin
J = jay	J = jelly	W = bubble	W = whale
K = key	K = kangaroo	X = eggs	X = xylophone
L = elbow	L = lamp	Y = wire	Y = yoyo
M = hem	M = mouse	Z = zen	Z = zebra

HERE IS A SHOPPING LIST WITH 25 ITEMS:

beef	eggs	fish	yogurt	cheese
potatoes	lettuce	tomato	cucumber	cookies
sugar	bread	soup	ketchup	meatballs
toothpaste	coleslaw	hummus	corn	bananas
gravy	apples	pizza	cauliflower	broccoli

To remember the list, associate the first item on the list with hay or apple (depending on which kind of alphabet you choose), the second item with a bee or ball, etc. You don't have to create a story, just make a strong association between the alphabet words and the groceries.

To recall the items, go through the alphabet letter by letter, recall the letter word, and the associated grocery item will come back into your mind. For example, picture beef wrapped in hay, a bee juggling with eggs, fish swimming in the sea, a deer with a yogurt container on its antlers, you with knees made out of cheese (rhymes as well!), and so on.

Don't spend too long creating these images; just think them up and move on to the next item on the list.

Go through all 25 items now and make an association as described. This should take you about three minutes.

Now close your eyes and run through the alphabet and you will be amazed how much you have retained. You should be able to remember 80 percent. By this time next week you will have forgotten it (without rehearsal), but you only need to retain the items in your memory long enough for you to reach the supermarket.

There are 35 objects on this page. Spend five minutes methodically going through the alphabet to create an association between each letter-word and object. When you reach "Z," start again at "A" and link a second object with your first image (so you'll have a pair of objects for the first nine letters of the alphabet). Then close the book and run through the alphabet, writing down as many objects as you can remember. *See* page 279 for your assessment.

MEMORY PALACE

This is the mother lode of visual memory techniques. It is used by professional mnemonists like eight-time World Memory Champion Dominic O'Brien to achieve world record feats of memory, but it is actually more than 2,000 years old and can easily be learned and used by anyone.

The earliest recorded reference to the "method of loci" (*locus* is Latin for "place") appears in ancient Roman and Greek writings, including the anonymous *Rhetorica ad Herennium*, Cicero's *De Oratore*, and Quintilian's *Institutio Oratoria*, which all date back to the first century BC. In Roman culture, orators were expected to speak without using notes, so the method of loci was very popular.

Its strength is based on visual-spatial and episodic memory and the fact that it is completely personal. The memory palaces that you create are unique because everybody has an internal spatial memory map representing their version of the outside world. Even if you think that your memory is weak, you will still be able to close your eyes and mentally walk through your house or other familiar locations noticing many of the objects that populate them.

You already have this wonderful three-dimensional matrix of memory hooks stored in your brain—that's your memory palace. To memorize a list of items, all you have to do is plan a route through it and then associate the objects that you want to remember with specific objects and locations (hook points) in your memory palace.

CHOOSE AND PREPARE YOUR MEMORY PALACE

Before you start memorizing, you must plan the route so that you can repeat the same journey every time without missing out any of the hook points. The best way to do this is by memory, rather than actually walking the route, because you need to work with what is already in your long-term memory. There is no limit to how many hook points you create. You might choose one per room or ten—it doesn't matter, so long as each one is distinct and you can repeat the journey accurately without leaving any out.

ASSOCIATE YOUR ITEMS

Mentally walk around your memory palace placing the items you want to remember at your hook points. Really make them interact with the environment. Suppose one of the things you had to remember was a dental appointment and your hook point was a lamp in the corner of your living room; you could place your dentist in the corner, holding the lamp. Make the images fun because your brain likes fun. If you want to remember bacon on a list of groceries, don't just place a package of bacon in your hook point—have hundreds of slices of bacon and drape them all over the hook point. If the hook point is your television, stick slimy bacon all over the screen, stuff bacon into the speakers, pile bacon on top until you have a bacon TV—object and hook point totally integrated.

Bizarre images are easier to remember than common material (this is known as the "Von Restorff effect" or "isolation effect") but the most important factor is to establish a strong link between image and hook point. To recall your items, simply retrace your steps and perform the exact same journey.

Establish your memory palace *first* and then test run it by committing these 25 items to memory. If you forget any items it will either be because your route or hook points are not firmly established, or because you didn't make the object interact strongly enough with the environment.

MEMORY LINK SYSTEM

The story of the wasp and the butterfly that helped you to remember the 24 chocolates on page 209 is an example of a memory link system.

This simple method involves using images to link, in a sequence, all the items that you want to commit to memory. They don't have to tell a story, but you might find that this happens naturally anyway. The plot of the story or tableau doesn't have to follow any of the normal rules of storytelling; it is created solely to link the images in the most memorable way. The images can be purely visual or they could have a phonetic/auditory component (like the lettuce below).

The planet Jupiter has over 65 moons. Suppose you wanted to learn the first ten in order by their distance from Jupiter: Metis, Adrastea, Amalthea, Thebe, Io, Europa, Ganymede, Callisto, Leda, Himalia.

You could do this using either the basic link method or the story link method. They are slightly more labor-intensive than other mnemonics, so they are most suited to memorizing facts that are unlikely to change and that you want to remember forever (as opposed to a shopping list, which is redundant as soon as you've been shopping).

REMEMBERING WITH THE LINK METHOD

- A LETTUCE with an M on it (**Metis**) has a DRASTIC TEAR in it (**Adrastea**)
- The DRASTIC TEAR was made by a MOUSE with a LISP (**Amalthea**)
- SLEEPY (**Thebe**) is one of the Seven Dwarfs who sings "IO, it's off to work we go to Europe" (**Io, Europa**)
- In Europe everyone drinks MEAD (**Ganymede**)
- MEAD makes Calista Flockhart (**Callisto**) tipsy, so she asks Harrison Ford to LEAD HER (**Leda**) to the HIMALAYAS (**Himalia**) to sober up

The story link method is very similar, but has more of a narrative structure.

REMEMBERING WITH THE STORY LINK METHOD

A LETTUCE with an M on it (**Metis**) had a DRASTIC TEAR (**Adrastea**) because a LISPING MOUSE (**Amalthea**) accidentally stepped on it as he was SLEEPILY (**Thebe**) singing "IO, it's off to work we go" (**Io**) while on his way to EUROPE (**Europa**) where he hoped to find everyone was drinking MEAD (**Ganymede**), especially his favorite actress Calista Flockhart (**Callisto**), who was so drunk that she asked husband Harrison Ford to LEAD HER (**Leda**) to the HIMALAYAS (**Himalia**) to sober up in the fresh air.

Here are some more lists that are well suited to the memory link method. Alternatively, you could use the acronym method on page 228, the number shape memory hook (*see* page 217), or the number rhyme memory hook (*see* page 219). Use whichever works best for you, but experiment with all of them.

TUDOR MONARCHS OF ENGLAND AND IRELAND

Henry VII , Henry VIII, Edward VI, Lady Jane Grey, Mary I, Elizabeth I

THE FIRST TEN U.S. PRESIDENTS

George Washington, John Adams, Thomas Jefferson, James Madison, James Monroe, John Quincy Adams, Andrew Jackson, Martin Van Buren, William Henry Harrison, John Tyler

THE FIRST TEN AMENDMENTS TO THE U.S. CONSTITUTION

1. freedom of religion, speech, press, and assembly; right of petition

2. right to bear arms

3. limit on quartering of troops

4. protection against unreasonable search and seizure

5. due process, double jeopardy; self-incrimination

6. right to speedy trial

7. trial by jury in civil cases

8. no excessive bail or fine; no cruel or unusual punishment

9. people retain rights

10. powers not delegated to the U.S. states or people

MNEMONICS
AND ACRONYMS

A MNEMONIC IS ANY METHOD OR DEVICE THAT HELPS MEMORY. HERE ARE SOME EXAMPLES OF VERBAL MNEMONICS, NUMERICAL MNEMONICS, AND ACRONYMS.

VERBAL MNEMONICS

1. Colors of the rainbow in order:
   red, orange, yellow, green, blue, indigo, violet

   Richard Of York Gave Battle In Vain

2. Color codes used in electronics, in numerical order:
   black (0), brown (1), red (2), orange (3), yellow (4), green (5), blue (6), violet or purple (7), gray (8), and white (9)

   Bill Brown Realized Only Yesterday Good Boys Value Good Work

3. Names of the planets:
   Mercury, Venus, Earth, Mars, Jupiter, Saturn, Uranus, Neptune

   My Very Educated Mother Just Served Us Nachos

4. The notes on the spaces on the bass clef stave:
   A, C, E, G

   All Cows Eat Grass

5. Order of Mohs hardness scale from 1 to 10:
   Talc, Gypsum, Calcite, Fluorite, Apatite, Orthoclase feldspar, Quartz, Topaz, Corundum, Diamond

   Toronto Girls Can Flirt, And Other Queer Things Can Do

6. The first eight U.S. presidents:
   George Washington, John Adams, Thomas Jefferson, James Madison, James Monroe, John Quincy Adams, Andrew Jackson, Martin Van Buren

   Will A Jolly Man Make A Jolly Visitor?

7. How to spell POTASSIUM:

   one *t*ea, two **s**ugars

8. When to use the spellings "stationery" and "stationary":

   There is an "e" in envelope = station**e**ry

9. The royal houses of England:
   Norman, Plantagenet, Lancaster, York, Tudor, Stuart, Hanover, Windsor

   No Planes Landed Yesterday, Ten Stewardesses Have Warts

10. Order of geological time periods:
    Cambrian, Ordovician, Silurian, Devonian, Carboniferous, Permian, Triassic, Jurassic, Cretaceous, Paleocene, Eocene, Oligocene, Miocene, Pliocene, Pleistocene, Recent

    Camels Often Sit Down Carefully. Perhaps Their Joints Creak? Persistent Early Oiling Might Prevent Painful Rheumatism.

11. The notes on the lines on the treble clef stave:
    E, G, B, D, F

    Every Good Boy Deserves Fruit

12. Reactivity of metals:
    Potassium, Sodium, Calcium, Magnesium, Aluminum, Zinc, Iron, Lead, Copper, Mercury, Silver, Platinum

    Please Send Cats, Monkeys, And Zebras In Large Cages Make Sure Padlocked

13. The notes on the lines on the bass clef stave:
    G, B, D, F, A

    Good Boys Deserve Fruit Always

14. Order of biological classification:
    Kingdom, Phylum, Class, Order, Family, Genus, Species

    King Philip Came Over For Great Soup

15. Bactrian camel has two humps, Dromedary camel has one:

16. The order of operations for math:
    Parentheses, Exponents, Multiply, Divide, Add, and Subtract

    Please Excuse My Dear Aunt Sally

17. How to spell NECESSARY:

    Not Every Cat Eats Sardines (Some Are Really Yummy)

18. The eight facial bones:
    Vomer, Conchae, Nasal, Maxilla, Mandible, Palatine, Zygomatic, Lacrimal

    Virgil Can Not Make My Pet Zebra Laugh

19. The order of the earth's atmospheres:
    Troposphere, Stratosphere, Mesosphere, Thermosphere, Exosphere

    Tropical Storms Make Their Exit

20. Countries around the Adriatic Sea (in clockwise direction):
Italy, Slovenia, Croatia, Bosnia and Herzegovina, Montenegro, Albania

    Incredibly Slimy Cockroach Bit My Aunt

21. Stala**g**mites are on the **g**round, stala**c**tites are on the **c**eiling.

22. What happened to the six wives of Henry VIII:

    divorced, beheaded, died, divorced, beheaded, survived

23. How to spell RECEIVE:

    It's better to g**ive** than rece**ive**.

24. Number of days in month:

    Thirty days have September,
    April, June, and November.
    All the rest have 31,
    Except February alone,
    And that has 28 days clear,
    And 29 in a leap year.

    Knuckles = 31 days, hollows = 30 days (except Feb. = 28 or 29)

25. First ten chemical elements:
Hydrogen, Helium, Lithium, Beryllium, Boron, Carbon, Nitrogen, Oxygen, Fluorine, Neon

    Happy Henry Likes Beer But Could Not Obtain Four Nuts

26. How to spell BELIEVE:

    Do not be**lie**ve a **lie**.

27. The next eight chemical elements:
Sodium (NA), Magnesium, Aluminum, Silicon, Phosphorus, Sulfur, Chlorine, Argon

    Naughty Magpies Always Sing Perfect Songs Clawing Ants

28. The 12 cranial nerves
Olfactory, Optic, Oculomotor, Trochlear, Trigeminal, Abducens, Facial, Vestibulocochlear, Glossopharyngeal, Vagus, (Spinal) Accessory, Hypoglossal.

    Oh Once One Takes The Anatomy Final Very Good Vacations Are Heavenly

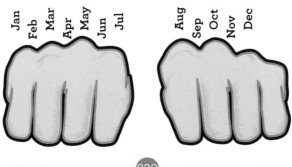

NUMERICAL/MATH MNEMONICS

1. First 15 digits of the mathematical constant pi:
   3.14159265358979

   Now I need a drink, alcoholic of course, after the heavy lectures involving quantum mechanics.

   (The number of letters in each word corresponds to a digit.)

2. The Roman numerals 50, 100, 500, 1000:

   Lazy Cats Don't Move (L, C, D, M)

3. Sine = Opposite over Hypotenuse; Cosine = Adjacent over Hypotenuse; and Tangent = Opposite over Adjacent

   SOH-CAH-TOA

   (Sine, Cosine, and Tangent are trigonometric functions which relate the angles of a right-angled triangle to the lengths of its sides.)

4. Speed of light in meters per second: 299,792,458

   We guarantee certainty, clearly referring to this light mnemonic.
   (The number of letters in each word corresponds to a digit.)

5. Three basic trigonometry relationships in triangles:
   Opposite = Adjacent x Tanθ;
   Adjacent = Hypotenuse x Cosθ;
   Opposite = Hypotenuse x Sinθ

   Old Aunt Tabatha, And Her Cat, On Her Ship

   (Sine, Cosine, and Tangent are trigonometric functions which relate the angles of a right-angled triangle to the lengths of its sides.)

ACRONYMS

1. The colors of the rainbow in order:
   Red, Orange, Yellow, Green, Blue, Indigo, Violet

   ROY G BIV

2. The position of the North American Great Lakes on a map:
   Superior, Huron, Ontario, Michigan, Erie

   SHO ME

3. In English, the eight parts of speech:
   Pronouns, Adjectives, Verbs, Prepositions, Adverbs, Nouns, Interjections, Conjunctions

   PAVPANIC

4. Scuba diving predive safety checklist:
   Buoyancy, Weights, Releases, Air, Final check

   BW RAF

5. The notes on the spaces on the treble clef stave:

FACE

6. In English, the seven coordinating conjunctions:
For, And, Nor, But, Or, Yet, So

FANBOYS

7. The most salient interrelated factors that explain the decline of a civilization:
Water, Energy, Climate, Agriculture, Population

WECAP

8. The stages of cell division:
Interphase, Prophase, Metaphase, Anaphase, Telephase

IPMAT

9. The order of operations for math:
Parentheses, Exponents, Multiply, Divide, Add, or Subtract

PEMDAS

10. Seven deadly sins:
Pride, Avarice (greed), Lust, Envy, Gluttony, Anger (wrath), Sloth

PALE GAS

ACROSTICS

An acrostic is a form of writing, usually a poem, which contains a secret word or message, spelled out with the initial, final, or another chosen letter of each line, sentence, or paragraph. The word "acrostic" comes from combining the Greek words ἄκρος (extreme) and στίχος (line/verse). Acrostics can be used for encryption or as powerful mnemonics (devices to aid memory retrieval); they are a great way to invent passwords you'll never forget (because you've already learned them).

Acrostics have been around for millennia and were particularly popular with the Greeks of the Alexandrine period, the poets of the Italian Renaissance, and the Elizabethans. The first printed version that survives of an acrostic poem is "The Strife of Love in a Dream," written at the end of the fifteenth century by a smitten monk to record his clandestine love for a woman. The initial letters of the first words of each section spell out in Latin the message, "Brother Francis Colonna passionately loves Polia."

Acrostics also feature in the Hebrew Bible and the Greek exclamation "Ἰησούς Χριστός, Θεού Υιός, Σωτήρ; Iesous CHristos, THeou Yios, Soter" (Jesus Christ, God's son, savior) spells out ICHTHYS (ΙΧΘΥΣ), Greek for fish. Christians adopted this as their secret symbol to avoid persecution by the Roman Empire.

One of the most famous ancient acrostics is the 25-letter Roman "Sator Square" (see right).

The earliest datable square was discovered in the ruins of Pompeii, but many others have been found in locations around the world, including Cirencester in England, beneath the church of Santa Maria Maggiore in Rome, and in Syria.

S	A	T	O	R
A	R	E	P	O
T	E	N	E	T
O	P	E	R	A
R	O	T	A	S

It reads the same upward, downward, backward, and forward. It appears in a lot of occult literature and records of medieval magic, because of its unique symmetry. It means "The farmer Arepo holds wheels for work" or "The farmer uses his plow to work."

Acrostics make convenient passwords—you can create one by taking the initial or final letters of words of a song that you already know. For instance, this password was created by taking the initial letters of words in the first two lines of a famous Elton John hit: gNJtinkyaa.

It's "Candle in the Wind" (the original version). Everyone has a unique catalog of favorite song lyrics stored in their long-term memory, so using them to create acrostic passwords is easy because you've already memorized them. If you want to keep track of which songs you've used, simply create a playlist or write a list of songs. Anyone seeing it won't realize that it's highly sensitive information.

Here's an example of an acrostic poem, by Edgar Allan Poe. Its title and the first word are a giveaway:

AN ACROSTIC
by Edgar Allan Poe (written ca 1829)

Elizabeth it is in vain you say
"Love not"—thou sayest it in so sweet a way:
In vain those words from thee or L. E. L.
Zantippe's talents had enforced so well:
Ah! if that language from thy heart arise,
Breathe it less gently forth—and veil thine eyes.
Endymion, recollect, when Luna tried
To cure his love—was cured of all beside—
His folly—pride—and passion—for he died.

ACROSTIC PASSWORDS

Here is a list of 12 initial letter acrostic passwords; see if you can crack them. The only clue is the artist.

nfnfwkhtdi (Bee Gees), bymiwtl (Johnny Cash), gsiybwgpliyb (50 Cent), ittrlitjfcialnefr (Queen), wwwmwdifltigcn (Rihanna), latslhtsfy (Coldplay), hygciyc (Arctic Monkeys), Lcttftnwidabcd (The Clash), yanbahdcatt (Elvis Presley), inmtcyasinmtcyap (Prince), icfyhhhicsyhhh (Beyoncé), haisimtcfatM (David Bowie)

REMEMBER
NAMES AND FACES

If you are hopeless at remembering names and faces, don't worry, you're not alone. In fact, studies have shown that most people find it harder to remember a name than an occupation and other biographical details, which hold more interest and meaning so they are easier to remember. Most of us don't have any trouble recalling a face (although as many as 2.5 percent of the population suffer from prosopagnosia—genetic face blindness).

A name is just an abstract label, so unless you use imagery to make names concrete, you will always struggle to remember them, like the vast majority of the general population.

1. Pay attention and don't get distracted. When you are being introduced to someone for the first time, concentrate on listening and remembering their name rather than getting so distracted by all the social niceties—handshaking, cheek kissing, smiling, trying to look interesting and/or interested—that you don't listen properly.

2. If you don't listen properly or don't catch the name, ask for it to be repeated. It's better to do this immediately than have to spend an entire conversation hoping you aren't going to have to introduce them to anyone else.

3. Try to link the name with a concrete image. If the person's name is Jerry, that might remind you of jelly, so link Jerry with the jelly—imagine it smeared all over his face, or that a jar of jelly is stuck on top of his head.

4. Identify the person's most distinctive feature—big nose, recessive chin, freckles—and link your image to this feature. If Jerry has big ears that stick out, imagine spreading strawberry jelly on them before sticking them to the side of his face.

5. Introduce the name at least once into a conversation (any more than this might appear insincere).

6. After the initial encounter has finished, spend a few minutes consolidating in your memory the names of people you have just met. This brief recap will deepen the encoding.

7. Don't smoke. Studies show that nonsmokers remember names and faces better than smokers.

USING THE STRATEGIES YOU HAVE JUST LEARNED, SPEND TEN MINUTES MEMORIZING THE NAMES OF THESE PEOPLE, THEN TURN THE PAGE AND SEE HOW MANY YOU CAN REMEMBER.

This only allows you 24 seconds for each face, to simulate what you might experience at a social gathering where you are introduced to a lot of people one after the other. So work quickly and try not to leave anyone out. If you can remember more than seven names, you are already above average, but with practice this should rise to between 15 and 25.

Caleb	Sota	Richard	Tony	Luigi
Mark	Sean	Jordan	Warren	Leonard
Ryan	Akio	James	Richard	Cameron
Jane	Tong	Gabriella	Penny	Lisa
Mary	Alyssa	Rachel	Grace	Yimei

FACIAL RECOGNITION

The fusiform gyrus runs along the underside of the temporal and occipital lobes of the brain, across both hemispheres—although it is larger in the right side. This area of the brain deals with facial recognition and it also communicates with the occipital lobe, where visual input is processed. Damage to the fusiform gyrus or to the neural pathways that lead from it to the occipital lobe usually results in impaired facial recognition, even of family and friends.

The facial recognition system, like language acquisition, becomes specialized as children grow older. Just as the ability to learn a foreign language like a native speaker drops off in infancy, recognizing faces from other ethnic groups also declines without regular exposure. We find it easier to recognize faces from our own culture, so growing up in a multicultural environment has lasting benefits for facial recognition abilities in later life.

Studies have also shown gender differences in face recognition. Men tend to recognize fewer female faces than women do, but there are no gender differences associated with male faces.

Facial recognition also has an emotional memory component, because when we see a face, we need to recall how we feel about that person and assess whether they are an ally or a threat. Damage to this system (e.g. a communication failure between the temporal cortex, which processes faces, and the limbic system, which deals with emotion) can lead to a condition called Capgras syndrome (or the Capgras Delusion), in which a person is convinced that a friend or relative has been replaced by an identical-looking imposter. Imagine recognizing your mother, but without any of the emotions that you would expect to feel; it's easy to see how this could lead you to think that something about her was "off."

If you can remember half of the names, very well done. As you can see, it's a challenge, but with practice you will be able to speed up the process (which is essential) and improve your hit rate in busy social situations.

USING BOTH SIDES
OF THE BRAIN

Since the 1960s, popular psychology has propagated the concept of "left-brained" and "right-brained" personalities. You are probably familiar with the idea that right brained people are creative, impulsive, intuitive, imaginative, and subjective, while left-brainers are analytical, attentive, detail-oriented, objective, and rational. In fact our brains are much more sophisticated than this. However, the concept can still be used to help you highlight some of your broad personality traits since they have a direct impact on how best you learn. It is important to recognize what kind of learner you are so you can adapt your learning style and/or work on your weaknesses. Fortunately, the brain is remarkably malleable even into late adulthood, so if you are impulsive, risk-taking, and big-picture oriented by nature, you can learn to be more logical, risk-aware, and detail-oriented (and vice versa).

COMMON CHARACTERISTICS OF A LEFT-BRAIN LEARNER

Memorizes best by repetition (auditory or writing)

Has no difficulty processing information that is presented verbally

Likes structure, making plans, timetables, routine

Prefers to work alone in a quiet environment

Happy with a lecture format (being talked at)

Can learn without requiring an emotional attachment to the material

COMMON CHARACTERISTICS OF A RIGHT-BRAIN LEARNER

Memorizes best by using meaning, color, pictures, story, or emotion in material

May have difficulty processing information that is presented verbally; needs visual input

Does not plan ahead regularly, likes to keep options open

Prefers to work in a group in a busy, even noisy environment

Prefers hands-on activities (doing) over a lecture format

Needs to feel emotionally involved with the material

ARE YOU RIGHT- OR LEFT-BRAINED?

1. Draw a Q on your forehead with your finger. Which direction did you draw the tail?

    a. Pointing toward your finger
    b. Pointing away from your finger

2. What does your desk/bedroom look like?

    a. Tidy
    b. Cluttered

3. If you could choose an assignment topic, would you rather:

    a. Describe the planets in the solar system
    b. Write a story about a flea that saves the world

4. I base important decisions on:

    a. Logic
    b. Intuition

5. I am a risk-taker.

    a. No
    b. Yes

6. It is easier for me to remember faces than names.

    a. No
    b. Yes

7. There is a right and a wrong way to do everything.

    a. Yes
    b. No

8. I am usually on time for my appointments.

    a. Yes
    b. No

9. If I lost something, I'd try to remember where I saw it last.

    a. No
    b. Yes

10. If I had to assemble something, I'd read the directions first.

    a. Yes
    b. No

RESULTS

Mostly (A): You are left-brained

Mostly (B): You are right-brained

Roughly equal (A) and (B): You do not have a dominant side and have attributes of both.

HOW TO MINIMIZE
MEMORY LOSS

As already discussed, the best way to improve your memory is to stay healthy by exercising regularly, getting plenty of sleep, eating healthy food, and keeping your brain active by doing memory exercises. However, several other lifestyle factors affect your mental and physical well-being and, with it, your memory.

POSITIVE SOCIAL INTERACTION

Surround yourself with friends and family and cultivate an active social life. Older people who maintain close ties with others have better mental performance than those who are more isolated. Social interaction stimulates the brain, but it is important to associate with people who encourage and make you feel good and allow you to self-actualize.

Scientists have studied how relationships can affect cognitive performance. In one study, nursing home residents were asked to complete a jigsaw. One group was given verbal encouragement, a second group was actively shown where the pieces fitted, and the third group was given no support. Later, they all attempted another puzzle independently. The people in the group that had been encouraged (while remaining independent) improved their performance; the second group performed worse; and those who had received no support remained the same.

STOP SMOKING

Smoking constricts the arteries, damages the lungs, and increases the risk of high blood pressure and stroke, all of which reduce oxygen flow to the brain, which affects memory.

CHALLENGE YOUR BRAIN WITH NEW EXPERIENCES

Your brain thrives on new input, new sights, sounds, and smells, breaks in routine, and interesting novel experiences. Variety isn't just the spice of life, it's also a memory booster—cross-training for mind and body.

CHECK YOUR MEDICATION

If you take medication to reduce anxiety, help you sleep, or treat allergies, it could affect your memory. Dr. Cara Tannenbaum, research chair at the Montreal Geriatric University Institute and associate professor of medicine and pharmacy at the University of Montreal, has found a link between certain kinds of medication and memory issues, including benzodiazepines (used to treat anxiety and insomnia), antihistamines, and tricyclic antidepressants. Don't stop taking your meds, but do discuss any memory concerns with your doctor.

SEEK HELP FOR DEPRESSION

If you think you might be suffering from depression, seek help. It has long been known that depression weakens the memory. Recent research by Brigham Young University published in the journal *Behavioural Brain Research*, indicates that depression impairs the ability to distinguish between things that are similar, a skill called "pattern separation." The more depressed a person is, the harder it becomes for them to differentiate similar experiences they have had.

Depressed people don't have amnesia as such, they are just missing the details, which impairs their ability to form long-term memories. One of the physical effects of depression is a measurable decrease in the growth of new brain cells in the hippocampus, a crucial part of the brain involved in memory formation and storage.

TAKE UP A CRAFT HOBBY

Researchers from the Mayo Clinic in Minnesota compared nearly 200 people aged 70 to 89 with mild memory problems, with a group with no impairment. Those who had read books, played games, enjoyed puzzles and crosswords, or pursued a craft hobby such as knitting or quilting had a 40 percent reduced risk of memory impairment.

REDUCE SUGAR IN YOUR DIET

A recent UCLA study with rats, published in the *Journal of Physiology*, showed a link between a diet high in fructose and memory and learning impairment. Fernando Gomez-Pinilla, a professor of neurosurgery at the David Geffen School of Medicine at UCLA, says, "Eating a high-fructose diet over the long term alters your brain's ability to learn and remember information. But adding omega-3 fatty acids to your meals can help minimize the damage."

MIND MAPPING

Creating a mind map is an effective way to visualize and organize ideas and create a network of associations. This also makes it an ideal way to encode and test your recall of factual information from your declarative memory (*see* page 173).

A mind map usually consists of a single word or idea, placed in the center of a page. Ideas and related information are then added, branching out from the center. This creates a page of information that is nonlinear, free from Western sinistrodextral (left-to-right) word formation. You can also use different colored ink to categorize information visually.

Mind maps can also help you to understand concepts, which is an important first step in memorizing; it's very hard to learn something that you don't properly understand, so if you are struggling to learn and understand information, write it down as a mind map.

Before you learn how to create a mind map, here are three important details to remember:

- They should only contain keywords and short phrases. They are a way to organize ideas, not to write reams of notes.
- They encourage and strengthen associations and connections.
- They can use color, images, and symbols as well as keywords and short phrases.

HOW TO MAKE A MIND MAP

1. Start with a blank sheet of paper, at least 8 ½ x 11 inches. Turn the paper so that it is landscape oriented.

2. Write the keyword or draw the key image in the center of the page.

3. Every time you add another word or image, draw a branch from the keyword to connect with it, or draw a branch from a branch. No matter how many branches you create, it should be possible to journey back along the branches to reach the center.

4. It will also be possible to travel from one word to any other word by traveling along the branches, so everything is connected.

5. Draw curved branches, not straight lines. Curves are more organic and flowing and encourage creative thinking; straight lines may encourage rigid thinking.

MIND MAPS: KEEP THEM SIMPLE

ATTENTION PLEASE

Attention is essential to effective learning. The best way to improve recall is to increase attention at the memory-forming stage. Without attention, retention is haphazard and beyond the learner's control. Attention must also target the appropriate areas of study, otherwise the retention will be strong but the information irrelevant. Effective attention involves being highly selective about what you consciously decide to commit to memory.

SEVEN WAYS TO IMPROVE YOUR ATTENTION

1. The learning task must have meaning and value, which can only be gained by understanding WHAT you are learning and WHY you are learning it.

2. Determine what is most important (*see* page 249).

3. Understand that attention is as much about deciding what to ignore as it is about focus. According to psychologist and philosopher William James, attention is "taking possession of the mind, in clear and vivid form, of one out of what may seem several simultaneously possible objects or trains of thoughts... It implies withdrawal from some things in order to deal effectively with others."

4. Eliminate distractions, especially those from digital media such as the television, internet, and cell phones. Psychologist Dr. Larry Rosen says that "solid research ...demonstrates how the technologies that we use daily coerce us to act in ways that may be detrimental to our well-being," causing what he calls an "iDisorder."

5. Time-limit and structure your internet activity to clearly differentiate between leisure browsing and research, so you don't waste half an hour under the pretext of "work."

6. Research has shown that self-discipline is more important than IQ in predicting academic success. Also, many people hamper their learning with the self-limiting belief that willpower is finite. In fact, studies by Stanford University psychology professors Greg Walton and Carol Dweck have shown that people who believe that willpower is unlimited and self-renewing are more effective learners than those who believe that willpower is a finite resource.

7. Reading is one of the most effective ways to increase your attention span and your attentional control—your capacity to choose what to pay attention to and what to ignore, how effectively you can engage and disengage your focus.

ATTENTION TEST

Only 20 of the symbols on these two pages look like this: 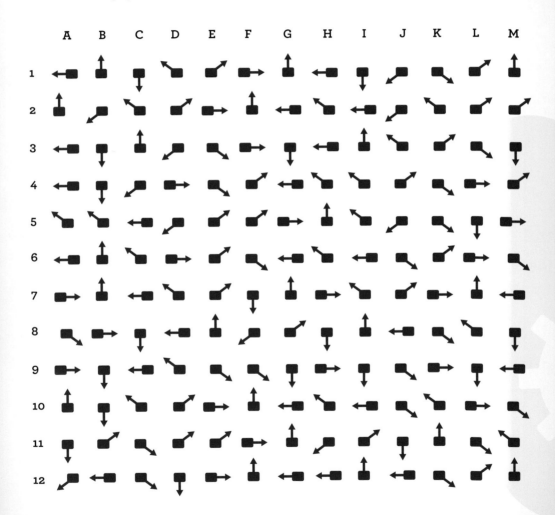 . Take as long as you need but time yourself. As quickly and accurately as possible, write down the coordinates of all 20 of them. Then *see* page 279-280 for your assessment.

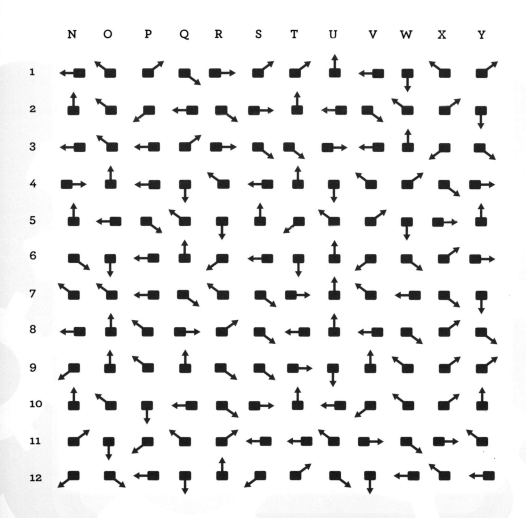

ESTABLISH REGULAR
STUDY SESSIONS

Learning is a habit, and memory works best when it can be refreshed a little every day. So it is better to study in several shorter study sessions than a single long one. You retain best what you study at the beginning and end of a session (these are known as the primacy and recency effects), so the longer the session, the less of the material you will retain in proportion to the time spent.

1. When planning six hours of study, schedule one hour every day for six days, then take a break on the seventh. If you have to learn two subjects in 12 hours, spend an hour a day on each subject for six days. This way you know that both subjects will gain the same attention.

2. Your learning will be less efficient if you split the week into two halves, focussing on one subject for half the week and the other subject for the second half of the week. Chipping away day by day at both subjects will make you feel more in control; otherwise the second subject can become a worry during the first half of the week and affect your concentration on the first subject.

3. The brain works best when it is rested. So it makes sense that each of your six study sessions spread over a week benefit from following a night's sleep (important for memory consolidation), whereas one single six-hour session only follows one night's sleep.

4. Use the Pomodoro technique to break up your study. Work for 25 minutes, take a five-minute break, work for another 25 minutes, then take another five-minute break. Every two hours, take a longer break of 25 minutes. So a two-hour study session would look like this:

5. For every 100 minutes you spend studying, you will spend 40 minutes resting. This might seem like a lot of rest, but the gains to your attention and memory more than make up for it.

DETERMINE WHAT IS
IMPORTANT

Be highly selective about what you study. Even if your willpower is unlimited, your time is finite, so you have to be decisive about where to place your attention. Effective learners don't know everything; they just figure out what they need to learn and what they can ignore.

When you are reading a text for the first time you need to be able to judge what information is important for the meaning and understanding, and what is extraneous, even though it may be interesting. You have to make a distinction between the most and the least important information in the text otherwise everything has equal value and you will be overwhelmed.

Reading and studying is like mining rock for precious metal. Gold miners can't mine gold unless they know that this is what they are supposed to be doing. Your task is to methodically extract the nuggets of meaning. Many readers just start metaphorically hacking away at a text without a clear goal, unaware that they need to sift and select and to use high-level reasoning skills to collect the important structural and material essence.

How to mine a text for meaning, to isolate supporting details, and to read for specific information:

1. Think about facts, ideas, and your own responses while you read. Search for answers to compelling questions. Write them down.

2. Identify key ideas or themes.

3. Monitor your comprehension, so that you are aware the moment a passage stops making sense.

4. Reread anything that doesn't make sense. Don't skim over it. Rereading for sense is normal and not a sign that you are either a poor reader or stupid.

5. Look out for the structural and semantic cues that signal importance: Headings, different fonts, framed text, captions, labels, lists, bullet points—all these things provide structure and point the reader toward the subtleties of meaning. Look out for key guiding words or phrases such as "for example," "however," "therefore," "in conclusion," "sometimes," "but," "never," "always," "represent the," etc.

6. Distinguish between interesting information and important information. The interesting information may be easier to learn and recall than the important information; it may also distract you from the important information. Don't let one crowd out the other in your long-term memory.

For example, say you need to learn and remember four things:

1. the etymology of the word "synapse"

2. the two basic types of synapse

3 & 4. the name and chemical structure of an important amino acid commonly associated with changes in postsynaptic signaling.

So you turn to the relevant page in your textbook and see this:

> *Comes from the Greek "synapsis" or conjunction. The word "synapse" comes from "synaptein," which Sir Charles Scott Sherrington and colleagues coined from the Greek "syn-" ("with," "together") and "haptein" ("fasten," "clasp"). There are two fundamentally different types of synapses: Chemical (via the activation of voltage-gated calcium channels) and electrical (with presynaptic and postsynaptic cell membranes connected by gap junctions). The amino acid is N-methyl-D-aspartic acid receptor (NMDAR). By altering the release of neurotransmitters, plasticity of synapses can be controlled in the presynaptic cell.*

First write down the important information. This is all you need to learn:

1. "synapsis" = conjunction, *syn-* (with, together) *haptein* (to fasten, clasp)

2. chemical, electrical

3. N-methyl-d-aspartic acid receptor (NMDAR).

4.

If you struggled to extract this information, reread page 249 to check which procedures you missed. *See* page 253 and how "elaborative rehearsal" can help you to commit this information to your long-term memory.

STRUCTURE AND ORGANIZE THE
INFORMATION

Organizing information and providing structure helps to package it, ready for your long-term memory. It's like sorting your groceries at the checkout into bags for the fridge, for the freezer, one for meat, another for fruit and vegetables, another for cleaning products or toiletries. When you get home you know where everything is and you can put everything in its correct place quickly and efficiently. Or you could throw it all into one hefty garbage bag and then dump it in the trunk. In both scenarios you get your groceries home, but only the first strategy is efficient and aids retrieval.

1. Group similar concepts and terms together. Use a highlighter to draw attention to important facts and ideas, then chunk them into smaller groups.

2. The "rule of three" is a popular rhetorical device used in writing and public speaking: Grouping ideas together in threes to clarify meaning, give the listener structural cues, and to give a satisfying feeling of closure. Many jokes, slogans, fables, and nursery rhymes follow this triune structure, as does Winston Churchill's famous utterance after the Second Battle of El Alamein: "Now this is not the end. It is not even the beginning of the end. But it is, perhaps, the end of the beginning."

    For instance, if you have highlighted 30 pieces of information, see if you can chunk this down, in a branching structure, to ten groups of three.

3. Arrange the material visually so that it can be represented in branches of information, like the mind map on page 244. This internal scaffolding and interconnectivity aid memory encoding.

Here are some more lists of information that seem impossible to remember. Impose the optimal structure to make memorizing easy (answer on page 280).

1. 58901234678012456379890156723 4

2. bird, calling, gold, turtle, bird, calling, gold, turtle, French, calling, gold, bird, French, calling, gold, bird, ring, dove, ring, hen, ring, dove, ring, hen, ring, hen, French, gold

3. table, knife, plate, spoon, cup, fork, jug, window, saucer, vase of flowers, cat, carrot, potato, chicken leg (hint: drawing a picture may be the best technique here)

4. Type your notes so that you can easily move text around to create the optimal structure. Use color and different fonts, to make the information more memorable.

Experiments at Princeton and Indiana Universities by **Daniel** Oppenheimer, an associate professor of psychology and public affairs at Princeton, Connor *Diemand-Yauman,* a **2010 Princeton** graduate, and Erikka **Vaughan** have shown that unusual fonts improve retention. They got one group of people to read information in 16-point Arial and others in 12-point Comic Sans MA and 12-point Bodoni MT.

The Arial font was easier to read, but it produced the worst retention.

The two fonts that were visually more challenging produced the best recall of information.

Then they conducted a bigger field trial with 222 high school students in *Chesterland,* Ohio. Some students were assigned material in three difficult fonts—**Haettenschweiler**, *Monotype Corsiva,* or *Comic Sans Italicized*—and other students were given material printed in the font that their teacher usually used, Times New Roman or **Arial**.

The students were tested on the material. Those who had been given hard-to-read fonts performed better than did their counterparts reading the same material in easier fonts.

The difficult fonts improve learning because of a concept called "disfluency." The reader has to concentrate harder to read the information, so retention is improved.

However, be careful that you don't use such wacky fonts that your notes become too difficult to read or even illegible. Illegible notes will not enhance your learning.

Cover the top of the page and then answer this question:

1. Write down the names of the three researchers. If you can't remember, write down your best approximation.

When you have finished, check your answers above and see if there was any connection between your retention and the choice of font. *See* answers on page 280 to see what you should have found.

ELABORATE AND
REHEARSE

Elaborative rehearsal involves taking the material and playing with it to create associations with different types of information. It means thinking about the meaning of something rather than just reading it over and over, repeating it mindlessly to yourself.

For example, say you need to learn and remember the etymology of the word "synapse," the two basic types of synapse, and the name and chemical structure of an important amino acid commonly associated with changes in postsynaptic signaling.

This is the basic important information that you mined from page 250:

1. "synapsis" = conjunction, *syn-* (with, together) *haptein* (fasten, clasp)

2. chemical, electrical

3. N-methyl-D-aspartic acid receptor (NMDAR).

4.

Committing all this information to long-term memory will be a challenge unless you elaborate to create meaningful connections. Having mined the important information from the morass of detail on page 250, the next task is to create personal scaffolding to bolt the facts into your memory. This is a highly active process (but no more time-consuming than conventional studying), that requires you to think about, reframe, and order the information in your head.

1. Think about other words you know that begin with "syn": "synthesis," "synergy," "synonym." Look them up:

   · synthesis: combination of two or more entities
   · syntax: the study of combining words to make sentences
   · synonym: words with the same or similar meanings ("with name")

Now consider "haptein":

haptics: nonverbal communication involving touch (fasten onto, touch). Your vibrating cell phone is an example of haptic technology. Now that you have made this connection with something familiar in your life, you will find it easier to remember the word "haptein" and its possible meanings more easily.

Not only have you encoded the information "syn" and "haptein," you have also increased your learning in other areas. You've ended up learning more information to support the original learning task, and deepened your interest and connectivity.

2. Chemical, electrical. This should be fairly simple to remember, because you already know that the brain experiences chemical reactions and displays electrical activity. But to reinforce the information you might imagine a chemistry flask with an electric plug inside and then quickly draw a picture of this idea.

3. **N-m**ethyl-**D-a**spartic acid **r**eceptor (NMDAR) for postsynaptic signaling.

If you learn the acronym, NMDAR, first, this will help you to remember the full name. You know it's an amino "acid" and also a "receptor," so the only words you have to learn are "methyl" and "aspartic" (the rest are letters). Simply making the effort to make these kinds of observations will make your brain pay more attention to the material.

Look up "aspartic acid" on Wikipedia and you'll see that aspartate was originally derived from asparagine, and isolated from asparagus juice. Now you have something concrete to fix your memory to: asparagus stalks.

Methyl is derived from methane. Cows produce large quantities of methane by farting and burping, so draw a picture of a cow eating asparagus and farting. Write NMDA in a gas bubble. Or print off a picture of a cow and a picture of some asparagus and a speech bubble, cut them out, and make a collage yourself.

The physical activity of making this little collage will enter your episodic memory and also provide kinesthetic and visual reinforcement of the information. This sounds time-consuming, but it doesn't have to be. It's actually more time-efficient in the long run because you won't have to relearn the information.

4. Finally, it's time to learn the skeletal formula of NMDA.

Lucky for you that it looks like a cow! When you start creating memory boosters, you'll find that coincidences like this will happen more often, because you are priming your brain to look for patterns and find meaning. Now you can add more details to your collage (if your cow is facing to the left). Write HO next to the horn, write "OH dear!" next to the methane. The cow's udder might remind you of a hand (like a blown-up rubber glove), so hand = HaNd = HN. Doodle in the two Os and you have the structure.

This may all seem like a lot of effort to learn a few bits of information, but there is no easy way to learn. You can either stare at the page of facts and repeat them mindlessly to yourself until you are so bored you want to chew off your own arm (and then find you haven't actually retained anything), or you can have a little thinking adventure that is fun, feels a bit silly, and feels a bit as if you're wasting time (you're not—studying doesn't have to be dull and masochistic, you know).

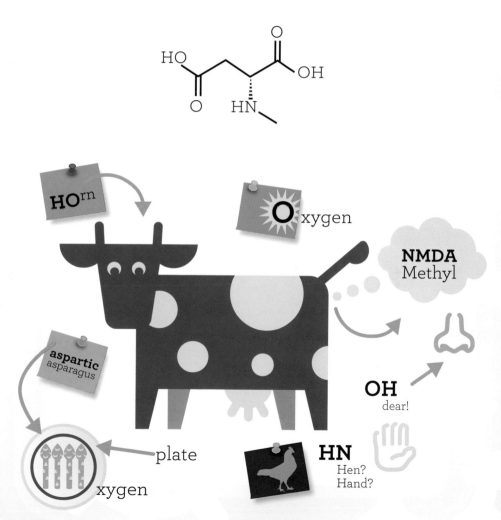

ASSOCIATION:
RELATE NEW INFORMATION TO EXISTING KNOWLEDGE

In the previous section, we saw how connecting new information to familiar imagery (e.g. cell phone, cow, asparagus) provides a hook on which to hang your new memories. This is because it is very difficult to learn anything without a context, and what you already know has a major impact on what you can learn. Your prior knowledge affects how you perceive new information.

To demonstrate this, here is a simple experiment. What is the first thing you think of when you see the word "FESTIVAL"? This will depend entirely on your upbringing, culture, and age. Some people will think of Christmas, others Diwali, Passover, Ramadan, birthdays, harvest, Newport, Woodstock. But the important thing is that you understand what a festival is without further explanation: It involves celebration, food, it is often associated with worship and commemoration, and it is usually fun, challenging, a test of faith, and a time for reflection. Now read this sentence:

"The festival of La Tomatina is held every year in the Valencian town of Buñol, Spain. The first event is the 'palo jabón,' when brave youths climb a greasy pole to reach a ham after which tomato battle commences with a cannon shot."

Because you have prior knowledge of festivals, you can understand the sentence and you can add this new information to your existing knowledge of festivals.

However, incorrect prior knowledge, or incorrect use of prior knowledge to give context, can also mislead. For example the phrase "battle commences with a cannon shot" would lead you to think that a weapon was used to start the tomato fight (since you associate cannons with battles in your memory); in fact a water cannon is used.

As you can see, prior knowledge has a huge impact on your future learning and how you make memories.

An analogy is a good example of this prior knowledge in action. In an earlier section, determining important meaning within a text was compared to mining for gold (*see* page 249). this analogy tapped into a shared understanding of the things most commonly associated with gold mining, namely that gold is precious and needs to be removed from the surrounding rock, which is hard work but potentially very rewarding. The inference was that key important facts are like precious nuggets of gold and digging them out of the text is necessary and potentially very rewarding, justifying the hard work and conscientious effort put in to acquire them.

So, when you are learning new information, use strategies to link and associate the material with your existing knowledge.

1. Consciously think back to situations in which you dealt with similar material. Ask yourself, "What is this like that I already know and understand?"

2. Briefly recap some key points from your prior knowledge to inform how you learn. For instance if you were learning about La Tomatina, you could research to find things in common with your own familiar festivals. So you might look to see what traditions, rules, and rituals are observed, or if there are any special costumes or pole decorations. This will guide how you search for information, and make it easier to learn.

3. Be aware that some of your prior knowledge can lead to incorrect assumptions about the new knowledge.

4. Always try to improve and deepen your understanding of ideas. View your ideas as testable, improvable objects.

5. Be curious; the more you let your curiosity flourish, the more connections and associations you will build as you research a new subject. For instance, aren't you curious about the total number of tomatoes used and who supplies them? This would lead you to discover that the estimated 150,000 tomatoes come all the way from Extremadura on the other side of the country, where they are grown specially for the festival (rather than for taste)...

WHILE WE TEACH,
WE LEARN

The benefits of teaching someone else have been known about for centuries: It was the Roman philosopher Seneca who said, "While we teach, we learn." Albert Einstein famously said, "If you can't explain it to a six-year-old, you don't understand it yourself," which is worth bearing in mind whenever you are tackling complex ideas. However, LDL ("Lernen durch Lehren" or "learning by teaching") has really only gained traction in modern teaching since the 1980s, when Jean-Pol Martin popularized it as a method of foreign language teaching in Germany.

Studies into LDL and "cascading mentoring" have found that when people have to teach a subject to someone else, they are more motivated to understand and learn the information themselves, plus the gaps and weaknesses in their understanding and knowledge are highlighted by trying to explain the concepts to a third party. LDL has also been found to improve self-esteem, self-confidence, and a sense of belonging.

One such 'cascading' mentoring program has recently been introduced at Penn Engineering, along with the Graduate School of Education, which has received a three-year, $600,000 grant from the National Science Foundation "to spur interest in computer science with a first-of-its-kind, 'cascading' mentoring program in which college, high school, and middle school students will learn with and from each other."

Undergraduates will teach and mentor high school and middle school students; the high school students will teach middle schoolers. "This learning-by-teaching approach will improve all of the students' understanding of computational thinking and purposes by exposure to a variety of hands-on software design activities and materials," said Susan Davidson, principal investigator and Chair of the Department of Computer and Information Science, University of Pennsylvania.

Computer scientists at Stanford and Vanderbilt universities are currently developing "Teachable Agents" called "The Betty's Brain System" which has been trialed with fifth grade science pupils. The children can teach the virtual agent to solve problems and the study found that "This motivates the students to learn more so they can teach their agent to perform better." The study also observed that "Beyond preparing to teach, actual teaching can tap into the three critical aspects of learning interactions—structuring, taking responsibility, and reflecting." So the children structured their learning more effectively, took responsibility to improve their own understanding, they reflected on how well they had taught the agent, and were more motivated to better prepare for future learning on related topics.

RESTRUCTURE AND REPOSITION
DIFFICULT INFORMATION

THE NINETEENTH-CENTURY GERMAN PSYCHOLOGIST HERMANN EBBINGHAUS, PIONEER IN THE EXPERIMENTAL STUDY OF MEMORY, DISCOVERED A LEARNING PHENOMENON WHICH HE CALLED THE "SERIAL POSITION EFFECT." HE OBSERVED THAT THE RECALL ACCURACY VARIES DEPENDING ON THE POSITION OF ITEMS WITHIN A LIST.

Spend one minute reading this list three times and trying to memorize all the items. Then write down as many as you can remember, before you continue reading:

circle, film, thermometer, album, vulture, rifle, gloves, signature, coffee, hammer, meteor, parachute

According to the serial position effect, you will remember more of the items at the beginning and end than those in the middle of the list. You also retain more information from the beginning and end of a study session than the middle.

That is why it's important to move information around, and vary the structure as you learn, so that you don't create the same memory blind spots. Flashcards (*see* page 266) are a great way to do this because you can shuffle them to change the order.

You must also work harder and pay more attention to difficult information, because your brain wants to take the path of least resistance; it wants to remember or recall the easy information and ignore the complicated information. This is called "availability heuristic" and we succumb to it all the time—interpreting the world around us based on immediate examples that spring to mind. However, basing judgments on the notion that, "if you can think of it, it must be important" is sloppy thinking that will often lead you astray.

ANSWER THIS QUESTION:

If you were to open a book at random and find the letter "K" in the text, which is more likely:

a) the word would start with a K;

b) K was the third letter?

The correct answer is b) but most people choose a) because several words spring to mind that start with K, but it is harder to think of words with K as their third letter. It's the same reason why people buy lottery tickets and overestimate the frequency of shark attacks or the danger of air travel.

People prefer data that is easy to obtain and they make decisions based on this limited information. Politicians know this, which is why they routinely quote dubious data and repeat sound bites to support their political arguments, because the electorate are all too eager to let themselves be spoonfed information rather than to engage their critical faculties and find out for themselves.

So, take the extra effort to learn the difficult material because otherwise you will shrink the world to fit your limited knowledge, when you should be motivated to increase your knowledge to understand its complexities.

Have you noticed how poorly educated people can speak with boorish certainty on matters about which they know very little? That's the availability heuristic, with an extra helping of "confirmation bias" (the tendency to favor information that confirms one's beliefs).

Consciously fighting against the availability heuristic will encourage you to be more rigorous in your learning:

- Be critical about your knowledge, ask yourself what specific observations are forming your belief, and examine reasons why you *shouldn't* believe it

- It is always better to spend time gathering data and researching than guessing or looking for material to support your limited knowledge

- Don't stop with an initial estimate; keep researching and looking for more information

CONSOLIDATION

CONSOLIDATION IS THE SINGLE MOST IMPORTANT MEMORY PRINCIPLE. MOST PEOPLE ARE FAMILIAR WITH IT, BUT STILL MANAGE TO IGNORE IT, FAVORING CRAMMING OR EXTENDED STUDY PERIODS OVER DISTRIBUTED LEARNING, WHEN THE LATTER IS LESS PAINFUL AND MORE EFFECTIVE.

The first recorded reference to the idea of memory consolidation appeared in the writings of the Roman teacher of rhetoric, Quintilian. He discussed the "curious fact... that the interval of a single night will greatly increase the strength of the memory," and observed that "the power of recollection... undergoes a process of ripening and maturing during the time which intervenes." The word "consolidation" was first applied to memory at the end of the nineteenth century by German researchers Georg Müller and Alfons Pilzecker, who conducted studies into the concept that memory needs time for "Konsolidierung."

Rehearsing or recalling information over spaced intervals reinforces neural pathways; synapses and the communication between brain cells become stronger the more frequently the same signal passes between them. If you doubt this, you have only to consider all the music you can hum and song lyrics you can recall without effort; you never sat down and learned them, you have simply heard them over and over again.

So you think you know all about consolidation. Did you know that caffeine enhances memory consolidation? In a recent study, published online in the journal *Nature Neuroscience*, 160 volunteers were shown 200 pictures of everyday items and asked questions about them. They were then given a pill containing 200 mg caffeine, or a placebo. In a memory test the next day, the caffeinated participants performed better than the control group. Senior author Michael A. Yassa, in an interview with *Medscape Medical News*, said, "My message from this study is that if, like me, you have a coffee habit, and drink several cups a day, this is another reason not to stop it."

TRY THE CAFFEINE MEMORY TEST

Spend three minutes memorizing these 25 objects. Tomorrow, take recall test number 1 on page 264 (no peeking). Then an hour later, look at page 263 and spend three minutes memorizing the other 25 objects. Then drink a cup of coffee and the day after tomorrow take recall test number 2 on page 137. Good luck—turn to the answers on page 265 to see what should have happened.

RECALL TEST NUMBER 1: WHICH OBJECTS ARE MISSING?

RECALL TEST NUMBER 2: WHICH OBJECTS ARE MISSING?

FLASHCARDS

You are probably familiar with flashcards but you may have overlooked them up to now as a learning and memory tool. They are a very powerful technique, but their simplicity and familiarity mean learners ignore them in favor of more novel and faddy studying methods.

Paper flashcards have been used since at least the early nineteenth century, when Favell Lee Mortimer, an English evangelical author of educational books for children, devised a set of phonics flashcards to teach children to read, called *Reading Disentangled,* in 1834.

Most flashcard systems rely on spaced repetition to consolidate information, as well as varying the length of review for cards for which the learning material appears to be secure, shortening it for material that is less secure. If you are a kinesthetic learner, you would benefit from making paper flashcards, but you can also create them digitally with apps like Quizlet, StudyBlue, Anki, and FlashCardMachine.

HOW TO MAKE AND USE FLASHCARDS

1. Your flashcards should be index cards about 4 x 6 inches (fold an $8\frac{1}{2}$ x 11-inch sheet of paper in half vertically, then horizontally).

2. Write a question on one side.

3. Write your answer or answers on the other side.

4. Keep the content brief. Don't overcomplicate with hoards of information. Have only one term or concept per card. If the question asks for a list, try to keep the answer to a minimum of three items. If you need a longer list, split the question over two or more cards.

5. Color code your flashcards for different subjects.

6. Writing or typing the cards benefits tactile learners, and color-coding is good for visual learners. Just creating the cards helps you learn the material but don't spend so long creating them that you run out of time to perform memory games with them.

7. When the information is totally new, limit the number of cards to 50, otherwise you won't be able to go through all of them in one learning session.

8. Every time you start a new pile, shuffle the pack so that your learning remains independent from the order of the cards.

9. Read a question and write or recite your answer (writing is best because it's harder to cheat yourself into thinking you've given an adequate answer).

10. Look at the answer. If you are correct, place your card on the "correct" pile. If wrong, place on the "needs to study more" pile.

11. When you reach the end of the cards, pick up the "needs to study more" pile and go through them again.

12. Keep going until all your flashcards are on the "correct" pile.

LEITNER SYSTEM

This was devised by the German science journalist Sebastian Leitner in the 1970s. Keep the cards in five boxes labeled 1 to 5. In Box 1 keep the cards that you often get wrong and need to review. Keep in Box 5 the cards which you consider yourself to have securely learned.

Quiz yourself on the flashcards in Box 1 every day, Box 2 every 3 days, Box 3 every 5 days, Box 4 every week, and Box 5 once a month. Every time you get an answer right, promote the card to the next box.

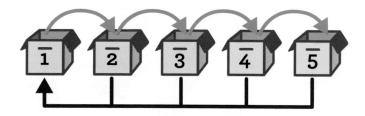

INCLUDE PICTURES IN YOUR ANSWERS

Studies show that pictures with words are more memorable than pictures alone. This is especially useful when using flashcards to learn foreign language vocabulary.

Congratulations, you have completed the first stage of your memory expanding adventure! If you have tried out all the puzzles and techniques, you will already be enjoying improved retention and recall, and more productive study. Now it's over to you. Using your new knowledge and regular daily practice, there's no limit to the incredible cognitive gains you can achieve.

BIBLIOGRAPHY

Train Your Brain

HOW TO DEAL WITH INTRUSIVE THOUGHTS

1. Wegner, Daniel. *White Bears and Other Unwanted Thoughts: An Exploration of Suppression, Obsession, and the Psychology of Mental Control*. New York: Viking, 1989.
2. Israel, Richard and North, Vanda. *Mind Chi: Re-wire Your Brain in 8 Minutes a Day, Strategies for Success in Business and Life*. Capstone, 2010.

AWAKEN YOUR SENSES

1. Nittono, H., Fukushima, M., Yano, A., & Moriya, H. "The Power of Kawaii: Viewing Cute Images Promotes a Careful Behavior and Narrows Attentional Focus." *PLoS ONE*, September 26, 2012.
2. Sanders M. A., Shirk, S. D., Burgin, C. J., Martin, L. L. "The Gargle Effect: Rinsing the Mouth With Glucose Enhances Self-Control." *Psychological Science*, 2012.

DIGITAL DISTRACTIONS

Rosen, Larry. *iDisorder: Understanding Our Obsession with Technology and Overcoming Its Hold on Us*. New York: Palgrave Macmillan, 2012.

THE 'FIVE MORE' RULE

Walton, Greg and Dweck, Carol. "Willpower: It's in Your Head." *New York Times*, November 26, 2011.

SOLUTION-FOCUSSED THINKING

Beck, Aaron. "Self-Focus in Cognitive Therapy", Beck Institute. YouTube, September 4, 2013.

LATERAL THINKING

de Bono, Edward. *The Use of Lateral Thinking*. London: Jonathan Cape, 1967.

PARALLEL THINKING

de Bono, Edward. *Six Thinking Hats*. London: Little Brown and Company, 1985.

VERBAL REASONING

Flower, Sydney B. Brinkle, John R. *The Goat-gland Transplantation, As Originated and Successfully Performed by J. R. Brinkley, M. D., of Milford, Kansas, U. S. A., in Over 600 Operations Upon Men and Women*. Chicago: New Thought Book Department, 1921. Released by The Project Gutenberg, EBook #29362, July 2009.

SPOT THE RELATIONSHIP BETWEEN NUMBERS

Du Sautoy, Marcus. *The Number Mysteries: A Mathematical Odyssey Through Everyday Life*. London: Fourth Estate, 2010.

PRIME NUMBERS AND THE HUMAN BRAIN

Bershadskii, A. "Hidden Periodicity and Chaos in the Sequence of Prime Numbers." *Advances in Mathematical Physics*, 2011.

ALGORITHMS AND ARTIFICIAL INTELLIGENCE

Wolchover, Natalie. "As Machines Get Smarter, Evidence They Learn Like Us." *Quanta Magazine*, July 23, 2013.

VISUAL DISCRIMINATION

Sachs, Oliver. *The Man Who Mistook His Wife for a Hat*. London: Duckworth, 1985.

VISUAL MEMORY

Press release from the website of The Stephen Wiltshire Gallery Ltd, 2011.

ACROSTICS

Godwin, Francis. *Rerum Anglicarum Henrico VIII, Eduardo VI, et Maria Regnantibus, Annales*. London: John Bill, 1616.

ENJOYABLE AMBIGUITY, PARADOXES AND OPTICAL ILLUSIONS

1. Rock, David. *Strategies for Overcoming Distraction, Regaining Focus, and Working Smarter All Day Long*. New York: HarperCollins, 2009.
2. Bayles, David and Orland, Ted. *Art & Fear: Observations on the Perils (and Rewards) of Artmaking*. Santa Barbara, California: Capra Press, 1993.
3. Cheung, Alexander. "10 Ways of Approaching Life to Help Anyone Embrace Ambiguity."

   Alexanderous (blog), March 28, 2013.

KILL THE ANTS

1. Levinson A. J., Fitzgerald P. B., Favalli G., Blumberger D.M., Daigle M., Daskalakis Z.J. "Evidence of Cortical Inhibitory Deficits in Major Depressive Disorder." *Biological Psychiatry*, March 2010.
2. Centre for Addiction and Mental Health. "Critical Brain Chemical Shown to Play Role in Severe Depression." *ScienceDaily*, March 6, 2010.

TRUST YOUR INTUITION

Ogas, Ogi. "Who Wants to be a Cognitive Neuroscience Millionaire?" *Seed Magazine*, March 2014.

Improve Your Memory

HOW THE BRAIN REMEMBERS

Bridge, Donna J., Paller, Ken A. "Neural Correlates of Reactivation and Retrieval-Induced Distortion." *The Journal of Neuroscience*, August 29, 2012.

MYTHS ABOUT MEMORY

Gamerman, Ellen. "The Brain Is Mightier Than the Camera When Remembering Art." *The Wall Street Journal*, December 17, 2013.

YOU REMEMBER MORE THAN YOU THINK

Spock, Benjamin. *Baby and Child Care*. New York: Duell, Sloan and Pearce, 1946.

MEMORY ABILITY IS DEVELOPED, NOT INNATE

Chase, William and Simon, Herbert. "Perception in Chess." *Cognitive Psychology*, 1973.

SHORT-TERM MEMORY

Miller, George A. , "The Magical Number Seven, Plus or Minus Two: Some Limits on Our Capacity for Processing Information." *Psychological Review*, 1956 vol. 63, pp. 81-97.

TOPOGRAPHICAL MEMORY

Berthoz, Alain. *The Brain's Sense of Movement*. Cambridge: Harvard University Press, 2000.

DECLARATIVE MEMORY

Ogas, Ogi. "Who Wants to be a Cognitive Neuroscience Millionaire?" *Seed Magazine*, March 2014.

PROCEDURAL MEMORY

1. Gladwell, Malcolm. *Outliers: The Story of Success*. New York: Little, Brown and Company, 2008.
2. Colvin, Geoff. *Talent Is Overrated: What Really Separates World-Class Performers from Everybody Else*. Portfolio, 2008.

EMOTION AND MEMORY

Easterbrook, J. A. "The effect of emotion on cue utilization and the organization of behaviour." *Psychological Review* 66 (3): 183–201, 1959.

EIDETIC MEMORY

Shafy, Samiha. "The Science of Memory: An Infinite Loop in the Brain." *Spiegel Online*, November 21, 2008.

MUSICAL MEMORY

1. Groussard, M., Viader, F., Hubert, V., Landeau, B., Abbas, A., Desgranges, B., Eustache, F., Platel, H. "Musical and verbal semantic memory: two distinct neural networks?" *NeuroImage*, Volume 49, Issue 3, February 1, 2010.
2. Janata, P. "The neural architecture of music-evoked autobiographical memories." *Cerebral Cortex*, 19, 2579-2594, 2009.
3. Macmillan, Jenny. "Successful Memorising." *Piano Professional*, September 2004.
4. Kageyama, Noa. "Does Mental Practice Work?" from the Bulletproof Musician website
5. *Jan Lisiecki – The Reluctant Prodigy*. You can see the video on the YouTube website.

TALENT IS OVERRATED: DELIBERATE PRACTICE BRINGS SUCCESS

Ericsson, K., Prietula, M. J., Cokely, E. T. The Making of an Expert. *Harvard Business Review*, 85, 114-121, 2007.

LIVELY REPETITION VS. ROTE LEARNING

1. Herzberg, Frederick. "One More Time, How Do You Motivate Employees?" *Harvard Business Review*, 1968.
2. Pink, Daniel H. *Drive: The Surprising Truth About What Motivates Us*. New York: Penguin, 2009.
3. Chua, Amy. *Battle Hymn of the Tiger Mother*. New York: Penguin, 2011.

MUSCLE MEMORY AND MINDFUL PRACTICE

1. Tom Dowie website.
2. From the Bulletproof Musician website.
3. Powell, Michael. *Acting Techniques: An Introduction for Aspiring Actors*. Methuen Drama, 2010.
4. From the Better Movement website.

CHUNKING AND PATTERNS

1. McCurry, Justin. "Chimps are making monkeys out of us." *The Observer*, September 29, 2013.
2. Bor, Daniel. *The Ravenous Brain: How the New Science of Consciousness Explains Our Insatiable Search for Meaning*. Basic Books, 2012.

OBJECT RECALL

McNamara, T.P., Rump, B., & Werner, S. "Egocentric and geocentric frames of reference in memory of large-scale space." *Psychonomic Bulletin and Review*, 10(3), 589-595, 2003.

HOW TO MINIMIZE MEMORY LOSS

Agrawal R., Gomez-Pinilla F. "Metabolic syndrome in the brain: deficiency in omega-3 fatty acid exacerbates dysfunctions in insulin receptor signalling and cognition." *Physiology*, May 15, 2012.

ATTENTION PLEASE

1. James, W. *The Principles of Psychology*. New York: Henry Holt, 1890.
2. Rosen, Larry. *iDisorder: Understanding Our Obsession with Technology and Overcoming Its Hold on Us*. New York: Palgrave Macmillan, 2012.

CONSOLIDATION

Borota, D., Murray, E., Keceli, G., Chang, A., Watabe, J. M., Ly, M., Toscano, J. P., Yassa, M. A. "Post-study caffeine administration enhances memory consolidation in humans." *Nature Neuroscience*, January 12, 2014.

ANSWERS

P13: INCREASE PRODUCTIVITY

Keg of beer: Tilt the keg until the beer touches the lip. If any of the bottom of the keg is visible, it is less than half full.

Three lightbulbs: Press the first switch, leave for one minute, and then turn off. Press the second switch, then enter the room. The illuminated bulb is switch 2, the warm bulb is switch 1, and the cold bulb is switch 3.

Good Samaritan: Choose the old lady. Ask your friend to drive her in your car to the hospital, so you can wait at the bus stop with your perfect partner.

P15: ATTENTIONAL CONTROL

Count the squares: 40

How many Fs?: 6, 9, 6

P17: HOW TO DEAL WITH INTRUSIVE THOUGHTS

Remove earworms: Jennifer Aniston, Eric Clapton, Cameron Diaz, Robert De Niro, Albert Einstein, David Letterman, Wolfgang Amadeus Mozart, Marie Osmond, Julia Roberts, Arnold Schwarzenegger, Serena Williams, Miley Cyrus

P31: SOLUTION-FOCUSSED THINKING

Digital dilemma:

12 + 3 - 4 + 5 + 67 + 8 + 9 = 100

P34: DEDUCTIVE REASONING

Barbara: All penguins have beaks.

Celarent: No penguins have teeth.

Darii: Some pets have feathers.

Ferio: Some animals are not dogs.

Cesare: No hotel is a horse.

Camestres: No carrots are horses.

Festino: Some women are not bald.

Baroco: Some pink things are not carrots.

Darapti: Some tasty things are nutritious.

Disamis: Some delicate things are colorful.

Datisi: Some endangered things are agile.

Felapton: Some of the yellow items in this bowl are not fresh. (There may be items in the bowl other than fruit.)

Bocardo: Some animals have no tails.

Ferison: Some green things have no wheels.

Bramantip: Some ostentatious clothing is in my drawer.

Camenes: No flowers grown indoors are colored.

Dimaris: Some friendly dogs are big.

Fesapo: Some neighborly people are not Hollywood actors.

Fresison: Some evil creatures are not pandas.

P39: INDUCTIVE REASONING

Which comes next in the series?

Question 1

Rule 1: The square moves from bottom right to middle to top left. This sequence then repeats.

Rule 2: The circle moves three squares counterclockwise around the edge of the grid.

Answer: D

Question 2

Rule 1: The triangle pointing upward follows the sequence top left, bottom right, bottom left, top right. This sequence then repeats.

Rule 2: The triangle pointing downward follows the sequence top right, bottom left, bottom right. This sequence then repeats.

Answer: E

Question 3

Rule 1: The number of dots predicts how many triangles there will be in the next box.

Rule 2: The triangles are red if the number of triangles is even, blue if the number of triangles is odd.

Answer: A

Question 4

Rule 1: The shapes move one corner clockwise each time.

Rule 2: The shapes alternate between square and circle.

Rule 3: The shading changes between shaded and unshaded every other step. i.e. shaded, shaded, unshaded, unshaded, shaded, shaded, etc.

Answer: E

Question 5

Rule 1: The shapes shrink from large, medium, to small, then start again.

Rule 2: The shapes alternate between triangle and circle.

Rule 3: The colors go white, to red, to blue, and then repeat.

Answer: D

Question 6

Rule 1: The shape is rotated 45 degrees clockwise.

Rule 2: The shape loses a line and then an arrow each time.

Rule 3: A circle is always purple unless an arrow is pointing at it.

Answer: E

Question 7

Rule 1: The face changes in sequence from smiley to ambivalent to sad.

Rule 2: The shape alternates between square and circle.

Rule 3: The shape symbol is green for two steps then clear for two steps.

Rule 4: The shapes move one corner clockwise each turn.

Answer: D

Question 8

Rule 1: The square appears every third step.

Rule 2: The triangle alternates between rotating clockwise 90 degrees around the middle of the square and being mirrored vertically.

Rule 3: The circle alternates between being present and absent.

Answer: A

Question 9

Rule 1: If the number of purple dots is greater than the number of red dots, subtract a purple dot.

Rule 2: If the number of purple dots is smaller or equal to the number of red dots, add two purple dots.

Rule 3: Add a red dot each step.

Answer: D

P43: ABDUCTIVE REASONING

Base rate fallacy: 1a, 2b

Prosecutor's fallacy: c

P46: BOOLEAN LOGIC

1. Since one of them is lying and one of them is telling the truth, Bonnie must be lying. So Clyde is telling the truth, and Bonnie stole it.

2. John is a liar and his wife tells the truth. They can't both be liars, because if John was a liar he can't make a truthful statement. If only his wife is a liar, then John would be lying about himself being truthful.

3. Pick from the one labeled "NUTS AND BOLTS." Since it is wrongly labeled, it must contain either only nuts or only bolts. Once you've labeled this box correctly, you can deduce the other two (e.g. if you pick a bolt, then the box labeled NUTS must be NUTS AND BOLTS since it can't be NUTS or BOLTS; if you pick a nut, then the box labeled BOLTS must be NUTS AND BOLTS since it can't be either BOLTS or NUTS).

P49: GEOMETRIC REASONING

1:

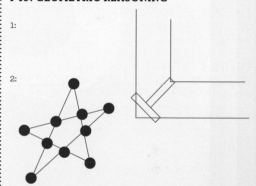

2:

3: A square manhole cover can be dropped diagonally through the hole, while a circular one cannot.

4: White. It was a polar bear and the hunter's camp was at the North Pole.

5: 15.92cm. The radius of a circle is always approximately 1/6.28 (or 0.1592) of its circumference, so increasing the circumference of any circle by 1 meter increases the radius of that circle by (0.1592 x 100cm) = 15.92cm.

6:

7: The pizza is rectangular. Make two horizontal and three vertical cuts.

P51: SPATIAL THINKING

1. C, A, D
2. A
    C and E
    D
    D
    B
    B
    E

P56: LATERAL THINKING

1. There is no soil in a hole.
2. Eight
3. John

P57: LATERAL THINKING CONTINUED

1. Window
2. During a forest fire, a fire-fighting plane had scooped water from the lake, including a swimmer.
3. He lives in a houseboat in the middle of the ocean.
4. The baby fell from a ground-floor window.
5. He asks each builder to name the best builder other than themselves. He then employs the one with the most recommendations.
6. The glass was empty.
7. He was walking.
8. He was in a balloon with several other passengers; it was losing height and about to crash so they drew lots; he drew the broken match and jumped to save the others.
9. The last person took the basket with the last egg still inside.
10. The poison was in the ice cubes, which hadn't melted when he had his drink.
11. The Archduke Ferdinand was sewn into his uniform so that he looked smart, but it could not be opened.
12. The room is the ballroom of an ocean liner. The man ran out of air while diving in the wreck.
13. Police uniform; Tommy had been kept all his life in the cellar.
14. The woman had already put sugar into her tea.
15. The date reads the same upside down; will next happen in 6009.
16. He had just visited his wife who was on a life-support machine in the hospital. As he walked down the stairs the lights went out, indicating a power cut.
17. Exactly twice the distance from one end to the middle.
18. The rest of the poker players were women.
19. She was a woman driving in Saudi Arabia.
20. If it is someone she likes, she can say she has just arrived; if it is someone she doesn't like, she can pretend she is about to go out.
21. Sister.
22. You don't bury survivors.
23. At least one with any certainty.
24. The man had jumped from a plane but his parachute had failed. It was the unopened package.
25. She was a circus tightrope walker who walked blindfolded over a high wire. The band used to stop playing to tell her when she had reached safety at the other end, but a stand-in conductor didn't know this and stopped the music too early. She stepped off the wire to her death.
26. The man had hiccups.
27. The taxi driver had heard his original instructions at the beginning of the journey.
28. The first tattoo artist must have done the superior eagle tattoo since it was on the other tattoo artist's back.

P62: SIMPLE SOLUTIONS ARE BEST

The seven bridges of Königsberg: No, it is impossible.
Five room puzzle:

Only if he walks through corners.
Four forward-thinking camels: First a camel from one side moves forward; then two camels from the other side move forward, then three camels from the other side, etc.

1. Throw it vertically into the air.
2. The words rhyme with 1, 2, 3, etc.
3. Copernican revolution: 16, the number of dots around a center dot.

P66: VERBAL REASONING

Make no assumptions

1. pushover, rugby; maiden, duck; drizzle, precipitate
2. cheese, slow, kick
3. classification
4. soporific, soothing
5. tribulation, contentment
6. marsh, swamp
7. aerobatics
8. car = carton, scarab, vicars, trocar
9. t
10. t, p; z, r
11. m, s, a; a, a, i
12. 1 true; 2 cannot say; 3 false; 4 true; 5 cannot say; 6 cannot say; 7 cannot say; 8 false; 9 cannot say; 10 cannot say

P72: THE HUMAN SPELLCHECKER

On opening the little door, two hairy monsters flew at my throat, bearing me down, and extinguishing the light; while a mingled guffaw **from Heathcliff** and Hareton put the copestone on my rage and **humiliation**. Fortunately, the **beasts** seemed more bent on stretching **their** paws, and yawning, and flourishing their tails, **than** devouring me alive; but they would suffer no **resurrection**, and I was forced to lie till their malignant masters pleased to deliver me: then, hatless and trembling with wrath, I ordered the miscreants to let me out—on their peril to keep **me** one minute longer—with several incoherent threats of retaliation that, in their indefinite depth of virulency, smacked of King Lear.

The vehemence of my agitation brought on a copious bleeding at the nose, and still Heathcliff laughed, and still I **scolded**. I don't know what would have concluded the scene, had **there** not been one person at hand rather more rational **than** myself, and more benevolent than my entertainer. This was Zillah, the stout housewife; who at length issued **forth** to inquire into **the** nature of the uproar. She **thought** that some of them had been **laying** violent hands on me; and, not daring to attack her master, she turned her vocal artillery against the younger scoundrel.

P75: VOCABULARY

argand, lerret, testiculate, exultion, flunge, scrutable, tribution, perchery

Wordsearch:

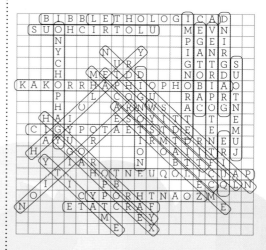

Word deduction:

abacinate	to blind using a red-hot metal plate
balaniferous	acorn-bearing
caducity	being of a transitory or impermanent nature
decastich	ten-line poem
eclogue	pastoral or rustic poem
fabulist	one who invents fables
ganoid	having shiny smooth scales
habilable	capable of being clothed
ignify	to burn
janitrix	a female janitor
keloid	hard scar tissue which grows over injured skin
landau	horse-drawn carriage with folding top
macrotous	big-eared
nevus	birthmark
octad	set of eight things
palpebration	winking
quadrilocular	having four compartments
ranivorous	frog-eating
sanative	healing
tardiloquous	slow in speech
unguligrade	walking on hoofs
vaticide	killing of a prophet
widgeon	freshwater duck
xanthic	yellowish

yelm	a straight bundle of straw used for thatching
zymosis	process of infection

P80: RIDDLES

The Riddle of the Sphinx: Man, who crawls on all fours as a baby, walks on two feet as an adult, and uses a walking stick in old age.

Einstein's riddle: The German

Twelve riddles

1. If Zeheratzade doesn't know the answer, that must mean that Soraya and Peri-banu are wearing different colored hats; so now Soraya knows what color hat she's wearing because it must be a different color to Peri-banu's.
2. two
3. footsteps
4. an umbrella
5. a snail
6. a chick in an egg
7. The four men were pallbearers; the other stayed dry inside the coffin
8. a cloud
9. a candle
10. the letter R
11. a nail in a horseshoe
12. the moon

Dingbats: back draft, all around the world, paradox, right under your nose, look both ways, scrambled eggs, overwhelming odds, goatee, three square meals, West Indies, counting on you, up in arms.

P85: ALGEBRA AND THE VANISHING CAMEL

pumpkin = 30, alarm clock = 20, ice lolly = 6

car = 9, gift box = 1, guitar = 29

He added his camel to the herd. He then led nine camels (one half of 18) to the eldest son, six camels (one third of 18) to the middle son and two camels (one ninth of 18) to the youngest son. That just left his own camel, which he promptly mounted and rode away. The mathematician solved the problem by recognizing that the sum of 1/2, 1/3, and 1/9 is not 1, but 17/18. Adding an extra camel made the division possible because 18 is the lowest common denominator of 2, 3, and 9 and so 9/18 + 6/18 + 2/18 = 17/18.

P87: NUMBER SEQUENCES

1. $233 = 1, 1, 2, 3, 5, 8, 13, 21, 34, 55, 89, 144, 233$
2. a) 64, 81 (square numbers series $1^2, 2^2, 3^2 \ldots 8^2, 9^2$)

   b) 21, 28 (add a row each time to make a bigger triangle)
   c) 51, 70
   d) 3,125, 46,656 ($1^1, 2^2, 3^3, 4^4, 5^5, 6^6 \ldots$)
3. It is alphabetical:
   eight; four; four; nine; nine; seven; six; three; three; two; zero

P92: SPOT THE RELATIONSHIP BETWEEN NUMBERS

1.

Blue	7	14	21	28
35	42	49	**56**	63
70	77	84	91	98

Red	12	**24**	36	**48**
60	**72**	84	**96**	

Yellow	13	26	39	52
65	78	91		

Predator	8	16	**24**	32
40	**48**	**56**	64	**72**
80	88	**96**		

a) red
b) blue
c) yellow

2. Here is the grid with the 25 prime numbers highlighted. The sequence 4, 4, 2, 2, 3, 2, 2, 3, 2, 1 refers to the number of primes in each row (going from top to bottom) and 5, 1, 7, 0, 1, 0, 6, 0, 5, 0 refers to the number of primes in each column (going from left to right).

1	**2**	**3**	4	**5**	6	**7**	8	9	10
11	12	**13**	14	15	16	**17**	18	**19**	20
21	22	**23**	24	25	26	27	28	**29**	30
31	32	33	34	35	36	**37**	38	39	40
41	42	**43**	44	45	46	**47**	48	49	50
51	52	**53**	54	55	56	57	58	**59**	60
61	62	63	64	65	66	**67**	68	69	70
71	72	**73**	74	75	76	77	78	**79**	80
81	82	**83**	84	85	86	87	88	**89**	90
91	92	93	94	95	96	**97**	98	99	100

3. $2,584/1,597 = $ phi

P95: PRIME NUMBERS AND THE HUMAN BRAIN

1. 13, 29, 53
2. He proved that the set of prime numbers is infinite.
3. 15,485,863 is the one-millionth prime.

P100: VISUAL DISCRIMINATION

1. Spot the difference
   1. Lady's red swimsuit changed to olive.
   2. Yellow umbrella changed to pink.
   3. New umbrella added beside the Nestlé wind break.
   4. Swimmers in the water have been deleted.
   5. "Simonis" wording has been flipped.
   6. Blue tent changed to green.
   7. Shark fin added to the water.
   8. Duplication of striped umbrella.
   9. Lady's red top has changed to purple.
   10. Duplication of boy in long green shorts, walking.
2. Shape matching
   1 is D rotated
   2 is A flipped
   3 is E flipped
   4 is B flipped and rotated
   5 is C rotated
3. Crime scene
   1 is 1, 2 is 4, 3 is 6, 4 is 7, 5 is 9.

P102: CONTRAST DISCRIMINATION

1. They are the same. If you don't believe it, cut them out and put them beside each other – the shading on the front center square causes this amazing illusion!
2. They are the same.

P106: VISUAL MEMORY

1. two; 2. blue, pink, and yellow; 3. red short-sleeved polo shirt; 4. nothing; 5. pink and green; 6. left; 7. row four; 8. Africa; 9. four; 10. green coin purse; 11. top right to bottom left; 12. calculator and socks; 13. yellow; 14. red; 15. two; 16. purple; 17. a book; 18. blue; 19. left; 20. orange.

P109: FIGURE GROUND

Hedgehog in plantpot on shelf; bell on light stand; bat bottom right of carpet; pineapple in chair cushion; bread on bookshelf; pencil horizontal on bookshelf; boot and hat on the wall in between plants; ear on the plant outside; paperclip on cushion on sofa; butterfly on the cookies; tie on bookshelf.

1. All of them
2.

P113: VISUAL CLOSURE

Left to right: Taj Mahal, The Colosseum, Hollywood Sign, Leaning Tower of Pisa, London's Tower Bridge, Statue of Liberty, the Erechtheion on the Acropolis, Elizabeth Tower (Big Ben), Eiffel Tower

P124: TRUST YOUR INTUITION

1. Hyper Text Markup Language
2. New Zealand
3. Demeter
4. Maria Callas
5. Neil Simon
6. Eggplant
7. Diego Velázquez
8. Paris and Istanbul
9. The science of kissing
10. Pieces of bread

P136: HOW THE BRAIN REMEMBERS

Most people will get between five and ten questions correct. If you got more than 12 correct, then well done indeed. This memory test is very challenging because we retain surprisingly little detail unless we are specifically looking for something (this shows how important attention is for forming memories).

Also, did you notice how easily you can be made to doubt your memories or create fake ones? How long did you spend wondering which animal was asleep on the armchair, or considering the position of non-existent apples and pairs of shoes? Did you name a key as one of your three metal objects in question 14 (immediately after reading the word "key" in question 13)?

In a week's time, take the test again and notice how your prior memory of the questions directs your attention. Naturally, you should perform much better this time, because now your attention is guided by your declarative memory (*see* page 173).

The other exercises in this section are to give you hands-on experience of some of the principles being explained (rather than give you a memory score), so don't despair if you found some of them tough. Use your scores as a benchmark to track your progress.

P154: YOU REMEMBER MORE THAN YOU THINK

The fourth image is the correct Madagascar.

P166: SENSORY MEMORY

The big tree in the middle is missing.

P175: SEMANTIC MEMORY

1. Apple
2. Red
3. a,d
4. Cyanidin
5. True

P176 DECLARATIVE MEMORY

1. Libra
2. South Korea
3. James Bond; climbing accident in the French Alps.
4. knee joint
5. Reginald Dwight
6. wind velocity
7. chocolate, vanilla, strawberry
8. Detective Comics
9. it knocked over a lantern
10. almond

P180: EMOTION AND MEMORY

1. Most people will notice yellow on the weapon as this is the brightest color and at the front of the weapon.
2. Most people will notice that the outfit was black but will not be able to give any further detail such as the shape of the necklace or that the makeup is pastel.
3: The ears have been removed! However, in the shock of looking at the picture you wouldn't focus on this otherwise very noticeable feature.

Most people will be able to give some detail to questions 1 and 2, but will totally miss the answer to question 3.

P208: CHUNKING AND PATTERNS

The nine squares of a tic-tac-toe board, going from top left to bottom right.

If you number each face of the Rubik's cube like this:
123
456
789
you can describe the positions of each color, so for example, left face, top face, right face

267	3	5	GREEN

so the answers for BLUE, WHITE, and YELLOW are:

3	18	9	BLUE
0	24	167	WHITE
18	5	3	YELLOW

The word DRAGON is an acronym (*see* page 231)

Dog
Rabbit
Anteater
Gorilla
Octopus
Newt

P220: MEMORY HOOK NUMBER RHYME

Top ten safest countries.

P223: MEMORY PEG ALPHABET

Most people should get over 20 using this method, which is considerably more than if you just used your normal nonassociative recall.

P234: ACROSTICS

The initial letter of the lines spell Elizabeth.
Acrostic Passwords: Night Fever, I Walk the Line, In Da Club, Bohemian Rhapsody, Disturbia, Yellow, Do I Wanna Know?, London Calling, You Ain't Nothin' But a Hound Dog, Purple Rain, Halo, Space Oddity

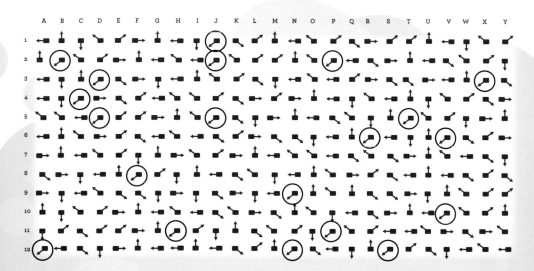

P246: ATTENTION PLEASE

 1J, 2B, 2J, 2P, 3D, 3X, 4C, 5D, 5J, 5T, 6R, 6V, 8F, 9N, 10V, 11H, 11P, 12A, 12N, 12S

You should be able to spot all 20 within two minutes with 100 percent accuracy. If you have made any mistakes, pick another icon and try again, only this time slow down and concentrate on accuracy instead of speed. Here are the coordinates for all the icons, so you can practice:

(42) 1B, 1G, 1M, 1U, 2A, 2F, 2N, 2T, 3C, 3I, 3W, 4O, 4T, 5H, 5N, 5S, 5Y, 6B, 6Q, 6U, 7B, 7G, 7L, 7U, 8E, 8I, 8O, 8U, 9O, 9Q, 9V, 10A, 10F, 10N, 10T, 10Y, 11G, 11K, 12F, 12I, 12M, 12R

(39) 1E, 1L, 1P, 1S, 1T, 1Y, 2D, 2L, 2M, 2X, 3K, 3Q, 4F, 4J, 4M, 4W, 5E, 5F, 5V, 6E, 6K, 6X, 7E, 7J, 8G, 8R, 8X, 9X, 9Y, 10D, 10X, 11B, 11D, 11E, 11I, 11N, 11R, 12L, 12T

➡️ (34) 1F, 1R, 2E, 2S, 3F, 3R, 3U, 4D, 4L, 4N, 4Y, 5G, 5M, 5X, 6D, 6L, 6Y, 7A, 7H, 7K, 7T, 8B, 8Q, 9A, 9H, 9K, 9T, 10E, 10L, 10S, 11F, 11V, 11X, 12E

🔲 (42) 1K, 1Q, 2R, 2V, 3E, 3L, 3S, 3T, 3Y, 4E, 4K, 4X, 5K, 5P, 6F, 6J, 6M, 6N, 6W, 7Q, 7S, 7X, 8A, 8K, 8S, 8W, 8Y, 9E, 9F, 9J, 9R, 9S, 10J, 10M, 10R, 11C, 11L, 1W, 12C, 12K, 12O, 12U

🚩 (33) 1C, 1I, 1W, 2Y, 3B, 3G, 3M, 4B, 4Q, 4U, 5L, 5R, 5W, 6O, 6T, 7F, 7Y, 8C, 8H, 8M, 9B, 9G, 9I, 9L, 9U, 0B, 10P, 11A, 11J, 11O, 12D, 12Q, 12V

⬅️ (48) 1A, 1H, 1N, 1V, 2G, 2I, 2Q, 2U, 3A, 3H, 3N, 3P, 3V, 4A, 4G, 4P, 4S, 5C, 5O, 6A, 6G, 6I, 6P, 6S, 7C, 7M, 7P, 7W, 8D, 8J, 8N, 8T, 8V, 9C, 9M, 10G, 10I, 10Q, 10U, 11S, 11T, 12B, 12G, 12H, 12J, 12P, 12W, 12Y

🔲 (42) 1D, 1O, 1X, 2C, 2H, 2K, 2O, 2W, 3J, 3O, 4H, 4I, 4R, 4V, 5A, 5B, 5I, 5Q, 5U, 6C, 6H, 7D, 7I, 7N, 7O, 7R, 7V, 8L, 8P, 9D, 9P, 9W, 10C, 10H, 10K, 10O, 10W, 11M, 11Q, 11U, 11Y, 12X

P251–P252: STRUCTURE AND ORGANIZE THE INFORMATION

1. It's easier to remember as: 0123456789 0123456789 0123456789
2. Five gold rings, four calling birds, three French hens, two turtle doves.
3. Imagine a cat stands on the window drinking from a saucer next to a vase of flowers. By the window a table is laid for dinner: knife, fork, and spoon, cup and jug of water, and a plate with a chicken leg, potato, and carrots.

As with the research trials, the names or parts of the names in the harder or more unusual fonts should have been easier to recall. However, the font of one of the names is so hard to read that it may have hampered your encoding.
Daniel Oppenheimer: Daniel is written in Haettenschweiler font, which should have helped encoding. Oppenheimer is a famous name (J. Robert Oppenheimer was one of the "fathers of the atomic bomb") so that should have been the easiest surname to recall.

Connor Diemand-Yauman: The font for Diemand-Yauman makes it very hard to read, so this may have affected encoding, although if you had associated it with "Diamond" you would have encoded that part easily. According to the serial position effect, you will remember more of the items at the beginning and end than those in the middle of the list, so this name is the hardest of the three to recall.
Erikka Vaughan: The surname was written in Comic Sans Italicized font, and also came at the end of the list, so it should be more easily recalled.

P264: CONSOLIDATION

As with the study referred to on page 261, you should have a better recall of the images after the caffeine drink on the second recall test.

INDEX

This edition published by Parragon Books Ltd in 2016 and distributed by

Parragon Inc.
440 Park Avenue South, 13th floor
New York, NY 10016
www.parragon.com

Copyright © Parragon Books Ltd 2014–2016

Packaged by Susanna Geoghegan
Inside designed by Angela Wilkinson

ISBN: 978-1-4748-3811-5

Printed in China